MI VOZ, MI VIDA

MI VOZ, MI VIDA

Latino College Students
Tell Their Life Stories

EDITED BY

**Andrew Garrod, Robert Kilkenny,
and Christina Gómez**

Cornell University Press
Ithaca and London

First published 2007 by Cornell University Press
First Printing, Cornell Paperbacks, 2007

Printed in the United States of America

Library of Congress Cataloging-in-Publication Data

Mi voz, mi vida : Latino college students tell their life stories /
edited by Andrew Garrod, Robert Kilkenny, and Christina
Gómez.
       p. cm.
   Includes bibliographical references.
   ISBN 978-0-8014-4597-2 (cloth : alk. paper) —
ISBN 978-0-8014-7386-9 (pbk. : alk. paper)
   1. Dartmouth College—Students—Biography.   2. His-
panic American college students—New Hampshire—Hanover
—Biography.   3. Hispanic American youth—Education
(Higher)—New Hampshire—Hanover.   I. Garrod, Andrew,
1937–   II. Kilkenny, Robert.   III. Gómez, Christina.
IV. Title.

   LC2670.6.M58 2007
   378.742'3—dc22
   [B]
                                                    2006101122

Cornell University Press strives to use environmentally responsible suppliers and materials to the fullest extent possible in
the publishing of its books. Such materials include vegetable-
based, low-VOC inks and acid-free papers that are recycled,
totally chlorine-free, or partly composed of nonwood fibers.
For further information, visit our website at www.cornellpress.
cornell.edu.

Cloth printing   10 9 8 7 6 5 4 3 2 1
Paperback printing   10 9 8 7 6 5 4 3 2 1

In recognition of their bravery and insight, this book is dedicated to the fifteen student autobiographers whose essays are presented here.

Contents

Preface

"Memoir is how we try to make sense of who we are, who we once were, and what values and heritage shaped us," writes William Zinsser, the editor of *Inventing the Truth: The Art and Craft of Memoir* (New York: Mariner Books, 1998). "If a writer seriously embarks on that quest, readers will be nourished by the journey, bringing along many associations with quests of their own" (1998, 6). The stories included in *Mi Voz, Mi Vida: Latino College Students Tell Their Life Stories* are essentially memoirs in which the student autobiographers—all late adolescents between the ages of eighteen and twenty-two at Dartmouth College—reflect on formative relationships and influences, life-changing events, and factors that helped shape their values, educational outcomes, and sense of personal identity. Each author brings to this book his or her own unique experience of growing up Latino or Latina in this country. It is our hope that readers of this anthology are engaged by the particularity and detail of these stories while at the same time connecting with the individual human experience.

Almost all the student essays in this book—with the exception of "Living between the Lines" and "On Being Canela," which are older—were written in the last three or four years. Though Dartmouth College was the site for the collection of the narratives, this book does not focus on Dartmouth per se or on its educational impact on our contributors, but rather on their evolving lives and Latino identities. All fifteen autobiographers worked one-on-one with Andrew Garrod in weekly one-hour meetings over the term's ten-week period. Typically, the student would submit seven or eight pages to Garrod prior to each meeting; these pages then became the focus of attention when they met. Teacher and writer also discussed how to proceed with the next portion of the narrative. Garrod made no assumption that the story was already formulated in the student's head and conveyed to the student that each story had to be found, piece by piece. Because the emphasis was on process—helping the writers with that most complex of all writerly tasks, finding their voice, a task further complicated for those whose first language was Spanish—no editorial interventions were made during the generative stage. Although the parameters were necessarily established by the editors, we encouraged the writers to develop their own themes and make analytical sense of their experiences in ways that gave them back a significant meaning for their own lives. Not infrequently, a writer was halfway through the process before he or she came to understand what the essay's central concerns and themes were, which led to the paper's being reordered to reflect the writer's new insight. "Memoir writers must manufacture a text, imposing narrative order on a jumble of half-remembered events," writes William Zinsser. "With that feat of manipulation, they arrive at a truth that is theirs alone, not quite like that of anybody else who is present at the same events" (1998, 6).

In helping our writers articulate their stories, we offered just a few guiding questions: What gives purpose to your life? What relationships have been of major significance to you? When and how did you become aware of the concept of ethnicity? What have been some of the major struggles in your life? How do you account for your academic success? What are the racial and ethnic backgrounds of some of your closest friends? Would you say that you were politically active in the college community? What role does your "Latinoness" play in how you identify yourself? Is "Latino" a useful categorization in your mind? We made no assumption that their ethnicity was a vital element in self-definition for all. Some only became aware that they were Latino or were viewed by others as such when they came to college.

The completed manuscripts were most often in the fifty- to seventy-page range. After careful consultation and discussion, over months or occasionally even years, cutting and editing reduced and sharpened the text to a manageable length of eighteen to twenty-four double-spaced pages. Editors' changes to the text were minimal. The variations in tone, degree of self-analysis, and style of expression reflect our commitment to respect each writer's story and life.

After the draft had been reduced to approximately twenty-five pages, the essay was sent to Robert Kilkenny, who had not worked with this student and who could offer a more objective reaction to the reading. This was done to bring the essay to another level of psychological cohesion in the hope that areas that seemed to be avoided or mysteriously unaddressed were brought to the attention of the writers. Suggestions were made as to why the story would be better understood if some of these lacunae were engaged or explored more thoroughly. This was a conscious process of pushing the writer to the edge of his or her ability to reflect on his or her own life history. It was not unusual to have a writer balk or say that further exploration was too painful, or that they were genuinely unable to reflect further about experiences still subjectively raw and unresolved.

Almost all of the students in this book were enrolled in the sociology course, Complexity of Latino Identity, taught by Christina Gómez and in Andrew Garrod's education classes. These courses offered students a resource to explore theoretical, experiential, and historical concerns, often functioning as a sounding board for the authors. Expanding the students' understanding of Latino history, politics, and public policy was a central goal. The Garrod courses embrace a developmental perspective and examine issues of race, ethnicity, class, and gender.

Although fifteen essays—ten by men and five by women—appear in this book, they represent only a portion of the essays, fewer than half, that were developed and completed. Some students withdrew their essays from consideration for this anthology, because the writing of the essay and the self-reflection it had necessitated was the primary reason they embarked on the venture in the first place; others hesitated to make suggested changes or to engage in further self-exploration and editing. In such cases, we made an editorial decision as to whether the case could stand as a whole without further elaboration or whether its coherence was insufficient to merit publication. At times, the student's self-understanding was not sufficiently developed to merit the essay's inclusion in the book. Nevertheless, the editors are deeply grateful for all the essays so diligently worked on over the years, whether included in the book or not.

To encourage the frankest possible exploration of their lives and relationships, we offered the writers the option of remaining anonymous. For those who have chosen that option—often in deference to the dignity and feelings of other people in the narrative—details of identity and location have been altered.

For many of the authors, the process of putting their experiences into words has acted as a catalyst for further self-reflection on their life history.

A life consciously reflected on is changed by this process of deep intro-spection. It has been the editors' consistent observation over seventeen years of encouraging this type of work that the process of autobiographi-cal writing can have a profound transformative effect on the spiritual, moral, and emotional domains of a person's life. We have found would-be contributors overwhelmingly open to the invitation to make sense of their childhood and adolescent experiences, which up to then may have been in-choate and unintegrated. This opportunity to reflect can reconcile them to trauma and lend emotional resolution and understanding to the primary relationships and vicissitudes in their lives. As editors, we have felt deeply privileged to be guiding the student writers through deeper levels of self-understanding and helping them gain purchase on the world through self-analysis and articulation.

The introduction to this book identifies, in sequence, four major themes in the essays—Resilience, Biculturalism, Mentoring, and Identity. We have chosen to arrange the memoirs to reflect this organization. Although certain motifs are indeed prevalent in the chapters identified in the intro-duction and pervasive in the book, each essay explores a multiplicity of themes. We want readers to appreciate the complexity of these as they play themselves out in the fifteen essays. Taken together, these memoirs offer the reader a rare opportunity to understand from the inside the experiences of students from a minority group, formerly small, but now the largest minority group in the United States. We are invited here to appreciate the courage, resilience, and insight of some remarkable young men and women.

The editors are deeply indebted to many friends and associates for the realization of this book. Alexander Hernandez-Siegel, the advisor for Latino students at Dartmouth College, has been a staunch supporter of our project since its beginning and has offered, invaluably, names of potential student writers. Misagh Parsa, Annelise Orleck, Deborah King, and Dean of Ad-missions Karl Furstenburg offered valued moral support and advice. Dody Riggs supplied essential editorial suggestions as manuscripts achieved their final forms, and former and present students at Dartmouth have served crit-ical roles in the essays' preparation and the book's production. These stu-dents include Michael Holmes, Adam Tapley, Kate Szilagyi, Allan Klinge, Daren Simkin, January Moult, Annie Delehanty, Ben Young, Erika Sogge, Licyau Wong, Rafael Mendez, Pavel Bogdan, and Nathan Raines. All have helped markedly to improve and edit the text. Our heartfelt thanks to Can-dace Akins and Katy Meigs for fine-tuning the text for publication.

The editors of *Mi Voz, Mi Vida: Latino College Students Tell Their Life Stories* particularly want to recognize *all* the students who worked with such industry, openness, and courage to bring their stories from the realm of the strictly private into more public view. Those who do not show up here have given no less generously of themselves. Finally, we salute the perseverance, insight, and honesty of all those whose essays make up this book.

MI VOZ, MI VIDA

Introduction   Being and Becoming Latino

Latinoness does not equal weakness. I want to be seen as successful, proud, and honest. And when people see that in me I want them to associate it with being Latino.
—David Ralos, "One Life, Many Lenses"

Latinos are now the largest minority group in the United States, forty-two million individuals, or approximately 14 percent of the population. By 2050, the U.S. Census estimates, one out of four individuals living in the United States will be of Latino heritage. Latinos are everywhere, and their influences have become staples of American culture. Latinos have made their mark on big cities like Los Angeles, New York, and Chicago, but also on smaller towns like Omaha, Nebraska; Little Rock, Arkansas; and Raleigh, North Carolina. They have become the new players in the political arena, taking an active role in national, regional, and local politics.

In the fifteen essays in this book, the authors, our Latino students, tell their stories. There is no one model, but what does come through is how powerful each writer has been in shaping his or her own life. Almost all of these authors were born after 1980. They grew up during the Reagan-Bush era, long after the civil rights movement, long after many of the heroes that inspired earlier minority cohorts were gone. Yet, it is clearly evident how much these earlier events shaped these young peoples' lives. We have often heard our colleagues lament that the youth of today lack the knowledge or passion to get involved in social or political issues, to fight the powers that be. These authors clearly understand the importance of their forebears, both family members and political activists. Although still young, all of these Latino authors connect the past with their present and future.

Each chapter of this book tells the compelling story of a young Latino or Latina student. Many of these students are the first in their family to attend college. Because they are entering highly selective institutions, almost every experience is new and fraught with uncertainty. Like other first-year students, they are anxious and nervous. They have the same concerns and questions that other students have: Will they fit in? Are they smart enough? Will they make new friends? Is there anyone else like them? But, unlike most other students, they also carry a history of being marginalized, isolated, and invisible.

These "superstar" students are deeply human; they feel insecure, lonely, and isolated. Some come from troubled families, others from happy homes; some are poor while others are rich; some are gay and others straight. They are of Mexican, Puerto Rican, Cuban, Dominican, Central American, and South American ancestry. Some identify as white, others as black, and some merely as Latino. In many ways, theirs are stories that many other college students could tell, but they share their identity as Latinos in a time and place where little is expected from them. As their teachers, however, we expected a lot from them, and they delivered. These stories continue this circle of sharing and learning.

Although it would be easy to claim that sheer merit brought these students to a prestigious institution and that their backgrounds do not matter, that would be naive. In the United States, race and ethnicity enter our consciousness and affect our experiences at every level. These students understand the structural forces that have impeded them, the ways they have been portrayed in the media, and the stereotypes that surround them. Regardless of their backgrounds, Latino students in predominantly white institutions are aware of how they might be viewed by other students and of the assumptions made about them.

With this book, we share the firsthand experiences and challenges of growing up Latino.

The Stories/*Los Cuentos*

Each chapter in this book tells a story of resilience, negotiation, self-definition, and strength of family. When reading these stories, it is easy to forget that these are young people struggling against unknown and unseen systems of racism, poverty, and oppression. They do not yet have the full vocabulary to contextualize their experiences.

The stories in this collection are united by four main themes. The first, resilience, focuses on the struggles these individuals have had against hard times, crisis, poverty, and sometimes tragedy. The second theme, biculturalism, is rooted in these students' ability to move in and out of different worlds, sometimes smoothly but often at great personal cost. The third theme, mentoring, shows how important adults are to these young people. Whether from their parents, teachers, or close friends, mentoring has been a vital factor in their academic and life success. The fourth theme, self-identity, focuses on the ongoing questions these students have about themselves, their Latinoness, and how it fits in with their sense of identity, issues of racism and stereotypes, and their place in society.

Resilience: The Struggle to Be Strong

Resilience is the ability to bounce back, to not succumb to failure, substance abuse, mental illness, juvenile delinquency, or other problems when exposed to great stress or adversity in life.[1] A lack of resilience can cause serious setbacks for many young people. For these Latino students, entering higher education presented unprecedented challenges and exposed them to extreme stress, yet they were able to recover quickly from their setbacks. In most cases, their resilience had already been tested long before they entered college. Like the general U.S. Latino population, many of these students have experienced poverty and economic challenges, single-parent households, dangerous neighborhoods, racism, and other equally stressful factors.

Although the Latino population is large and quite diverse, all Latino groups have experienced a less than promising educational future. Latinos have the lowest educational attainment and the highest dropout rates of any racial or ethnic group in the United States. Forty-two percent of all high school dropouts in 2002 were Latinos, while Latinos made up only 17 percent of the population of youth aged sixteen to twenty-four. The dropout rate for non-Latino whites was 12 percent.[2] According to the 2002 U.S. Census, only 11.1 percent of Latinos received a bachelor's degree or better, compared to 29.4 percent of the non-Latino white population.[3] Yet these students, represented in this book, are not special cases or pampered individuals; they are the young Latino men and women we meet in our everyday lives. Each of them has overcome their uniquely personal challenges and achieved remarkable personal and academic success against the odds.

There are four main characteristics of resilient youth: social competence; problem-solving skills; autonomy; and a sense of purpose and future.[4] Resilience theory suggests that all these attributes are present in most individuals, but whether they actually allow an individual to cope with adversity depends on protective factors during that person's childhood.[5] Protective factors include family support, effective teaching, school success, and resources from the surrounding community and schools. However, "it is important not to specify too exactly how that may be enacted or interpreted—different families in different historical and social contexts will do it differently."[6] In other words, resilience occurs in many different shapes and forms, and what works for one individual may not work for another.

The authors of these stories understood early on how important it was that they be able to endure hard times and come out of them even stronger. This factor was vital to this group's survival and success. They are survivors; time and time again they have overcome difficult circumstances and found solutions when many others would have simply given up. They have carried these lessons with them into higher education, which helped them succeed.

Eric Martinez relates the harrowing problems he experienced with his family as a young boy growing up in Southern California. His parents' physical abuse, drug use, and alcohol addiction led to an almost impossible existence for him, which ended with the death of his mother:

> I was thirteen years old when I stood over my mother and watched her fade away. Tears streamed down my face and my heart ached. A unique and inexplicable pain gripped my chest. I looked at her sweet mouth and thought of the loving words and kisses that had surfaced from those full lips. She looked beautiful as she slipped into eternal sleep.
>
> All those years of wishing for my mother's death had finally come true, and guilt streamed through my veins. Though my mother had been unpredictable and at times violent, I still had a deep love for her.

Even while he mourned his mother's death, Eric recognized that his life would have new possibilities, and once those possibilities became available to him he took full advantage of them.

In his essay "Dignity and Doubt," Joseph Rodriguez tells of his experience of becoming poor. After living an upper-middle-class life, his father was incarcerated and the family was evicted from their home and forced to live in a motel:

> I realized then that poverty is terribly unkind—especially because I was not used to it. For the most part I dealt with the situation as a type of adventure—an unfortunate circumstance, certainly, but one that we could overcome. However, it became difficult at times, as reminders of our lack of resources came to the foreground.

Joseph's ability to understand his situation, adjust to it, and find new friends was vital to his success. Instead of becoming bitter at his parents, he found creative ways to handle the situation. His rage at not having enough money fueled his desire to get a better education and find financial security for himself and his family.

Being resilient came at a price for Sarah Fox, a Cuban-Jewish student from Florida. A recovering alcoholic, changing her ways was a difficult struggle:

> My philosophy had always been to resist feeling guilty and invest energy in learning from the experience after making a mistake. But the possibility of learning from a mistake assumes some logical cause—something solvable. When drinking became the source of my mistakes, my habit of avoiding guilt became a perpetuating force for my irrational addiction. If I didn't feel guilty about the negative consequences of my drinking, what would motivate me to quit?

Despite spending her high school years getting drunk, Sarah managed to do exceptionally well in school. She continued drinking while in college but eventually realized that her addiction had a heavy cost. Meeting her future husband changed her and led her to quit drinking. She transformed herself from party girl to wife, mother, as well as student, and she finished her senior year with a newborn daughter. Sarah's ability to understand the consequences of her actions and pull herself together to complete her college education while caring for her new family shows her tremendous ability to overcome her personal demons. She understands that it is an everyday struggle to keep herself away from alcohol and from her destructive past behavior, and that even though she has changed she is still the same girl who partied hard.

Biculturalism: On Both Sides of the Border

To be bicultural means to exist within two cultures and to be able to adapt to both ways of being. Neither culture needs to be more important or all encompassing; rather, an individual can move from one space to another, learning and deciding what to take or leave behind from each. Biculturalism exemplifies a move away from the either/or conception of acculturation, which presumed that the more immigrants become Americanized, the more they discard the behaviors and values of their culture of origin.[7]

All students in this book are bicultural. Many of the students are children of immigrants, or immigrants themselves, living their lives in the United States but with a foot in their home countries. Miguel Ramírez lives on the border, watching Mexico from his backyard, being part of both worlds simultaneously:

> From my earliest memory of Mexico—that place over there—I knew it was where I belonged, though we didn't live there. The United States was my home, but it wasn't mine. When you cross the international border into the United States you are asked to declare your citizenship; I always thought that they only asked Mexicans.

Like Miguel, many of our students felt like outsiders; they are border crossers, both literally and figuratively. They enter new spaces, learn new ways, and try to adjust. They are migrants; some have moved to different countries, different neighborhoods, and different schools. Each has moved from their own home and family to a majority white institution, and this transition was not always easy or fluid. Disconcerting differences between the two spaces quickly became apparent. Many of the authors had trouble fitting in and belonging to their new world, while others felt at home and even a bit guilty for enjoying their new surroundings. Sometimes having two cultures brought out new personalities in the students, allowing them to experiment with their identity.

Abiel Acosta, in his essay "The Double Life," describes this "new side" he discovered while at college. After the student newspaper carried an article about him and his party habits, he wrote:

> My parents do not know the "partying" side of me and would be shocked to hear me be so vulgar and see pictures of me looking so stupid. My parents learned that I drink not that long ago, and they still think I have never been

drunk. They do not know anything about my sex life and the ridiculous things I do or say in college. I am naturally a quiet, well-mannered introvert, but when I am at school, I tend to be outgoing and wild. My personality does a complete 180, and I force myself to be extroverted to entertain people and get along with others. I live a double life.

But did Abiel lead a double life in order to fit in to this environment? Did his clownlike personality, which included drinking, having sex, and becoming a campus character, really prove that he had assimilated into college life? Like many minority students, Abiel's decision to totally immerse himself in college life came at a personal cost. Latino students' ability to be accepted "like any other white person" also often means that they keep their home life hidden.

Unfortunately, for many of these students the two spaces of their biculturalism have come to mean Latino versus white, poor versus rich, uneducated versus educated, lazy versus hard working, and illegal versus legal. Our society has so clearly demarcated both spheres that even individuals who inhabit both worlds daily can become confused and feel the need to express their differences. José García, in trying to come to terms with his ethnicity and school, wrote:

I recall a white friend telling me I was more white than he: I acted white, I dressed white, I talked white. In essence, to him I was normal, and normal was white. You're not part of a gang? You must be normal, you must be white. You don't shoot up every morning or carry a gun? You must be normal, you must be white.

In order to fit in, José had to deny his Latino identity. He is ashamed of his parents' accent, his dark skin that tans easily in the summer, and his immigrant background. He is a U.S. citizen and a child of Honduran immigrants, and he struggles to embody both selves. His story is one of learning, developing, and finally accepting his bicultural self.

Marissa Saldivar also struggled with biculturalism, but for her it had more to do with "growing up" and becoming her own person in her own way. Marissa, who comes from a Chicano family in Los Angeles that was involved in civil rights, fell in love with Antonio Rodríguez, a Cuban-Colombian student from an upper-middle-class New York family. Her family worried about the changes they saw before them, and like many Latino families, they worried about Marissa leaving home:

In order to combat his sorrow, my father immediately began his long process of letting me go—a process that was finally completed when I announced my pregnancy. At first he didn't know how to go about the letting go. I had changed so much and so quickly that he was conflicted. In front of him he saw a confident woman whom he could be proud of, but he was not ready to let go of the little-girl image he had associated with me.

Her family's fear that Marissa would not return home did actualize. After college, Marissa moved to New York City to raise her newborn baby with Antonio. Her biculturalism has given her the ability to cross into new worlds, to transform herself, and to leave her home. Marissa worries that she will never return home and about her own loss. She questions whether the privilege she has gained is worth it. As a new mother, she desires the best for her daughter, but she also understands that her daughter's life will be different from her own. Ironically, Marissa's educational success will move her daughter further away from Marissa's own Chicano family. While Marissa's biculturalism allowed her to enter new worlds, it has also placed her child directly in a life of tremendous advantage and one that might be monocultural.

Mentoring: The Someone in My Life

The literature on the role of mentoring students has been growing in the areas of education, human resources, psychology, and ethnic studies. Mentoring is defined as the process that strengthens an individual through a personal relationship with a more experienced and caring person. Positive life goals are built through these relationships, and the individual being mentored can be guided onto a successful life track. For students at risk, mentoring can help prevent dropping out of school and/or involvement with drugs, crime, and violence.[8] For the students in our book, mentoring has often been a life-saving experience. Although it is often thought of as a deliberate activity—adults sign up to mentor an "at-risk youth"—mentoring comes in a variety of ways.

For students Viana Turcios and Robert Cotto, their lifelong mentors have been their mothers (both their fathers left the family). Contrary to the literature that finds that Latino families do not value education, these mothers dedicated themselves to giving their children the best opportunities possible.[9] Even though they may not understand the educational process in the United States in detail, these mothers took risks and encouraged their children to succeed academically. Viana Turcios relates how when she was accepted at Exeter, an elite private high school, her mother had the courage and foresight to allow her to go:

> I just thank God for giving my mother the strength to leave my father when she did, because I cannot even imagine what my life would have been like if we had stayed with him any longer. Although my mother has been human and thus not perfect, she has been my fuel, my inspiration to accomplish all my goals. I have never met a woman with my mother's relentlessness and strength, and I hope to emulate even half of it.

Robert Cotto's mother is also a constant force in his life. Raising her three sons as a single parent doesn't stop her from giving her children the strength to believe in themselves. As Robert explains:

> A turning point came when my mother saw me throwing an application to a summer college program in the trash and yelled at me, asking why I was doing so. I began to rethink my decision to ignore the program—perhaps this was an opportunity I should not pass up. More than anybody else in my life, my mother has shown me not to let opportunities slip through my hands; she has always pushed me to seize chances, no matter how unreachable the goal may seem.

These stories add to the literature debunking the myth that Latino families do not value education. Based on pseudoscientific notions of "deficit thinking," this myth "refers to the idea that students, particularly students of low-SES [socioeconomic status] background and of color, fail in school because they and their families have internal defects, or deficits, that thwart the learning process."[10] Disputing this mythology, numerous studies have found high parental involvement within Latino families. Latino parents might not always have economic resources, but they express a strong desire for their children to succeed academically.[11]

In Angelita Urena's essay "Orgullo Dominicana," she opens by describing fifty family members coming to her graduation:

> I thrust my dorm room window open and found myself surrounded by loud Spanish chatter and music. I knew they were coming, but they caught me by surprise. My mom looked up at my window and screamed, "La trulla llego, pero no podemos entrar" (The troops have arrived, but we can't get in).

Her family's excitement and pride in her graduation are evident. Angelita's mother, grandmother, aunts, and even her father help her in achieving her goals. Angelita graduates with a roar from her family, a Dominican flag wrapped around her, and the love of her family dancing around her.

Latino Identities: Becoming and Unbecoming Latino

What it means to be "Latino" has been a struggle for many young people. Stereotypes of Latinos as poor, uneducated, and unassimilated to U.S. culture are ever present in the American media. This caricature of Latinos was asserted once again in the spring of 2004, when Harvard political science professor Samuel P. Huntington wrote:

> The persistent inflow of Hispanic immigrants threatens to divide the Untied States into two peoples, two cultures, and two languages. Unlike past immigrant groups, Mexicans and other Latinos have not assimilated into mainstream U.S. culture, forming instead their own political and linguistic enclaves—from Los Angeles to Miami—and rejecting the Anglo-Protestant values that built the American dream. The United States ignores this challenge at its peril.[12]

In his article and subsequent book, Huntington warns that "the cultural divide between Hispanics and Anglos could replace the racial division between blacks and whites as the most serious cleavage in U.S. society."[13] His concerns about language and culture ignore research on immigrants and English-language acquisition, on the cognitive achievement of students with fluency in two languages, and on the "Americanization" of Latinos in the United States.[14] Huntington's exaggerated "us versus them" rhetoric fuels an anti-Latino agenda and perpetuates Latino stereotypes.

The students in this book have encountered these stereotypes too. Their classmates assume they come from poor *barrios*, received inferior education, and speak Spanish. Yet, these Latinos come from diverse backgrounds. Not only are they from various Latino groups, but they are from different socioeconomic backgrounds. Some Latino students in fact are concerned about not being Latino *enough*. Their lack of Spanish fluency, as well as their middle-class lifestyle and physical features, place them outside the circle of "typical" Latinos.

David Ralos clearly wrestled with these images. After being accepted by an Ivy League college, his classmates questioned his ethnic credentials. David writes, "I'm sick of feeling like I am not a true Latino simply because I was not poor or disadvantaged."

In his essay "Me against the Wall," author Antonio Rodríguez, who describes himself as "a pale-skinned upper-middle-class white Latino" also struggles with the stereotypes that other Latinos face:

> As a white Latino who has grown up in a different class than many first-generation Latinos in the United States, I have lived among Latinos who share a different set of cultural values, tastes, and beliefs.

Antonio writes of his first encounter with his racist roommate's father, who refers to Antonio as a "spic." Later, when applying for a job with an investment bank, Antonio was again confronted with stereotypes about Latinos. Even though Antonio's upper-middle-class background and lighter skin might have protected him from some racism, it clearly did not provide a complete safeguard.

Alessandro Meléndez tells how he first became aware of his identity as being both black and Latino. Because the United States has "de-categorized" racial identity in the Latino community—individuals can identify as non-Hispanic white, non-Hispanic black, *or* Hispanic, but not as black *and* Hispanic—Alessandro had particular trouble identifying as both:

> Until I reached the United States, and particularly college, I was not aware of the politics of skin color. Even in the Latino organization and community, I noticed I was the only dark-skinned male in the group.

His realization that he can be both black and Hispanic helped him achieve his full potential. Latino identity comes in many shapes, colors, and sizes. The stereotypes that permeate U.S. society place boundaries around who belongs and who doesn't, but it only takes one person to question those boundaries and open the borders to allow new possibilities of identity.

For other Latinos, learning about their Latino identity comes during and through their college education. Some Latino students have never associated with their culture. Alejo Alvarez, a young Puerto Rican man from New York City who grew up in a predominantly white, upper-middle-class neighborhood, felt that he was invisible within his own culture:

For me, Latinos, Hispanics, and minorities were groups labeled *them*. I knew on some level that I was one of *them*, but for all my daily purposes, I lived in a world where my Latinoness was simply unnecessary.

Alejo understood that discovering his Latino identity is a journey. Although he was surrounded by his culture while growing up, he didn't connect to that identity—to him it was foreign. Later, during a college summer, he began to contemplate his Latino identity, and his relationship to that identity changed:

> Being Latino has been a recent process of creating a cultural definition that comes to terms with who I was, who I am, and who I hope to be. It is a journey both of *being* and *becoming* that allows for a cultural placement from which I can look toward everything that is Puerto Rican, while shedding my cloak of cultural invisibility so everything Puerto Rican can also see me.

His ethnic identity grew as he grew and became more comfortable with who he is.

Norma Andrade, in her essay "On Being Canela," also learns to identify with her Latinaness. She struggles with her family's expectations of what it means to be a woman. She has had to pave a road for herself and create her own definition of what it means to be Latina, even though it might be different than that of her mother:

> After twenty-one years of living, I have learned a lot about myself and continue to do so every day. Becoming Latina is one facet of myself that I am still learning about, because I know that it has built barriers between me and the world that I grew up in.

The Journey/*El Viaje*

We conceived this book because we believed it was important to uncover stories of Latino and Latina students that are seldom heard. These *cuentos*, these stories, are different from the stories about Latino failure, and although we offer only fifteen portraits, they are colorful, revealing, and promising. These students come from both wealthy and poor backgrounds, from inner cities and suburbia, from intact families and single-parent households, from private and public high schools; they are children of

Mexican, Puerto Rican, Ecuadorian, Honduran, Cuban, Colombian, Dominican, and Peruvian parents. Missing from the many studies that describe Latino students are the stories of those who have succeeded, who have "made it against the odds." This book tells some of those stories, and we hope it will inspire many more.

In a world of debates about immigration, poverty, and education in the United States, these stories allow us to reflect on how young people who might be most affected by those decisions are actually navigating their lives. Their ability to face difficult times and persevere should give us hope. Their resilience and biculturalism are skills that allow them to succeed. Their stories should make clear how important mentoring is for our children. Our young students need guidance, support, and role models from those of us who are parents, teachers, and friends. These students, and the many who are like them, need to be acknowledged and celebrated, and understood for who they are—and that includes being Latino.

We hope future Latino students will see themselves in these stories and realize that they are not alone in their struggle for education and self-fulfillment.

Notes

1. Robert Linquanti, *Using Community-Wide Collaboration to Foster Resiliency in Kids: A Conceptual Framework* (San Francisco: Western Regional Center for Drug-Free Schools and Communities, Far West Laboratory for Educational Research and Development, 1992).
2. Data for 2002: "Child Trends' Calculations of U.S. Census Bureau, School Enrollment—Social and Economic Characteristics of Students: October 2002: Detailed Tables: Table 1." Available online at http://www.census.gov/population/www/socdemo/school/cps2002.html.
3. U.S. Census Bureau, "Annual Demographic Supplement to March 2002 Current Population Survey."
4. Bonnie Benard, "Drawing Using Community-Wide Collaboration to Foster Resiliency in Kids: A Conceptual Framework," *Reclaiming Children and Youth* 6, no. 1 (1997): 29–32.
5. Nancy Feyl Chavkin and John Gonzalez, *Mexican Immigrant Youth and Resiliency: Research and Promising Programs* (Charleston, W. Va.: ERIC Clearinghouse on Rural Education and Small School, 2000).
6. Sue Howard, John Dryden, and Bruce Johnson, "Childhood Resilience: Review and Critique of Literature," *Oxford Review of Education* 25, no. 3 (1999): 307–23.
7. Dina Birman, "Biculturalism and Perceived Competence of Latino Immigrant Adolescents," *American Journal of Community Psychology* 26, no. 3 (1998): 335–55.
8. Theresa Barron-McKeagney, Jane D. Woody, and H. J. D'Souza, "Mentoring At-Risk Latino Children and Their Parents' Impact on Social Skills and Problem Behaviors," *Child and Adolescent Social Work Journal* 18, no. 2 (2001): 120.
9. Richard R. Valencia, "'Mexican Americans Don't Value Education!' On the Basis of the Myth, Mythmaking, and Debunking," *Journal of Latinos and Education* 1, no. 2 (2002): 81–103.

10. Ibid., 83. See also Richard R. Valencia, "Genetic Pathology Model of Deficit Thinking," in *The Evolution of Deficit Thinking: Educational Thought and Practice*, ed. Richard. R. Valencia, 41–112 (London: Falmer, 1997).

11. See Richard R. Valencia, *Chicano School Failure and Success: Past, Present, and Future* (London: Routledge/Falmer, 2002).

12. Samuel P. Huntington, "The Hispanic Challenge," *Foreign Affairs* no. 141 (March–April 2004): 30–45.

13. Samuel P. Huntington, *Who Are We? The Challenges to America's National Identity* (Cambridge: Harvard University Press, 2004), 8.

14. Alejandro Portes and Dag MacLeod, "Educational Progress of Children Immigrants: The Roles of Class, Ethnicity, and School Context," *Sociology of Education* 69 (1996): 255–75.

RESILIENCE

THE STRUGGLE TO BE STRONG

Eric Martinez   The Devils Within

On Saturday nights back home during my high school years, I would hear my name come on over the loudspeakers as I rushed for another touchdown. The announcer had a flair for putting an emphasis on the Mexican name that was so common in my neighborhood. "Mar-tiii-nezz," he would scream. Our team roster had a diverse mix of ethnicities including Filipinos, Anglos, and Latinos. I was fond of my teammates and the camaraderie that we shared, and the sports that I played gave me a platform to excel in high school. I enjoyed every minute of the excitement when I got the snap and took off running for the end zone or when I dove for that screaming line drive coming down the baseline. Growing up as a Latino in Southern California I was able to enjoy my adolescence and escape many of the prejudices that I had heard about from my grandparents and mother. Things had changed since they had come to the States, and I liked how everything had ended up. Many doors had opened that were not open to them in their youth. Although these advantages helped me in many ways, a downside existed. Being Latino created a duality of lives for me throughout my adolescence, and the hardships that I endured shaped me into who I am today.

As a small child, I viewed my lovely Mexican-born mother sustain blows from my father's bronze-colored hands. I have wondered about the impact of having a stereotypical abusive Latino male as my role model for relationships. The abuse that my Latina mother endured created a fear that I believe has made me gravitate toward relationships similar to that of my parents. I wonder, do I look for chaotic and unstable relationships in an attempt to replicate the one I viewed in my childhood? How did growing up in the midst of poverty in Southern California suburbia, the son of abusive, alcoholic, drug-abusing parents form me into the man I have become? Have I managed to transcend the difficulties of my childhood and reach manhood unscarred? Did being adopted by new parents in my early adolescence undo some of the harmful effects of growing up in a chaotic family? After all I've experienced, how is it that I am about to graduate from an Ivy League college and enter a prestigious job with a bright future ahead?

When I was nearly five years old and my sister Kelly was two, my parents decided that their marriage had run its course. After several weeks of separation, my parents divorced. Looking back on the situation, I know that they made a good decision; neither one of my parents could have continued in the relationship without increasing conflict. I did not want my parents' divorce to occur, but it seemed the path of separation had been blazed by years of unhappiness.

At the age of two, when I had a limited understanding of the world around me, I sensed that I wanted a father and a mother in my life. Yet, I did not want to grow up around and learn from the type of marriage my parents had. I have vivid memories of the growing tension of their failing marriage.

I was four and a half years old and tears streamed down my cheeks as I screamed at my father. My small feet seemed glued to my parents' bedspread as I stood, bouncing, on their bed, my hands and arms outstretched as I pleaded with them. My little sister crouched by my side and her eyes begged for my parents to stop fighting. All the while we both cried and yelled, "Daddy, please stop! I just want you guys to stop. Stop! Stop!" I must have repeated those words a thousand times. My body would not—rather *could* not—move to stop my father although he and my mother were only inches away from my grasp as they stood between the worn, brown dresser and the bed. The mirror on the dresser reflected the beads of sweat that gleamed on his forehead and the veins that seemed ready to explode in his tensed arms. My mother's mascara ran down her cheeks and her hair had become a tussled mess. She looked so small as my father dug his fingers into her shoulders. Instead of ceasing their argument, my father, with a fire in his eyes, knocked my mother to the ground with a forceful blow to the side of her head. The thud of her body slamming into the ground ended the noises that had been erupting from my sister and me. My father stepped over my mother and out of the room. My sister and I gasped in horror as we jumped off the bed to console my mother. Her arms embraced us and her eyes called after my father even though his angry fists had just clobbered her to the floor. She gingerly raised her bruised head as she begged, "Honey, please don't leave! I know that we can work this out. Sean, please don't leave me like this. Don't leave your kids like this. We can work this out. I am sorry. Please!" Her words broke into sobs as my father walked out the door. Her body crumpled to the floor and the three of us huddled on the ground in a pile of tears and sadness.

So many factors had brought my parents to this point in their marriage. The constant fighting and unhappiness had stemmed from many things that I did not comprehend at the time—addictions, mental illness, and incompatibility. At the time, my sister and I were simply caught in the middle.

The addictions that added to the turmoil in my parents' relationship were brought to my attention during a harmless search for treasure. When I was about eight, I went into the bathroom to explore all the nooks and crannies for treasure. My vivid imagination created images of buccaneers, pirates, and swords protecting a mystical "X" that marked the spot of discovery and a booty of gold and jewels. I found a spoon. The spoon was just an ordinary soupspoon. Any young kid could find a misplaced soupspoon, but I found one hidden in a cupboard in the bathroom. "What the hell is this stuff on the spoon?" I thought to myself. Burnt, dark ashes hid the silver luster of the spoon's well. The bottom of the spoon had a multicolored hue that resembled oil mixing with water. I had not found any treasure, nor had I needed to fight off any pirates, but I had unlocked the door to one of my parents' hidden secrets.

While driving several months ago, in a moment of reminiscence, the time that I found the spoon crept into my consciousness. Sometimes elements of life are not understood until experience plays that cruel trick of stripping away the thin veil of naïveté. Thoughts of my childhood often slam into my head with the force of a bullet. Left in a state of confusion, I work to place the pieces of my jumbled memories into an aligned picture. The image of the spoon sprung up from a deep corner of my mind as I drove the car that day. I finally understood that the ashes that stuck to the spoon's silver tone had entered the veins of my family. My blood. My family had injected this fluid bliss into their blood, my psyche. The short high they reached forever scarred my cerebrum. A moment of pleasure, a lifetime of pain—this contradiction seems to be a common theme in the story of life. Small vials laced with white residue of private parties mushroomed around the house. The vials seemed to grow out of the cracks of the floor and suddenly blossom. Somehow my small hands found these little secrets. I hit the steering wheel so hard I thought I might have broken a finger. It's amazing how reality hits you as you mature. Scenes from the past, once gray and fuzzy, blend into a vivid interlude of clarity. My parents were drug addicts.

I recently saw a movie about drug use. I wanted to leave the theater when I saw the young girl cooking the heroin. A sledgehammer hit my chest and my heart fell onto the sticky theater floor. Tears swelled in my eyes from the pain. I am a man and I am not supposed to cry like a woman, I thought to myself. Trying to be the strong one that has a solid grip on reality has put great stress on me since my childhood. My grandparents and aunts and uncles understood what my parents exposed us to, yet they still expected both my sister and me not to fall into the temptations of drugs. I was supposed to set the example for my sister. Who was supposed to set the example for me?

I didn't want to be the father, husband, and son of the family. I wasn't ready for these responsibilities. "Mom, the kitchen is filthy and cockroaches are running all over the place. I guess I will just clean it; you go ahead and stay in bed," I said. Dirty pots, pans, and plates were stacked high in the sink. Moving a single item resulted in multitudes of cockroaches scurrying into the cracks on the walls and the disheveled drawers. I was about seven years old at the time. Some days, I came in from playing outside with my friends and my mother was very attentive and helpful. Other days, she had not gotten out of bed for three days and did not even know if I was in the house or not. On these days, my mother was physically present, but her mind had led her into complete darkness. She became unaware of everything around her. When she slipped into this state of delirium, I had to care for my sister and me. I got used to making Campbell's soup. Food stamps and welfare did not allow for gourmet dinners, but I still had food in my stomach. I cooked, cleaned, and went to school. I had food, a roof over my head, and I was a straight-A student. Yet, my mom would not get out of bed. When her eyes would finally open, in a look of complete despair and surrender, my mother would say, "Listen to me, I don't want to live like this anymore, you two." Even though I knew she would not take her life, I hated it when my mother talked about suicide.

I remember one incident clearly, when I was around five years old and my mother lost her temper. My parents had been arguing like they often did. This time my father screamed at my mother but his hands did not land any blows. His nostrils flared and spittle flew out of his mouth but he never raised a hand. He looked like a rabid dog ready to pounce. Luckily, he did not attack. He decided to slam the front door as he left rather than slam my mother against the wall like so many times before.

He barged out of the house and the wheels of his car left marks in the cement as he drove off. Everything happened so quickly that the door seemed to still be slamming as he drove off. Time froze during those abusive episodes. My father's car could be heard squealing around the corner. My mother could only plop down in a chair behind her. She crumpled into the corner like a pile of dirty clothes. Her bones seemed to melt within her body. Thick streams of mascara-stained tears rolled down her cheeks, she shook with quiet sobs, and her mouth quivered with pain and despair. She was lost. I could see her trying with all her might to keep her head from falling into her chest.

Her arms rose slowly and she reached out for the only support she could find—her children. Her actions begged for an eternal embrace—a permanent sanctuary. My mother said, "Kids, everything is going to be alright. Your dad and I will work things out. I will make sure that everything gets fixed. I do not want you kids to grow up in this kind of shit. You are good kids and don't deserve this!" Her voice shook with each sentence.

I asked her, "Why did Daddy leave?" To my dismay, her right hand suddenly flew into the left side of my face. My jaw dropped and a single tear ran down my cheek. "Why did you hit me, Mom? I didn't do anything," I said. She thought that I had blamed her for my father's departure. She had heard, "Why did you make Daddy leave?" I could only cry along with her, and she grabbed me and held me even closer than before. "I am sorry, I am sorry, I am sorry," she kept saying. My sister and I half stood, half sat while embracing our mother. We all wept.

Today, I wonder why my mother struck me; I was not hit often as a child, and I never received strikes to the face. I may have been spanked, but that did not even come in excess. The only explanation that I have is that my mother had transferred her anger toward my father into a blow to my face. The rage she felt needed to release itself somehow, and, as the nearest male, I fit the profile. I know that she could not find any alternative in her confused mind and I was the closest one, so she blamed me. I feel sorry for what my mother went through in those days. I forgive her for hitting me. It was out of her control—most things seemed to be out of her control in those days.

The devils that controlled my mother and kept her in bed all day wanted to crush the spirit of our house. I didn't understand why she was so tired.

She just kept crying. The sheets and blankets that enveloped her body became a refuge from the battle inside her mind. "Mom, are you okay?" She usually didn't answer me. One time, my grandmother tried to explain my mother's condition to me. "Your mother is a manic-depressive woman," said my grandmother. "She will be better when she starts taking her medication." I didn't know how the medicine was going to vanquish the devils that racked my mother's body with pain. How could pills get rid of a monster that lived inside her? Besides, my mother had a hard time remembering to take her Prozac, lithium, and Xanax. Either she refused to take them or she swallowed them down with big gulps of Bartle and James wine coolers. The names of the green, blue, and white pills had become common knowledge for me. I used to watch as she popped the handful of pills into her mouth. I knew that my mother needed to take these pills so she could take me to baseball practice. "I am going to be on the All-Star team this year. I need to make it to practice," I would say to myself. Looking back, it's funny to think that I was worried about making it to baseball practice. As my mother was going through a severe mental breakdown, I was worried about making the All-Star team. I realize now that I needed my times of ventilation from the stench of reality. I needed to run in the fresh air with other kids, to just *be* a kid.

I went to a private Catholic school in an upper-middle-class neighborhood from kindergarten through eighth grade. My classes consisted of mainly white students with a few splashes of brown and black. Even now, I believe that I am very much a product of the Catholic beliefs and practices that I imbibed in childhood. The colored rays of light that streamed through the stained glass windows of my church are forever etched into my memory. Making the sign of the cross over my body has always been a daily ritual. My religion has become a comfort and support in my times of need. Like breathing, it is an automatic, subconscious activity.

I think of my grandmother, my mother's mother, when I think of religion. How she loves being a Catholic and going to Mass! The greatest honor of her life came when she received an award from the pope. She glowed for weeks and still asks me if I have seen the award and all the pictures of the ceremony. I gaze at the award and the photos with a smile when she puts them in my hands.

If my grandmother had not always been around, I would not be where I am today. She knew when it was time to get us out of the house away from the devils of depression. "Come on kids, you are going to come over to my house for a little while." Those were the most beautiful words. "*Mijo*, are you hungry? I will fix you some *albóndigas*. That will warm you up." The magic of Grandma's food served as my escape from the constant bombardment of poverty, depression, and confusion. Looking back, I know that my grandmother's love and the faith she helped instill in me are two factors that saved me from ruin.

I was sitting in my grandparents' dimly lit dining room when the phone rang. I was about thirteen years old. My mother had left for the supermarket to pick up items for dinner. She and I had been having a small argument prior to her departure—something to do with my homework. Nothing about the disagreement suggested that we would not apologize to each other soon after. I asked as she hurriedly left, "Mom, where are you going?" "The store," she responded. "See ya soon," I said in my sweetest voice. I had tried to apologize and tell her everything was all right by the tone of my voice. I had never really said the words "I am sorry," but I felt that things were settled from our argument. I vividly recall watching her walk out the front door of my grandparents' house—her wavy brown hair picking up as she stepped down onto the porch. She had lost weight then and looked very healthy. She always had to fight the weight but had finally gotten to a point that she looked fit, even vibrant.

In a little over an hour, the phone rang. I was still sitting at the dining room table doing my homework. An unfamiliar man's voice asked if I was Mary's son. "I am your father's boss. He received a call from the hospital and was told that your mother is in intensive care. He wanted me to inform you of the situation. Someone had found her unconscious in her car at the supermarket," said the unfamiliar voice. I thanked the man. As I hung up the phone, I yelled to my grandfather and sister, "Mom is in the hospital. We need to get over there right away."

My mother was not a stranger to the emergency room. A combination of severe asthma, chronic health problems, and self-inflicted wounds had given her plenty of opportunities to visit the ER. Incidentally, the L.A. race riots of 1992 were in progress and many fires had erupted in the past few days. The smoke had turned the skies a dirtier color than usual. I wondered if the smoke had caused a severe asthma attack and she had not reacted quickly enough to take her medication. All these thoughts raced through my head as we drove to the hospital. Though the hospital was only several blocks away, the ride seemed to take an eternity. Every light signal would turn red as soon as we came near. My palms dampened with sweat as my nerves rose in anticipation of the worst. I gripped the door handle with white knuckles.

The hospital had become a familiar place to me because of my mother's frequent visits and because of my own asthma-related visits. As soon as my foot hit the hospital ground pavement, I took off running for the front desk. "Eric, don't run, and calm down! Everything is going to be all right!" my grandfather yelled after me. I knew that everything was not okay from the tone of the man's voice on the phone. I reached the information desk and asked for my mother's room.

Multiple wires, tubes, and needles ran into her body. Small strands of her hair fell across her pale face. My mother always had a beautiful bronze tone to her skin, but something had stripped away her familiar glow. Her full lips looked chapped and dry. I reached for her hand and felt her warm touch against my skin. As I touched her palm, the familiar smell of her skin seemed to float through the air. "Mommy, we are here. Please open your eyes if you can," I said as I stood over her. Her eyelids did not move. She remained completely still.

The physicians informed us that a man had found my mother slumped in her car. The doctors had done several tests upon her arrival and found that she had had an aneurysm. The aneurysm had burst in her brain and caused massive internal bleeding. "If she is to survive, then she will be heavily brain damaged," said the doctor. "If my mother gets out of this alive," I thought to myself, "then she will be a human vegetable—not able to use her limbs, not able to communicate, not able to even process thoughts." At that point, I pictured my beautiful mother sitting in a wheelchair and drooling on herself, unable to touch me again with her tenderness. I fought off the thoughts of wishing for her death and prayed only for her to live. I told myself that I could handle having a brain-damaged mother.

It seemed like I didn't leave the hospital for two and a half days. The reception room became a familiar place as I slumped into one of the cushy chairs. Friends and family would come in with a half-smile, half-frown on their faces as they entered the room. I remember a constant urge to break down crying, but forcing myself to stop. After my many hours of waiting and hoping for the best, the doctor entered the waiting room. His blue hospital scrubs swished as he walked through the door. As his lips began to part, I knew what his next words would be. "I am sorry, but she has no brain activity. We have officially pronounced her brain dead," the doctor said. As much as I did not want to hear those words, I knew it was coming. I had known as soon as the stranger's voice had asked me if I was Mary's son. Many times before, I had had premonitions of my mother's death, and now all my visions had become a reality. As I stood in the waiting room, digesting the news of my mother's death, I thought back on the years that I had dreamed of her death and why I had both dreaded and hoped for that day to come.

Pictures of my childhood slipped into my mind's eye. In one vision, when I was around nine years old, my mother had started having a "mental episode" and was intent on drinking away the effects of her chemical imbalance. With a fifth of Smirnoff vodka in her hand, she kept taking long swigs. The bottle would hit her lips and she would follow it with some orange juice. This started at the house and continued as she drove my sister and me toward the mountains. We started going up this winding hill in the foothills of our local mountains. I could see the glazed look in my mother's eyes as she stared out the windshield. Her hands gripped the steering wheel tightly. The old brown Volvo swerved left to right as she clumsily adjusted the wheels in the tight turns of the mountain road. She was out of control and she knew it. I could tell that she was torn between having us with her and leaving us with family. Every minute on the windy road, I worried that my mother would steer us toward a dramatic ending—images of the brown Volvo flying off the road and cascading down the mountain's granite face kept passing through my head. She often talked of suicide and sometimes included us in her plans of starvation or some other means of death. I was afraid that this would be an occasion when my sister and I were included in the plans.

As large pines whizzed by the car, the steep ravine kept pulling my eyes to the side of the road as we neared its edge many times. Death seemed so near as the car's wheels slid off the pavement and kicked up the dirt of the road's shoulder. My mother's arms tensed as she veered us back onto the paved road. A quick yelp of fear broke the silence. My sister usually became quiet when my mother went into these states. She had learned that keeping quiet was the best thing that she could do. Her little scared eyes looked at me from the back seat and her small voice called to my mother to stop the car. The terrified tone in my sister's voice begged for the wild ride to end.

Tears welled up in my eyes. Tears streamed down my poor sister's face and her body shook. "Eric, I want you to drive us down the hill. I can't do it anymore," begged my mother. "Mom, I can't drive the car. I don't even know how to drive. You can get us down the hill. You have to get us down the hill," I said and hoped. After pleading with my mother to stop the car, she finally pulled over and stopped. I climbed out of the front seat and into the back seat. My sister had decided to sit in the front; I lay down in the backseat and closed my eyes. As always, I had left my mother to her own devices and my sister with the burden of supporting her. My sister had always had the strength to be near my mother during these episodes. The strength she showed baffled me. When we finally reached the base of the hill, I opened my eyes and thanked God for our survival. My mother drove toward our house and I just hoped that we would make it home.

On the way, we stopped very near my father's house. My mother got out and crouched on the curb to urinate. She had simply pulled the car over, strolled from the driver's side, and used the car as a shield to the passing traffic. Thoughts pulsed through my head as she pulled her pants along her thighs. "Dad's house is only two blocks away from here. If we run, we can make it there before Mom even has time to catch us," I said to my sister. The frightened eyes of a beautiful young girl stared back at me with a look of apprehension. "We can't leave Mom like this all alone. She needs us to help her," my sister replied. "Screw that! I am makin' a run for it," I said. A trickling sound reached my ears, and my eyes moved toward the stream of liquid running over the curb's edge. Although the sun's light had long faded, I surveyed the area searching for some passerby that would see my mother pissing on the street. I knew that the opportunity had come for me to run.

My heart vigorously pumped blood into my legs. The dark, damp pavement flew by as I ran toward my father's house in search of an impossible solution. Tingles and shivers overtook my body as I ran in anticipation of capture from behind. I pictured my mother's hand reaching a distance of two blocks and clutching the top of my right shoulder. "Where the hell do you think that you are going?" she would have said. As my feet struck the concrete leading down my father's driveway, I knew that I had escaped a fretful episode.

When I reached my father's door, I breathed a sigh of relief. The brown wooden door was cool to the touch as my knuckles rapped a tune of despair. "Dad, are you in there?" I asked. "Yo, how is it going, *mijito*? What's up?" he replied. His eyes were reading my expression and his ears listened to my heavy breaths as my chest heaved and my eyes danced in confusion. "Dad, Mom is down the street and she is peeing on the curb. She is really drunk and she has been driving us all over the place. I don't know what to do. She stopped really close by so I decided to run over here," I said. His arm reached out toward my shoulder and I moved into his room. His familiar smell comforted me and his strong hand put me at ease. I knew that I had found a temporary refuge.

My mother's attempt to apprehend me was imminent and she would soon be knocking on the door for me. No longer than five minutes passed before my little sister came into the room crying. "Mom wants you to come out to the car and come home with us," she said. My mother, in a drunken stupor, followed close behind her. "Get your little ass in the car," she yelled in a burst of spittle. Strands of her hair fell in tangled masses over her eyes and her face was contorted from alcohol's poisonous power. The beauty of her face had melted away into a visage of my deepest fears—an intoxicated, lost soul.

My father lunged toward my mother. His angry hands forced her out of the room and toward the sloped driveway. Shutting the door behind him, he turned and told my sister and me, "Stay in here while I take care of your mother." Ugly, unforgettable sounds followed each push and shove as my father trounced my mother. The distinct clunk of a body hitting car metal rung out loud as my mother hit her head on the hood of my father's truck. Defeated by her ex-husband and betrayed by her children, my mother retreated in a battered state. My heart raced with satisfaction and self-hatred as I heard my father "take care" of my mother. My sister and I watched television for distraction from reality. Our role models, our confidants, our parents once again fell victim to abuse—both alcohol and physical.

In an attempt to assuage the situation, I reached for the phone on the wall. I heard my grandmother's voice through the line and I told her, "Grandma, Grandma. Mom is really drunk and can't drive the car anymore. We are at my dad's house and need you to pick us up. My dad says that she is okay but can't take us the way she is." "Okay, *mijo*, we will come and get you," my grandmother said.

Fifteen minutes passed as we anxiously waited for my grandparents to arrive. My sister, mother, and I climbed into the car and started driving down the hill toward our grandparents' house. My mother stunk of liquor and yelled at my grandparents: "You don't love me. My kids don't love me. Look what that bastard did to me. He hit me so hard. Look at my head. I have a fucking huge bump on my head. That bastard. Why did you go to him, Eric? Why? Why did you do that to me?" My mother continued ranting about her condition as the car's wheels rolled us toward our destination.

At a stoplight, she attempted to jump out of the car. My grandfather locked the doors, but my mother persisted on getting out of the car. "Let me out. I don't want to be with any of you. I don't want to be like this. I just want to die. Let me go," she yelled. With all of my strength, I grabbed her and held her against her seat. Sitting behind her in the backseat allowed me a quick hold on her arms as she reached for the passenger side door. "Stop it, Mom," I yelled, "Stop it. I am not going to let you go. Stop fighting against me. We are going home." My grandmother spoke to my mother in Spanish, "¡Mijita, cálmate!"

When we reached my grandparents' home, we all helped to get my mother into the house. Although she could walk, she stumbled and had a hard time staying on her feet. "I don't need your fuckin' help. I can do it on my own," she yelled. "Just get in the house, Mom. I don't want you to hurt yourself," I said. As I lay on my grandfather's bed watching television, my mother let out short gasps of pain from the back room. She called for my sister, "Kelly, come here honey. Mommy needs you." My sister has since recounted this scene to me. My mother had taken a large knife from the kitchen and cut open her stomach. Blood had splattered onto the bathroom floor and walls—red speckles of my mother's life had stained the whitewashed walls. In shock and horror, my sister helped my mother clean blood off the floor and walls of this horrible scene.

The night ended with my mother in the hospital. From that point on, I sensed that we would soon be back in the hospital to visit my mother in her last minutes of life. After this experience, I knew that my mother would die a young woman. I wanted this to happen because she was a danger to my sister and me.

I was thirteen years old when I stood over my mother and watched her fade away. Tears streamed down my face and my heart ached. A unique and inexplicable pain gripped my chest. I looked at her sweet mouth and thought of the loving words and kisses that had surfaced from those full lips. She looked beautiful as she slipped into eternal sleep.

All those years of wishing for my mother's death had finally come true, and guilt streamed through my veins. Though my mother had been unpredictable and at times violent, I still had a deep love for her. In my fantasy of her death, losing her did not hurt as much as it did in reality. I already felt the loss of those moments of tender caresses and loving words as I held her clammy hand and sensed her spirit drift away. As I cried, though, a growing excitement arose in my heart. The desire for personal safety and happiness, for my sister and me, overwhelmed the feelings of love for my mother. The legal documents that gave my mother custody would now fall into my father's hands. In losing a mother, I would gain a father that I only hoped could provide the consistent love and safety that my mother had not.

Following a few days of tears shed, my sister and I moved from my grandparents' home to live with our father. We both brimmed with enthusiasm about the new living situation. During the years of our parents' divorce, the weekends that we had spent with our father were filled with hours of entertainment. Going to the theater, riding ponies, and watching television were typical activities when we were with our father. My sister and I perceived those fun-filled days to be a normal week at our father's home. Living with our father looked very promising after the heart-wrenching loss of our mother.

When I moved in with my father, he and I shared a bedroom. We even slept in the same bed. I liked sleeping together—the feel of his thick, muscular arm over my body gave me comfort. Being a manual laborer for most of his life and working out at the gym had kept his body in good shape. As I struggled with the loss of my mother, I would reach for his arm when I needed reassurance that he would care for me. Since my parents' divorce, I had not spent a lot of time with my father. The only men that I had interacted with were the fly-by-night men that my mother had brought into the house. I longed for a male that I could love and emulate, and now I finally had a consistent man in my life. With tenderness and care, my father would scratch my back and put me to sleep—his masculine, callused hands felt good against my skin. These reassuring caresses put me at ease and made the new living situation seem that much better. The masculine love that I had been missing for all those years was now supplied by the man I wanted it from the most—my father.

In the midst of my mother's death and the move to my father's home, I was at the cusp of my adolescence. A growing curiosity about the opposite sex had sprung within me. To my delight, my father had no problem talking to me about sex and showing me his full collection of *Playboy* magazines from the bottom of the bookshelf. All my questions concerning sex and women were always answered. He would tell me about "pussy" and "tits" all the time. "Take a look at this set of tits. She has a great pair," my dad would often say. The excitement of seeing the nude pictures and having my father treat me as an equal made me feel like a man.

I remember an occasion when my older cousin had come to stay with us for a short time. He and my father talked about the first time that they had had sex. "I remember how nervous I was the first time," said my dad. "I had gone down to Mexico with my cousin and I had sex with this prostitute. That was the first time for me. This fuckin' broad had droopy tits, but she really knew what she was doing. She had a lot of experience and it showed." I remember listening to the story in awe. My eyes were fixed on my father's lips as he spoke these words of wisdom. My father and cousin had lost their virginity at around fourteen years old. Losing my virginity became a mental goal as I sat there listening to the two men's stories. I didn't want to be the only one that had not experienced sex. Having all this access to sexual material at the beginning of my adolescence changed my perception of sex. Although I had learned for years that it was a sin, I began looking at sex in a different light. I could not wait to slip myself into a girl's most secret part.

All these new thoughts raced through my head. My access to sexual knowledge seemed endless and my father's love seemed infinite. I often heard the words "I love you more than anything" spilling from his lips. Everything was perfect in our new house with our dad. My sister and I felt that we had finally reached a stable home with love and happiness. After only several weeks living with him, we would find out that every day would not be like the fun weekends. The daily duties of a parent would soon prove too difficult for my father. Lacking basic parental skills, my father began resenting me when I had questions about homework or school. "You are a smart kid," he said, "do your own damn homework." The added stress of raising children soon began to take its toll on him and he escaped his new existence through small bottles of tequila. The angry, alcoholic father that I had learned to fear during my parents' marriage reentered my life.

He often had the little plastic bottles by his side. When he felt the urge for a shot, he could simply sneak away and empty the bottle down his throat. Hearing the sounds of him heaving his guts into the commode became a common occurrence. Through his drunken fits of anger, my father's true existence became clearer to me. A man in his mid-forties who still lived with his parents in a converted garage—that was my dad. My grandmother, dad's mother, continued to cook for him, wash his clothes, and not charge him high rent. All the things I had hated about him when he beat my mother started springing back into my mind. The love and tenderness that he showed began to dwindle and the lack of parental support he offered with school and sports started taking their toll. Like my mother, my father had his weaknesses and could not care for his children. I knew that my time had come to try to find a better life, and for good this time.

The summer following my mother's death, I had begun spending a lot of time with my aunt, the younger of my mother's two sisters. She even offered to take me to work in her office. The days I spent with her and my uncle, her husband, did not resemble anything I had ever experienced in either of my homes. The polite and caring manner in which they interacted with each other and their daughter seemed so different than my parents' relationship with each other, my sister, and me. The growing problems with my father only made their home seem that much more inviting. After a few weeks of worrying and thinking, I asked my aunt if I could live with her and her family.

Leaving my father's home proved emotionally difficult. I always seemed to be turning my back on one of my parents. First I had left my mother for my father, and now I was leaving my father for another family. Even though these feelings of guilt rushed through my body, I knew that I could not live with another alcoholic parent.

Moving in with my new family became the best decision I had ever made. Worrying about being on time to school or having food to eat became things of the past. Consistent love and tenderness were offered in my new household and I knew that I had finally found my dream home. My sister had not joined me at first, but after several months of debate, I convinced her to move in with me. Finally, the two of us could live together in a stable, nonabusive household. The constant, steady love and attention that my "new parents" offered began stripping away the pain from my preadolescent years. The tense feeling of apprehension of another chaotic episode being around the corner finally left me. For the first time, I could focus my thoughts solely on school, sports, and my identity.

The four years I spent in high school differed immensely from my preteen years. Every morning, around 7, my adopted mother would open my door and say, "Rise and shine. It's time to get up for school." The sweet words became my alarm clock every morning. "Rise and shine" would ring through my ears for several minutes before my eyelids lifted and my eyes adjusted to the sunbeams streaming through the miniblinds. Reaching into my drawer, I would always find clean clothes and underwear. Every weekend, my adopted mother would make sure that my clothes were washed for the next week. She would never allow the piles of dirty clothes that used to build up in my old room. She always made sure that I had clean clothes and a clean room. "Eric, bring in your hamper and separate your clothes. I am going to start washing now," she would say. The prior lack of reliability and dependability in my life had been assuaged by my adopted mother's constant attention to the important details. Whenever I wanted something clean to wear, I had it. Whenever I was hungry, I was fed. I no longer worried about the simple procedures of life that had slipped by me on occasions during my childhood.

There were still a few aspects of my old life that I missed. Although I wanted the comfort of being a child under my new parents' wings, the jump from being treated as an adult to being treated as a child had come suddenly. I longed to talk like I had with my father about sex and women. Instead, I dealt with my sexuality and all the questions of my past on my own. Neither my sister nor I talked to each other or our adopted parents about our past. "Let your mother rest," my adopted mother would say. "She loved you very much, and that is all that matters. Your father loves you, too." I attempted to figure out who I had become because of all the things that had happened in my life, but my new parents did not wish to talk about it. Though they saved me from an impossible living condition, they did not help me overcome the internal questions I had. I struggled with my identity as a Latino male and the influences that growing up in a chaotic household had on me.

After high school, these questions would come into full blossom as I entered a new life at college. My successes in high school, both in sports and academics, ensured my access to a prominent college of my choice. After much searching and discussion with my adopted parents, I decided to head off for New Hampshire. The years I spent at the Ivy League institution allowed me to understand my ethnicity and openly speak with pride about my heritage. Through all the chaos of my childhood, I realize my mother had always instilled a deep pride for my heritage in me. "Never forget that you are Mexican American, Eric," she would say. "Don't let anyone take that away from you. That is who you are."

The years of my adolescence with my adopted parents had saved me from disaster, but they had also created new questions for me to answer. Living under the guidance of an Anglo father and a Latina mother gave me a new perspective on my culture. Although my Anglo father offered constant love, I could not speak to him about my questions of ethnicity. My adopted mother did not embrace her ethnicity as I did, so she did not offer advice on such topics. It finally dawned on me that I had to combine all the lessons I had learned through my life. My birth parents had both been unsteady and chaotic, yet they had instilled a pride for my heritage deep within me and given me the tools to succeed. My adopted parents had allowed those tools to blossom and ensured my success through their constant attention and love. Also, my grandmother's love and religion had served as beacons of light in my time of need. This collage of values and lessons would work as my guidance through life.

I have light-brown eyes, thick dark hair, nice full lips, and brown skin. My mother and father have passed these strong features on to me; yet I wonder how many of the internal demons that they contained have been passed to me as well. My slicked back hair and my manner of dress resemble my father's sense of style, but I hope that I have overcome the negative images of women and relationships that he taught to me. The influence of having a father full of machismo and anger toward women has been a daily struggle, yet I know that I have overcome many of those evils. Likewise, the control I have over my existence does not resemble the turmoil that my mother lived in; I do not seek continual excitement as she did. Having a meaningful relationship with love and tenderness is more important to me than the excitement of conflict that my mother looked for in her relationships.

Born the son of Mexican American parents, I am proud of my ethnicity, yet I strive to transcend the stereotypes of the Latino male. The turbulence that I lived through showed me the antithesis of my ideal life. My adopted parents' love, compassion, and dependability will serve as a guide to not replicate that environment for my children. All the influences of my life have shaped me into the man I have become; yet I am my own man now and dictate my destiny. I can finally take control. My entrance into a new chapter in my life will truly tell if I have succeeded in vanquishing all the devils that haunt my past and perhaps still dwell deep within me, but I feel secure that my own family and children will enjoy the stability and safety I sought as a child.

On graduating from Dartmouth, Eric Martinez accepted a position with a global real estate investment and property management firm in their Chicago headquarters. Working with a team of sales professionals, he advised Fortune 500 companies on the disposition of their real estate assets around the United States. Eric belonged to local sporting clubs in the Windy City. After four years of cold winters, Eric moved back to Los Angeles where he now lives and continues his real estate career, without the cold winters. The future still looks bright, and he is sure that big things are on the way.

Joseph Rodriguez   Dignity and Doubt

I was lost in Chicago. I had gotten off the subway at the station my father had named, but he had not been certain about the address of the building I should go to. He had guessed, and guessed wrong, and as a result I had been searching in vain for over an hour on one of the hottest days of the year—a mixture of frustration, exhaustion, anger, self-pity, and sympathy for my father all burning in my eyes.

I had not eaten since I left my house in Westmont, Illinois. I had taken the two o'clock Metro train one hour into the city, and switched at Union Station to the subway, which took me into this unfamiliar territory in the south side of Chicago. For suburban kids, the ethnic neighborhoods of Chicago are all an apparition; only downtown Chicago is real. I did not have more than a few dollars on me, so I stopped at a McDonald's and sifted through my school bag for loose change to buy something off the dollar menu. After walking an hour in the wrong direction, I stopped at an auto-repair garage and asked if there was a jail in the area. I got suspicious glances, but the people did not seem entirely unfamiliar with my predicament. They told me it was in the other direction—the direction I had come from. Grudgingly, I turned back.

I recall being terribly tired as I walked along the street for the second time. I passed the mini-mall, the Old Navy department store, the Chinese man selling watches on the street, and the woman selling purses next to him. Finally, I reached the Chicano neighborhood where I first got off the train, where booksellers were peddling books in Spanish. Any other time I would have welcomed the sights and sounds of the city, but this day my mind was occupied by only one thing. I stopped twice more that afternoon to ask where the Cook County Detention Center was. A man finally directed me to a tall building with metal bars on the windows. As I looked up, I understood why I had missed it the first time; its inconspicuous facade was covered by wooden signs painted blue. I walked around to the back, searching for an entrance, past a gate and some large trailers, and finally up a short set of stairs, also painted blue. I timidly stepped in. There was a barred window directly in front of me with a guard behind it. Someone was at the window speaking with the guard. I asked another guard where I could drop things off for an inmate, and they told me I had to get in line. I went to the back of the line and took my place among the roughs of Chicago—the high school dropouts, the large black women wearing spandex, the Latinas with children in their arms who had come to visit their husbands or boyfriends. I noticed that I was the only man in the line, and that with my collared polo shirt I was the best-dressed person there.

The guards moved with no particular sense of urgency. This gave me time to look at the "wanted" posters on the walls, exclusively featuring black and Latino men. I also saw a Polaroid photograph of a woman in handcuffs, and beneath it was a warning: "If you try to smuggle drugs in, you'll end up in here." It seemed a shocking warning when I considered that it was addressed to me. I was further saddened by the disheveled appearance of everything and everyone around me. The depressing conditions were overwhelming, particularly to someone who had never seen real deprivation. I remember thinking, "There is no hope here, and I am here," and those two thoughts together hurt me. I tried not to take this as a value judgment of me individually, tried desperately not to internalize anything. I wondered what my being there meant about my father and me, and how I could overcome it. At least I could take comfort in the knowledge that I would be leaving there that day.

Then I was suddenly hurt by the thought of my father, who would *not* be leaving, and I tried not to develop any solid mental images of him and this place as one. As I looked around and noticed the lack of any white faces, including the guards, I thought that perhaps this prison was just part of minority culture. The titles of disturbing books that I had read in the past—*Savage Inequalities, The Autobiography of Malcolm X, Makes Me Wanna Holler*—ran through my mind, along with upsetting statistics: blacks and Latinos represent "X" percent of the national population, but represent "Y" percent of the population incarcerated in adult facilities; there are more black men in jail than in college; black and Latino men are incarcerated at a higher rate than any other race. I was aware that these figures referred to me, and that this was not something I could escape. My father was a part of those figures, and that scared me. Then, above the noise of those figures buzzing in my brain, I could hear the words of Malcolm X's that I read my junior year of high school—something along the lines of the fact that every prominent black figure in America has been incarcerated at some point. This made me feel better about this experience and about my father and allowed me to believe, as I had believed for years, that there was something wrong with the system as opposed to there being something wrong with the people of my race.

All these thoughts ran through my head as I stood there in line with the frustrated, angry, self-loathing feeling still stinging inside me. I felt both pity and fear for and from all the people around me who had to endure a similar experience, visiting loved ones who had failed by society's standards. I tried to envision what their lives might be like; how they lived; how they survived; how they interacted with one another; how they coped with their unenviable predicament. These people, hardened by the American system, were still beautiful and glorious.

At last I crept up to the window, and the guard asked me unsympathetically for the name of the prisoner for whom I was dropping things off. I gave my father's name, then reached into my bag and pulled out a package of white socks and T-shirts, his sandals, and a pile of *New Yorker* and *Economist* magazines. The lady at the window told me I had to remove all the mail-away inserts from the magazines. I remember this because I could not see the reasoning behind it. Nonetheless, I began to go through each one, ripping out the cards. The guard gave me a receipt to fill out. I did this slowly, checking the appropriate boxes and filling in the correct information. Then I left, feeling relieved. I was glad I had been able to find the place on my own. I had time on the train ride home to think about what had happened and to get my thoughts in order. I have often found that order is more a state of mind than it is a state of affairs.

These events took place during the summer between my high school and college careers. I realized how difficult it had become to focus on things, since everything seemed to pale in comparison to my father's problems. I feared many things and didn't want my mind to linger too long on any of them because they hurt to think about. After all of my father's struggle to get out of poverty, to forge a new path, to find a better life after City College, law school, and Harvard Business School; after the army, and France, and Brooklyn, and struggle, he was here—in a detention center. It seemed that we had met society's expectations for us as Latinos; it hadn't mattered that I was the best-dressed (and probably best-educated) person in that line at the jail; I was still in that line and at that jail.

I left feeling bitter and angry—feeling I had learned something that day about the system and the way it is reinforced generation after generation. I recognized with fear the weight of being Latino. I wondered if my father's experience perhaps should not have been so unexpected. I had been quite sheltered and been taught to put my father on a pedestal. When news of his imperfections came to me in scattered fragments from familial sources, the experience was always shocking and upsetting. I knew that statistics suggested it was much more likely that my father would be in jail than on Wall Street. Still, from what I understood of his experience, I figured he was being held in the detention center because of some mistake he had unconsciously made. I did not believe (or did not want to believe) that he had committed some violation with malign intent.

That summer before college I hardly saw my father. The separation gave me time to think and to reevaluate my view of him, as well as my view of myself. Of course, it was not at the age of eighteen that I realized my father's fallibility for the first time. He was always my father, and I loved him regardless. But in my early adolescence I began to develop a conception of him as a person separate from his connection to me. Growing up, my father was absent a lot because of his job as a corporate lawyer in downtown Chicago, so my mother was the person my sister and I spent most of our time with. My father was home on weekends and was certainly a visible and important part of our life, but he was not there to discipline us, not there to pick us up from school, not there to take us to the doctor. This was my mother's role. By assuming the traditional male role of provider, he cleared space for himself as the dominant figure in the household, and we treated him as such. I think my father, largely because of his Puerto Rican background, took seriously the role of provider—if he failed to provide it was his fault, and he believed he had failed us. I recall thinking of him in this way, and know that it had an important influence on the development of my own conception of family, and on my view of the role that would one day belong to me.

Leading a sheltered life, it was not until middle school that I became aware of myself as an individual. Middle school was trying for me because of the changes I was undergoing physically and mentally. It was the closest I ever came to being rebellious. At the time, I recall feeling confused, as though no one understood me except for my friends, and this was true for the most part. It is only now, looking back, that I have the confidence to say that my teachers were not good teachers who fostered my interest in any subjects; instead, they went against me and made me feel as though I was perpetually wrong. When I was in need of support I was only offered criticism. I remember a feeling of being cast off. I truly felt as though I was more intelligent than they gave me credit for. Conjuring up memories of my father, whom the administration in his high school in Brooklyn had tried to place in vocational classes, I wondered if their treatment (or mistreatment) of me in turn was because I was a minority. Could the same thing have been true at my small, suburban private school as was true for my father at his large, urban public school a generation prior? Throughout my middle school years, I never had one minority teacher with whom I could identify. Though I was becoming aware of myself and others around me at this time, I don't think I was yet familiar with racism. If it had guided other people's decisions or their treatment of me as the "Latino kid," I was wholly unaware, and labeled their actions toward me by some other name.

My mother discouraged such sentiments. She is very light skinned and has always held to the American Dream that if you work hard, you can make it. With her Jewish heritage, she tried to instill in us Jewish cultural values. Though we adopted some of these, I found it easier (possibly due to my appearance) to identify as Latino. In the coming years I would have minor battles with my mom about her ideas and about the challenges that minorities face in society. She has always been a believer in the power of an individual to achieve, despite her experiences teaching in a poor neighborhood. The way she put it, blacks and Latinos, in order to progress, needed to stop making excuses. I recall one incident, years later while my father was in jail, where I had a disagreement with my mother about the role of race in society. Afterward, my dark-skinned uncle, Anthony, pulled me aside and told me, "You know, your mother will never be able to understand the way you feel." He was referring to the difference in our skin color, and his words in many ways reaffirmed the validity of my own experience and my own feelings in the face of racism.

During middle school, however, disagreements with my mother were based around my less than perfect grades and my relations with my teachers. Because I felt I was being pushed away by the adults in my life, I was drawn to my friends for support. The friends I had then were the first I had really chosen for myself without parental interference. I remember my parents telling me at the time that I should expand my circle of friends. They didn't understand that at the time I had no particular desire to do so.

I was content with them because they were there for me when I felt the rest of the world was not.

The end of middle school marked a turning point for me. I was physically and mentally separated from the world I had known growing up. I can trace this separation back to one moment, because it was, for me, the first in a series of events that would introduce me to adulthood.

The last day of classes, I played football with my friends after school and then went to town with them to get pizza and candy, and to generally declare our independence, as we always did on Fridays. My mother found me that day outside of Starbucks. She pulled up in her champagne-colored Lexus with my sister riding in the back. I could see that my sister was upset, as she questioned where I had been. "Something happened with the house," my mother stated suddenly. She allowed the silence to hang, and then said that moving men were relocating our furniture to storage: "We're not going to be allowed to go into the house, but we can pick up our things." As we made the familiar drive up to our house, I was met by unfamiliar faces—the large moving men who took our things out of our house did so with obvious unease. As they moved in and out of my house, I wondered what was happening. I knew that my mother did not know all the details, and I could not gather the courage to ask my father. In my memory he is absent from this scene. Whether or not memory serves me correctly, I do not know.

That night we drove to a cheap hotel in a neighboring town. The first night we spent there we were disoriented, confused, and tired. I was trying to be upbeat and supportive of my family, not showing that what was happening was bothering me. And for the most part it was not. Sure I had unanswered questions, but I could not imagine at the time how what was happening that day might affect my future. A sense of security and optimism has always been ingrained in my psyche. Perhaps this is why, in my own naive way, I never thought that a bad experience was necessarily negative. I remember being envious of people with difficult, dislocated lives, because I felt that they led the most interesting lives and had the best stories to tell. I was unable to imagine that anything could deter a person from their path. It was not so much a belief in fate as it was a belief in the resiliency of an individual—a belief that no matter how awful the circumstances, a person could always recover. So it was that I took this stay in the hotel as a break from my everyday life—an opportunity for a story, and nothing more.

My mother, sister, and I were scheduled to go to Puerto Rico in a couple of days, as we always did during the summer. At the time, we viewed the hotel stay as temporary until we could go to our other home in Puerto Rico. We spent our time on vacation mostly with each other. Here, at least, things could feel normal. I figured that we would go to Puerto Rico, my father would solve whatever problem had occurred, and we would move back to our house in Downer's Grove. I did not know at the time that it was the last trip I would make to Puerto Rico for many years.

When we finally did return from the island, it was not to the hotel we had been in, but it was not to our house either. My father had, again for reasons unknown, decided to relocate to a Howard Johnson hotel in West-mont, Illinois. I was disappointed, but this, too, I took in stride. The ho-tel looked as though it had been constructed in the 1950s. We got one room with two double beds for the four of us. My mother and sister shared one bed, my father and I the other. Our Spartan existence was interesting for some time. Several weeks later we moved into the sole suite at the ho-tel. Here we had two rooms—a bedroom and a living room with a kitchen. I observed that my father was somewhat humbled (though he had never been excessively proud) by the circumstances. I wondered, was it wrong to be embarrassed by this, and further, was it wrong to be embarrassed for my father? By this time it was clear to me that we were not going back to our old house, so when friends would ask where I was living and what had hap-pened, I would respond with feigned surprise, "Oh, I didn't tell you? We're moving!" Although I was far from sure where we were moving to and where I was headed, I wasn't concerned because of my belief that every-thing would go on. Whether I was living here or there, I believed it would not alter my direction in life. Still, I wasn't sure what had happened to the house, but I suppressed my curiosity partly out of reverence for my par-ents and partly out of a supposition that whatever answer I received would somehow be insufficient and unsatisfactory.

The first derailment came late that summer. My sister was preparing to enter her junior year of high school at our private school in Naperville, Illinois. A few weeks before the start of the school year, she went away for soccer preseason with the rest of her team. Because my father was away at work, my mother and I spent a lot of time together. The two of us went searching for houses. During this time, my mother slowly revealed to me the depressing state of our finances. We had lost the house due to compli-cations with the mortgage—the details of which were never made clear to me.

I knew at that time that we also owed my school a lot of money. This was made apparent to me several months before, when my mother had sat me down to explain that for my middle school graduation, instead of receiving a diploma, I would receive an empty folder. The school took this action with the intention of pressuring my parents to pay the outstanding bill, but this action completely neglected my feelings and was ultimately very hurtful to me. It was one of the first times (with many similar experiences to follow) that I felt like an outsider in a place where I was supposed to be most at home. To this day, I have never received my diploma. My mother told me afterward that she had had to argue with the administrators, since they had wanted to exclude me from the ceremony altogether. I never blamed my parents for their inability to pay their debts—particularly as it related to my schooling. How could I, since I was the one benefiting? On the contrary, I took it as an expression of their love that they were willing to suffer such anxiety for the sake of providing me with greater educational opportunity. The farthest I could get in my own attitude toward them was to consider them irresponsible, but never bad people, because I knew that they were well intentioned.

Already owing money to my school, my parents did not want to accrue more debt, and so they looked into the public schools in Westmont. My mother and I went to visit the high school. It seemed nice enough. It was huge, with two thousand students. It was also far more diverse than any school I had previously attended. It was only later that I learned, as is true in so many high schools in the United States, that the student body was, for the most part, segregated by race and class. I approached the idea of switching schools with flexibility. People are always hesitant when they encounter the unknown, but I knew that I had not particularly enjoyed the last couple of years at Naperville Country Day School because of the difficulties I had experienced, struggling to define myself throughout middle school. I tried to reassure my mother that it was okay for us to switch schools, that they should save that money, and put it toward some other thing.

My sister returned from camp expecting to go back to Naperville with her friends, and she was far less accepting of the change. I think this set a tone for her, as she did not like the rest of her time in high school. We went to the high school together several weeks before classes were scheduled to start. The woman at the office was Latina, and I remember being comforted by hearing her speak with my mother in Spanish. I have always had a similar feeling whenever I hear my parents speak to others in Spanish, as though the two of them (and me by association) were in on some secret—

with the same power as a wink and a smile or a head nod, speaking in Spanish (or having dark skin) in many places meant that you were not going to be mistreated by those who were like you. The Latina woman administered several tests to gauge what level classes we should be placed in. She put me in all honors classes—with my strong feeling of entitlement and confidence, I would have been disappointed by anything less. My sister was placed in all honors, except math.

When we started school, I found the place intimidating. Playing football, basketball, and baseball, however, I quickly found my niche among the popular kids. To my delight, several of my teammates were in my class, and I became close with them. The high school served students from several middle schools, so I took comfort in the fact that, as freshmen, most of the people did not know one another. I also found that, though this was a public school, the kids were very sheltered, far less versed in cultural literacy and slang than I was. I felt that this gave me some sort of advantage over them. My friends at Naperville had been wealthy, but many of them lived closer to the city, had grown up or spent time there, and were into "acting black." Most of my peers at Westmont were entirely ignorant in this regard.

I recall being treated like the smart kid who knew slang, and I would occasionally mention an experience that was racialized, which I knew none of my classmates could identify with. I think I encouraged this view of me, as I thought it gave me credibility, conferred some toughness. Knowing the mannerisms and the language provided a sense of belonging—cultural shibboleths by which we could distinguish "us" and "them." It was generally felt that the white kids who got good grades were stiff and not cool. Meanwhile, images in society reinforced the stereotype that minorities were meant to be the opposite of that. Doing well in classes put pressure on me, making it more difficult for me to identify with my culture. To compensate, I felt I had to behave a certain way. For the most part it felt natural, but it did bother me when I was treated as though I was supposed to act that way (mostly by white people), as though if I acted any other way, it would have been deviant from the image they had of me. Still, identifying as a minority allowed me to create some distinction between myself and the rich, white, conservative, and ambitious kids who were viewed unfavorably by most of the other students. My teachers at Westmont, unlike my teachers at Naperville, encouraged me to identify with my culture. I presented myself differently to my teachers than I did to my peers, but I did not abandon all aspects of myself and simply try to assimilate. My teachers gave me books that reaffirmed my identity and validated my sense of self, providing a huge boost in my confidence.

It was good that school kept me engaged, because tensions in my house during this time were constantly at an elevated level. My sister was having difficulties, and I was trying to be supportive of my family. I tried to calm the situation, but sometimes I would let my own frustrations out and rebel against my parents and my life. I recall being upset and angry often during this time. I still often feel angry when those memories creep back into my consciousness. Usually it is frustration over being misunderstood, or being labeled or stereotyped. At the time, I often wanted to escape—go for long walks, go on vacation, go to friends' houses.

I realized then that poverty is terribly unkind—especially because I was not used to it. For the most part I dealt with the situation as a type of adventure—an unfortunate circumstance, certainly, but one that we could overcome. However, it was difficult at times, as reminders of our lack of resources came to the foreground. From this period I developed a belief—one that I still hold—that it is psychologically harder to be poor in a rich area. I was more acutely aware of the contrast between my life and the lives of my wealthy friends with whom I had grown up. I often had to walk to school, or to games, or to the train station, bitter at all the people I saw passing in cars. Experiences like these changed the way I viewed the world, and my place in it. My friends from Naperville who had been supportive before could not understand these new problems. A few years later, when they were all getting cars, I was still walking, still riding the bus. I was now with a new group of people with whom I could identify. I remember one experience in particular. One of my best friends throughout high school, a poor black kid, told me of a time when he had asked his mother for ten dollars for school, and she had responded, "Sorry, Paul, I don't have it." This story had made me feel better, as though I were not alone. I learned from this the importance of determining your friends and the people you connect with. I believe that some people simply cannot be friends because they have no common ground. Because of this dislocation, my attempts at identity formation were usually frustrated.

We stayed at the Howard Johnson hotel for over a year and a half. My friends from Naperville would poke fun at me, asking me how long we were going to live at "HoJo's." When we finally did get a house, it was in a small working-class area of Westmont. At the hotel I would have friends over, but when we moved into the house, I stopped inviting friends (especially wealthy friends) over to my house. My mother used to criticize my father for having a similar attitude, as though he was ashamed of his home, but now I could understand his feelings. I think my father and I shared this sentiment because we always felt like something of an outsider no matter where we were.

Moving out of the hotel was nice, but having a house meant a whole new set of problems. There were several times when the power was turned off or our phone would get disconnected. It was never for long periods of time, but it served as a hurtful reminder of what we didn't have. Speaking from experience, needing something and not being able to afford it is one of the most difficult feelings I know. Partly out of shame, and partly out of a knowledge that they couldn't understand how I felt, I never told my friends about my struggle.

Most of the trying experiences I have faced in my life I have dealt with on my own. This has reinforced my sense of independence, but it has also left me feeling alone when I most needed help. The only experience I can compare it to would be years later, sitting at the financial aid office at Dartmouth, unable to come up with the money they were asking for. When the lights were turned off in my house, I never really minded. We brought out the candles and solved the problem relatively easily. In many ways, it filled that void I once wanted for some sort of disturbance that would alter the course of things just enough to make things interesting, to have a story to tell afterward, but not in any significant way.

At Dartmouth, not having the money for college had the potential to entirely disrupt my plans. I imagined with dread the ramifications of not being able to complete college. The people in the financial aid office told me that this was a real possibility and that perhaps I should think about "switching schools." I was and am deeply hurt every time I cannot find the money to check in for the term. I think this has contributed to my cynicism, to my dislike as well as my reverence for money. Throughout my adolescence, I was learning the power of money.

When the lights or the phone were turned off, my family became closer. I knew my mother and father were taking things hard, but I was building rage inside as well. To a large extent, this rage has not died down, since my troubles have persisted. The only thing that might allow me to fully abandon that rage (and even then, memory would not allow me to be unconscious of other people's problems) would be to make enough money to feel secure. There is irony in this statement, because early in my life, when I felt secure, I was hungry for some insecurity. Maybe security can only be appreciated when some insecurity has been experienced. This is, after all, the prototypical journey of the hero-warrior that Joseph Campbell talks about. A person must first descend into the abyss before they can emerge brighter than before, like a phoenix rising from the ashes.

My father believes (perhaps needs to believe) that all people go through some such trying experience in their life. He points to both great and common men when he tells me this theory. This struggle, he tells me, is his test. I wonder if he has ever thought of it as *our* test. My mother tries to make him aware that this has been hard on all of us. For my sister and me, it has been particularly hard because of the lack of answers that accompany most of these experiences. Any explanation must only be imagined.

When we were given a rare explanation, it was darker than I had supposed. The morning we were going to go to Chicago to discuss my father's case with his legal partner, while my father was already in jail, my mother came into my room at a particularly early hour. She sat down in my wooden chair and spoke in a calm voice, as though she had rehearsed what she was going to say. She knew we might hear things at the meeting that were unfavorable toward my father, so she wanted to prepare us for all the ugly parts of their past that might creep into the conversation. Your father, she told me, had a daughter when he was younger. I did not initially understand the full weight of this statement. She continued to explain that he had had an affair before my sister was born. She said the girl had grown up in Puerto Rico and that my father had no contact with the girl, but still she existed. My mother expressed great animosity toward the mother of the child, saying how rude and offensive she had been. I wondered what claims the woman had on my father, what she might have expected from my father that he had disappointed.

I could not imagine my father as a sexual being, much less a sleazy or sordid character. I felt the demon of machismo creeping up. I wondered to what extent this had to do with my father being Latino—to what extent he felt that his manhood was proved by the number of women he could sleep with. Then I thought of the fatherless girl in Puerto Rico. I imagined the hatred she must feel toward my father. I worry still how my father contributed to the trend that has bothered me so much, of single-mother households. It is difficult for me to reconcile my image of my father with the image I have of the delinquent fathers who neglect their responsibility, leaving the already oppressed minority women of this world to fend for themselves. I wondered if the girl, my half-sister, harbored any animosity toward my sister and me for being the children my father chose to stay with.

This ugly tradition of machismo never figured into my father's stories of Puerto Rico. One of the unfortunate aspects of Latino society is the staggering number of illegitimate children that machismo has spawned. I recall the disappointment I felt when my grandmother told me several years ago that my grandfather used to receive letters from girls around the world when he was home from the military. He had been stationed around the world and I suppose had sought the company of other women when my grandmother was not with him. I was surprised that my grandmother, an incredibly strong woman, would have put up with this behavior. However, I saw that the Puerto Rican tradition was not particularly kind to women. I saw that the stories my father told me when I was younger were all filtered versions of reality. Everyone, I saw, had aspects of their past that were much darker than anyone had supposed.

When my father would paint a vision of Puerto Rico for us through his stories, it was always filled with nostalgia for the undisturbed beauty of tradition. Never did he mention the parts of his past or of our family's past that were lackluster. He expressed regret for the Puerto Rico that was passing—the sweltering sugarcane fields, the dilapidated houses, the dirt roads, the rusted tin heaps, and the hand-painted boats. On our visits, we stayed in our apartment and interacted with our extended family but never really immersed ourselves in the culture or the community. We would observe the quiet towns with ancient women sitting outside on their porches in the stagnant afternoon heat. Puerto Rico for us was separate from the poor neighborhoods, the street kids, or the boom boxes blasting salsa music out of their cars by the beach. I don't mean to say that we were entirely separate from the natives of the island, as some of the gringos are when they visit the island. Our experience was much more similar to that of the Puerto Rican New Yorkers—the self-named Nuyoricans—who visit the island, feeling as though it is a part of them, but feeling as well that their culture has been filtered. Our apartment was certainly in the community, but we were not part of the community. If our minimal interaction with Puerto Rican kids did not give us away, our imperfect Spanish did. Interestingly, most of my identity as Puerto Rican has been learned in Chicago, specifically from my father, with whom I was never shy about going to the Latino neighborhoods.

Some of my earliest memories, in fact, are of car rides with my family where we would escape beyond our world. We would go down to Humboldt Park, or to Pilsen on Chicago's south side, or to drive past the *bodegas* on Division Street in the Puerto Rican neighborhood, where my father would stop for a cup of coffee because he swore it was the best in the city. My mother, predictably, saying, "Ay, Hector, I don't know why you insist on coming to these places." The four of us would sit in the car for the length of the drive—my mother in the passenger seat, my father driving, my sister and I in the back. It seemed routine on these trips that my mother would ask where we were, and my father would respond, smiling, that he had no idea, and that we were lost (something we never believed). Years later we discovered that we were lost in other ways, but the bond that we developed during those earlier years held us together through machismo and financial trouble and identity formation and change.

Those car rides were my father's time to translate to us the nobility of poverty. He wanted us to avoid the struggle of growing up Latino and colored in this country, and tried to shield us from many of the painful experiences he had had to go through. For the most part, sheltering us had worked: by the time I was in high school, the honors classes I was taking separated me from the few Puerto Ricans, Dominicans, or Cubans at my school. At the same time, however, my father wanted to instill in me a feeling of being Puerto Rican. After all of his attempts to separate himself from *el barrio*, he still cherished his identity and wanted us to share in that—to soak up some of the warmth and richness, the life and blood of our heritage. In some ways he had a difficult time assimilating into the corporate world he inhabited after he left law school and business school because he refused to sacrifice his Latino identity. It is an unfortunate state of affairs that in the most elite places, corporate boardrooms and wealthy country clubs, white culture dominates, and any variance from that culture is not warmly received.

My father's battle, one that I have largely inherited, has been the struggle of defining himself in relation to his environment. I think my father feels Puerto Rican, first, whereas I feel American. This struggle for identity led my father to question his place in relation to his race. On family car trips he would often quote for us a passage from one of his favorite books, James Joyce's *A Portrait of the Artist as a Young Man*:

> Mother is putting my new secondhand clothes in order. She prays now, she says, that I may learn in my own life and away from home and friends what the heart is and what it feels. Amen. So be it. Welcome, O life! I go to encounter for the millionth time the reality of my experience and to forge in the smithy of my soul the uncreated conscience of my race.

My father was always intrigued by the search for the conscience of his race. I think at times he even desired to be that conscience. My father has had to deal with the anxiety of leaving behind a race and a people, and trying to discover his own path along the way. I think he has always been haunted by feelings of "selling out," particularly when he has been surrounded by friends he grew up with whose experiences diverged from his own throughout the years. I think he has tried to define himself as Puerto Rican out of a desire to be grounded in something, even if he has not admired or internalized all of the stereotypical traits and mannerisms that accompany that identity.

For me the problem of identification has been even more complicated. Because I have never truly been either here (Chicago, Westmont, the United States) or there (Puerto Rico), I have been left with something of a divided identity. However, this anxiety has extended far beyond my identification with an ethnicity. I have had to think of myself in many different ways, never truly feeling like anything. I have at times simultaneously felt wholly a part of everything and entirely alienated from everyone—being the poor kid among the rich, the rich kid among the poor, the American in Puerto Rico, the Puerto Rican in America, the Jewish Puerto Rican honor student among people who have not yet managed to extend their thinking beyond one definition of an individual. Being an outsider has given me perspective and enriched me as a person, but it has also been a burden I have had to bear. I suppose, as with any burden, it has also made me stronger. Throughout my life I have had to search for the conscience of my race, even as I have changed and the conscience has changed. I think, perhaps, the more important goal is embodied in the mother's prayer that we may find what the heart is and what it feels. Once this is discovered, it lifts you beyond the herd mentality, the ugly parts of each culture, and it makes you entirely you. The process of discovering what the heart is, is uniquely individualistic, and success in this, my search, would allow me to incorporate all the complexities that comprise the "Me, myself" that one of my favorite poets, Walt Whitman, wrote about.

In light of the burdens (and privileges) of being Puerto Rican and Jewish and financially insecure and dark skinned and a million other things, I would not surrender any of these aspects of my identity. Identifying as Latino gives me a history, a grounding in a particular culture, but I would not have that be the defining aspect of me, and I would be averse to any attempts to encapsulate me. I have not had to struggle for my identity as Latino in the United States, only in Puerto Rico. While we have some flexibility with the identities we choose, those identities will only go unchallenged if they are believable to others. My challenge has been overcoming the images others have of me and finding room for my own definitions of myself.

A friend of mine, a poet, said to me that he was taught to "respect men who stand by their convictions, but are smart enough to see the signs and survive the fight." I think I have tried to be that person. My father has helped me, since I think he has fallen victim at times to not seeing the signs. Because it has often been said that history repeats itself, I am concerned every time that someone says of me, "He is just like his father." I approach this anxiety over his influence on me with mixed feelings. The comparisons are both an honor and a burden, a cause for pride and a cause for concern.

This story lacks a conclusion, because the events of my life (or even this part of my life) have not yet concluded. I spoke with my father the other day. I was feeling lonely, as I often do at college, and he told me of my great-grandfather, whom my father viewed with reverence. He spoke of this strong man who cut sugarcane all his life. This poor man's life, my father told me, could have been seen by some to be insignificant, but he was wealthy in his own way, with the children and grandchildren that surrounded him. My father has often told me when I complain about something being difficult, "Life is struggle." When a person ceases to experience any struggles, his or her life has become irrelevant. Thus I feel sorry for those who do not face the challenges, both physical and mental, that I face, and am grateful for my experience. I continue my struggle, which I hope will lead me toward the depth that comes from living and living well. I asked my father if there is one theme that has been recurring in his life, and he told me the importance of resilience. It seems from my father's words, that simply living—being aware of yourself and others and surviving the fight— is the best thing any individual could hope for.

Joseph Rodriguez graduated from Dartmouth College where he majored in government with a concentration in international relations. Currently living in Cambridge, Massachusetts, and working in consulting, he is looking forward to going to graduate school in the future.

Sarah Fox   Beyond the Euphoric Buzz

"Someone go find Luke. His girlfriend is puking."

I'm lying on the bathroom floor of the hotel room. Luke and I had been going together for only a month when he asked me to be his date for his junior prom. We had drunk together plenty in those four weeks, but this was the first time I got sick. In my excitement at the after-party, I disregarded the classic "beer then liquor, never sicker" rule, and so there I am.

I wake up to see Luke walking through the hotel room's bathroom door. "Oh, hi," I try to smile, but the room is spinning wildly, and I can't make it stop. I close my eyes. Oh, worse: I grab the toilet bowl to heave some more. I hate vomiting. It feels like my guts are being yanked out through my mouth for everyone to have a look at. But there's nothing I can do to stop it. I keep waking up, feeling the room spin, puking, then falling back asleep.

At some point Luke decides I need to get in the shower. I argue with him because I can't move without the entire room turning into a carousel gone mad. Eventually he ignores my whimpers; but as he props me up, dizziness overwhelms me. I begin to fall in slow motion. The world is tipping, like a bottle of tequila, and I'm stuck inside, sloshing back and forth sickeningly. . . .

I am lying in the bathtub. Every movement creates another current in the water and the bottle sways back and forth. I slosh from side to side, bumping my head on the glass side. Luke is trying to hold the small plastic trash bin for me to puke into. I stop throwing up as the waves die down. I move my arm to get comfortable. More waves. More vomiting. I knock the trash bin on its side and the vomit spills into the water of the bathtub. For just a moment I'm watching the room from above. I see myself lying in the bathtub, pitifully: sopping clothes, stringy hair, unable to control my bodily functions, bits of vomit floating around me. Then I'm back inside myself, inside the bottle that almost reaches the equilibrium necessary for me to stand up straight—but then something sets it rocking again. After what seems like hours I drift back to sleep, with Luke holding my head above the water. I'm too exhausted to keep up the fight.

Looking back at that night, I marvel that I never apologized to Luke. I remember feeling awkward because I had never become so ill from drinking and wasn't sure how to act. But apologizing had not been my instinctive response. Instead, as soon as I realized that I had ruined Luke's big night, I began making excuses: "It was only his *junior* prom," I told myself. My philosophy had always been to resist feeling guilty and invest energy in learning from the experience after making a mistake. But the possibility of learning from a mistake assumes some logical cause—something solvable. When drinking became the source of my mistakes, my habit of avoiding guilt became a perpetuating force for my irrational addiction. If I didn't feel guilty about the negative consequences of my drinking, what would motivate me to quit?

Today I can answer that question easily. I am finishing my last year in college; I am a wife and mother; and I comfortably identify myself as a nondrinker. I do not pretend that the person I am today is unconnected to my past; just two and a half years ago I drove home drunk with a six pack on the seat next to me and cruised into a tree in my front yard, putting a sizable dent in the hood of my mom's car. I had to ask, how did things get so bad? Did aspects of my personality allow me to sink so low, or was mine a simple case of alcohol addiction? In the present, what keeps me from having a drink tomorrow, starting the whole cycle over again? What I found was that the more I uncovered the complex networks of my mind, the more I saw how my recovery would be a lifetime process of realization and readjustment.

I am the youngest of four girls in my family, so I learned everything about growing up from watching my sisters go through it: adolescence, boyfriends, high school, alcohol, drugs. I saw it all—first through the eyes of a little girl, and then later through my own experience.

Lilliana, my oldest sister by six years, was my idol. She was a cheerleader; she made homecoming court; she was popular. She drank, she partied. After a while she even did drugs. Pot. Acid. Probably more. But I knew her only as my beautiful, glamorous sister, who I wanted to be just like when I grew up.

Her teenage years were extremely hard on the family. Lilliana was anything but subtle in her disobedience. She would yell and scream at my mother with the slightest provocation. It was not unusual to find my mother chasing her around the kitchen table, out the front door, and around the rickety old station wagon parked in the driveway, wielding a wooden paddle and a fierce look—intent not on hurting her but on disciplining her rebellious spirit.

My parents learned a lesson in dealing with Lilliana: you can't force your teenage child to do what you want. So they didn't take an authoritarian approach with the rest of us. Whereas my parents would try to tell Lilliana to come home at one—and she would purposely stay out all night—I never had a curfew. My parents' strategy with the rest of us was to persuade us to do what they thought was best by reasoning with us, discussing the issues, and telling us about their experience. But ultimately the decisions were ours. They understood that sometimes hearing about their mistakes wasn't enough; we needed to experience and learn for ourselves, too.

Such was our relationship: for as long as I lived in that household I respected my parents, obeyed their few rules, considered their abundant counsel, and made my own choices. I could say that not having a curfew was conducive to excessive partying. I could say that being allowed to drink at home was convenient for drinking heavily. But I don't. I do not blame my parents for any position I found myself in; I made my own decisions and hold myself accountable for all of the repercussions.

As my parents were in fact genuine hippies, drugs were never a taboo topic. I knew that my parents had lived on a commune with a diet consisting mostly of soy and pot for the majority of their young adult lives. I was raised on all the "psychedelic" music of the sixties, and by the time I was twelve I knew all about the allusions to drugs in the Beatles' songs.

Still, drug use was not a subject that I took lightly. A particular memory is imprinted in my mind not because of great meaning or emotional impact but from sheer repetition. My mother would be doing something around the house and talking to me at the same time. Suddenly she would stop—always mid-sentence, sometimes mid-word; it appeared that she was just pausing in order to better concentrate on what she was doing. I would wait for her to finish the task, expecting her to then complete the sentence, but she never would.

"Mom, what were you going to say?"

"What?"

"What were you going to say? You were just telling me to do something."

"Oh," she would say with surprise. "I was? I'm sorry, honey, I don't remember."

"But *Mom*!" I would reply, drawing out the "o" in exasperation. "You were *just* saying it."

"I'm sorry, sweetie." And the conversation was over.

For that to happen once would have been understandable; twice would have been forgivable; three times a little trying. But over and over and over . . . it was something I couldn't forget. When I later found out that this was a typical symptom of being "burnt out," the memory served as the greatest incentive I could ever ask for never to try pot.

By the time I was thirteen, both Lilliana and Rachel, a year and a half my elder, were heavily into drugs. Everyone in the family knew it, but there wasn't much we could do. I resented the huge role that pot played in my two sisters' lives. They totally dropped out of family life, not just by neglecting chores but also by retracting all emotional investment. They were always off in their fairy-tale land where everything was cool and chill and nothing really mattered. They couldn't stand to be around the family without the buffer of being high.

My mom could handle picking up the slack around the house, but their betrayal of the family was a much graver offense. My mother was born in Cuba, where she lived in a world saturated with family; her playmates were all relatives. Distant or near, it made no difference—cousin was synonymous with friend. And there was a comfortable balance of respect and intimacy with adult relatives, as well. So when my mother raised children of her own, it was incomprehensible that my sisters and I were not as instantly enamored with our extended family as she had been with hers.

Language was a nearly insurmountable barrier. While most of my mother's family spoke Spanish, my sisters and I knew only what we learned in school. My grandmother was confined to a wheelchair and refused to learn English. My grandfather knew enough to translate roughly, but Spanish was the language of their home. So while my grandparents lived only a few short miles from our house, visiting them was more of a chore than a pleasure. Instead of acknowledging this and adjusting her expectations, my mother felt that we could never see our grandparents enough, respect them enough, or love them enough. When my sisters stopped making even minor efforts at spending time with them, she took it hard.

And so did I. In fact, I was the only one of my sisters to actually develop a strong sense of family obligation. Whether it meant cleaning the kitchen without being asked, stopping by our grandparents' house to say hello, or noticing that something was bothering my mom and talking through a problem with her, I was always the most present of my sisters—a trait that earned me the moniker "Mommy's angel." To my mother's side of the family, I was the only one of the Fox girls that fulfilled their expectations of a good little Cubana. Even as I hit puberty, I was able to maintain a relatively positive relationship with the family.

High school was a wonderful time for me; it was filled with new experiences, new faces, and new challenges. Our freshmen class at the regional school comprised six hundred students. Wandering through the halls I saw many familiar faces from middle school and many new ones. I smiled brightly and said hello to everyone, without hesitation. On a whim I ran for treasurer for freshman board; I had fond memories of making campaign stickers for Lilliana years earlier: Vote for Lilliana Fox!—with little legs and a bushy tail drawn around the "Fox." I was soon making posters and stickers in the shape of a sun that read, "Vote for Sarah Sunshine!" To my surprise, I won.

The following week a freshman student assembly was called to introduce the freshman board. The four elected officers sat in four lonely chairs, an insignificant island on the vast gymnasium floor. The bleachers towering before us were like a mammoth beast crouched, muscles tensed, ready to spring at any moment. The kids who filled the seats were full of that fidgeting, bottled-up, first-week-of-school kind of energy. The assistant principal spoke (for too long) and then began introducing the board. Eventually it was my turn. "And here is your newly elected treasurer, Sarah Fox." Applause, stomping, yelling. Wow! Was that louder than they had cheered for the president? It sure sounded like it to me. But as I approached the microphone, the mob before me was still daunting.

"Thanks for electing us to freshman board," I said with a smile. "Our goal is to make school a more enjoyable place. And I think we've done good so far. We got you out of class today, didn't we?" Hooting, hollering! I was beginning to blush. They hadn't cheered during anyone else's speeches. As the gymnasium quieted again, Ted Williams, the hunk of the class, yelled out, "We love you, Sarah Sunshine!" starting another round of rowdiness. Realizing that I could control this great throng, I willed my bashfulness to disappear. "Okay, okay," I said, as if I was used to this, unimpressed. I continued with my speech, and glancing up, I saw it: people were actually listening to me! With this reassurance, I flashed smiles at faces I recognized. When I came to the end of my note cards, I headed to my seat. The compulsory applause followed. But I couldn't stand such a mediocre ending. Just before I reached my seat I dashed back to the podium. "Freshman class rules!" I cried into the microphone. They exploded! They stood on their seats, they went wild! And I wasn't just a participant in the excitement—I was the leader of it. Yes, that's right, follow my lead, I chuckled to myself as I sat down.

Looking back I saw that this experience had quite an impact on me. That feeling of power over the multitude was intoxicating. Until then I had lived each moment like a little girl, without a care about the impression of my words and actions. In the course of that speech I lived my first calculated moments. I did not smile or speak as I always had, out of an impulsive, friendly instinct; I acted in order to produce a desired effect. I was rewarded for my calculation with instant popularity. As my high school career progressed, I treated every action as a public statement.

Being on class board was not just about popularity for me, however. I quickly involved myself in every aspect of the school's inner workings. The principal once introduced me by saying, "This girl runs the school. She holds everything together around here with her sunshine smile." I once let a curse word slip out in class and was sent to the office. "Look," I said to the assistant principal, "I've heard you use that word how many times. How are you gonna punish me for it?" Not only did I have a certain degree of administrative immunity but I was making honor roll without trying terribly hard, and all my teachers loved me.

I seemed to spread the fairy-tale glitter of my life over everything and everyone that I came in contact with. And the better I became at playing to the crowd, the better my life seemed to get. I couldn't have asked for more. This was every girl's dream of high school. So why shouldn't I become totally immersed in it? Yes, it required some acting, putting up facades, surrendering my hopes to live life with childlike innocence. But it was worth it. Hell, it was more than worth it. What I had was better than innocence. It was perfection.

Throughout middle school and my freshman year of high school I never drank. I had always been firm in my refusal to do so, to the point that I no longer needed to mention it; it was assumed. I was confident in my role and I felt like I was being wise. When I decided to get drunk for the first time, I could honestly say it was a choice that I made for myself, when I felt I was ready. I wasn't just following the crowd. *I* wanted to try it. I set the date in my head and then told everyone else. "Next Saturday night I'm going to get drunk," I said.

All that week I looked forward to it. On Friday, a friend asked, "Why don't you just do it tonight?"

"Nope. Tomorrow. Don't worry, it'll be just as fun!" And was it ever! I drank a beer and felt giddy. I was talking and laughing, which was not really uncommon for me; but everything seemed to have an extra sparkle. I drank another and was off and running. Weighing a mere one hundred pounds, I knew it wouldn't take much alcohol to affect me. We were hanging out on the beach, as usual, but tonight I had new inspiration. "Let's go down to the water!" I said excitedly. I met with groans and sighs.

"Come on, come on! It'll be fun!" I urged. "Come *on*!" Finally I convinced a couple of people to go. "Race ya," I said and set off running. I arrived at the water's edge out of breath. My best friend, Diana, was trailing behind me, laughing.

"Sarah, you're such a nut!" she cried happily.

"Oooh!" I said, as I had another thought. "Let's go swimming!" And before she could respond I was running toward the water. As soon as it was deep enough I collapsed into the water. I felt it close in around me, hugging my body, making me warm. I moved and turned, feeling the water swirl around me. After a while I popped my head out of the water, took a gulp of air, then let the water envelop me again. I just lay there this time, letting the lull of the waves move my body for me, relaxed completely. And then I felt arms around me: real, human arms. Someone was dragging me out of the water.

"Oh, hi!"

"Diana thought you were drowning," explained the one who had "rescued" me. He didn't sound amused.

"Oh. Well, I wasn't." I replied. He set me on the ground. Then I caught sight of the sky. "Ooooh! Diana, look at the stars!" I said. "Let's spin!" I stretched my arms out, let my head fall back, and spun around and around and around, looking at the stars in the heavens. I was a little girl again—grinning so widely that my cheeks bulged to twice their normal size. No cares outside of the here and now. Ah life! What joy! I sat down and pondered with amazement while the world slowly stopped spinning around me.

And so I fell in love with the drunken state of mind—and still love it today. Being drunk is like being a kid again. I could experience carefree bliss. What I had lost by becoming a calculating political figure, I could regain by getting drunk. I could have my cake and eat it too. So why shouldn't I?

Sophomore year I was elected class president. I was passionate about the work I was doing to improve the school; the people around me seemed to sense this passion and became excited with me. It was the same with all the people I worked with: facilities personnel, administration, students, teachers. They worked extraordinarily well with me and for me because they respected me professionally, liked me personally, and thought that the final products of my work rewarded their efforts. Indeed, I wasn't just the president anymore; I had become a public figure. My success depended on my personal integrity as much as it did on my capabilities.

Sophomore year I was partying with all of the most popular kids on campus. I began to stand out even from that crowd, because when I wanted to have fun, I *really* had fun—no inhibitions, no quiet reservations. I always drank to get drunk. And I usually passed out sometime during the night. I knew people thought it was a big deal to black out, but it didn't seem like a problem to me. Passing out struck me as just like falling asleep—and when can anyone remember the exact circumstances of falling asleep? Everyone had a "Sarah was so drunk . . ." story to tell at school the following Mondays, and I thought it was great. I remembered my nights in the form of a flash: action and feeling. And the emotion from that flash would wash over me with an intensity that could hardly be paralleled in sobriety. Why dilute memories with specifics and particulars? In my eyes, I was sucking the marrow out of life.

As of the second or third time I got drunk I did begin to think about alcoholism. I still wonder, was my instinct warning me from the very beginning? Could I have known somewhere deep within my subconscious that I was *too* in love with being drunk—that it could become a problem for me? I wanted to find out more about alcoholism, but I was scared my student council career would be over if my secret concerns became known.

In eleventh grade the opportunity I had been waiting for finally came. The assignment was a film documentary on a topic of my choice. I didn't have to think twice; I immediately knew I wanted to interview recovering alcoholics and counselors for drug and alcohol abuse, then take what I learned from them and apply it to students who were known as fun partiers. I wanted to show that what most people thought of as harmless fun could be truly dangerous. Looking back I realize that I wanted to increase social awareness and change the norms about what was acceptable. More to the point, I already felt that I was getting away with too much; I wanted someone, any of the adults in my life, to set a boundary and tell me that I was going too far past it—that I should stop because I was in danger. I also wanted a clear definition of alcoholism that I could apply to myself. The best definition I heard from those interviews was, "Social drinking becomes alcoholism when your alcohol use is having a negative effect on more than one area of your life and you continue to drink." The problem, of course, is that the more addicted one becomes, the more subjective one's judgment becomes. The definition of what's "bad enough" keeps sliding.

Going into the summer before senior year I had it all made. I was managing to keep my school responsibilities and my drinking compartmentalized, balanced. At that time I had been involved with Luke for over a year and a half—my most serious relationship yet. But Luke's family was moving about six hours upstate, and he would be leaving for state university in the fall. We hadn't been getting along as well and I noticed myself starting to look at other guys. I was just hoping to stay faithful until he left, and then I'd be free. I had already convinced him it would be better not to attempt a long-distance relationship.

Moving day came and Luke left. Thursday came and Matt called. We went to a fantastic party. The end of the night found us skinny-dipping in the Jacuzzi; we made out passionately in the steamy water. He pressed himself against me, and for the first time in my life I seriously considered not saving myself for marriage. Luckily, I was too nervous about the whole situation—nude in a strange place, with my recent ex-boyfriend's good friend—to do anything.

Three days later I was at another party, where there was a guy who I had my eye on. He was tall, thin, and very attractive. When I introduced myself, he said, "I know. I used to watch you during lunch when you sat outside." I was flattered. He used to watch me from afar! I always wanted an admirer! As the party cleared out, Christopher and I were left on the fold-out couch. We started making out and it got pretty intense pretty quickly. At some point he asked me whether I wanted to "do it." I said I never had and he dropped it. A while later he brought it up again and after a few minutes of pondering I said sure. Just like that. That night seemed like it never ended. I don't know what girls are talking about when they say the first time hurts. I thought it was terrific. Over and over. At times I would forget his name, then the next time I woke up I'd remember it.

I awoke the next morning and knew right away that everything had changed. Why had I decided to go for it? I asked myself. I had no answer. Saving myself for marriage had been such an integral part of my positive self-image as a good, moral person—like a banner that I could point to and say, "See! I'm still pure!" I could feel guilt lurking, huge and dark, just around the corner. Without my virginity, my positive self-identity was thrown into question.

It took only a moment for me to formulate a response. I would not regret losing my virginity to Christopher. No regrets! I would make it a meaningful experience by developing a real relationship with him. And if that worked, wouldn't it be fantastic if I actually ended up marrying my first?

For the next month, we spent little time together without being drunk or having sex. But we were also getting to know each other a little more. I learned that he was much more uptight than I was; he had been a complete loser at school; he had been kicked out of two state universities in the past year; and none of his friends or family thought highly of him. In fact, anyone who knew about us tried to convince me that I shouldn't be with him. Not many people knew, though. I thought that if any of my friends from school heard I was with him, they might also hear that I was sleeping with him. And that, I knew, would be the end of my perfect reputation at school.

Our relationship was a constant roller coaster. Every time something came up that put us on less than good terms, I panicked. I could sense that guilt was just over the horizon, impending, threatening, and that if we didn't stay together it would come barreling down on me. It got to the point where the simplest interaction, like calling him up, required having at least a few drinks first to calm my nerves and rally my courage.

After about five weeks I stopped caring. I found what I needed in my drinking. I finally ended my relationship by kissing another guy. While I had been with Christopher, I told myself that he would be the only exception to my abstinence. But once we broke up, guilt again threatened to overwhelm me; and I still didn't want to surrender to it. The only alternative was to keep going without looking back. That's just what I did.

Aside from people at school, I knew that my mother's Cuban family would reject me if they ever knew about my choices. According to them, girls were to be protected from the lustful urges of men; sexuality was to be enjoyed exclusively by the male gender. For a woman to be sexually active, never mind spirited and assertive, was appalling to them. No one had ever told me this, but somehow I knew. Of course this is true in American culture as well to some extent, but perhaps in a more subtle way. So I almost felt like I was standing up for myself, not just to them but to society—saying, in my own self-defeating way, "No, I won't let you make me feel ashamed! I'm going to satisfy my desires and get something out of this."

All summer I partied every night. Drinking started to lose its excitement. My new thrill was hooking up with whomever I wanted. There was a certain satisfaction in knowing that I could seduce anyone, anyone at all. My conquests were always one-night stands and I had no emotional involvement. Looking back, it was as if I became a completely different person when I went out drinking. Never would I have done those things sober. I knew they were wrong, and I would have felt too ashamed. But as the summer went on I would plan who I would get that night before I even started drinking. By the end of the summer alcohol was not a necessary accomplice. Although it was still a large part of my lifestyle, I didn't have to be drunk to carry out my conquests.

I drank more and more during the day. Partying all night left me depleted of energy. Drinking made the daylight hours bearable; it made me feel physically better, more energetic, and happier. Yet not only was my physical health faltering but my emotional health was deteriorating as well. My sexual conquests required cutting off all emotions. And once I learned how to cut myself off, I found myself doing it all the time. Not only was it easier living life without a conscience, but there was a convenient after-effect: since everything but drinking was slipping down to the bottom of my list of priorities, even when alcohol was having a negative impact on all other areas of my life, in my mind things never became "bad enough" to quit.

When school started in the fall I hardly paused. I was president of student council, captain of the debate team, and treasurer of the National Honor Society. I was enrolled in two AP courses and three honors courses. I was dedicated to my academics, but somehow I still found the time to drink. On Wednesdays I arrived home from school at four o'clock; church orchestra practice started at six. On my way home from church, I would stop by the 7-Eleven and buy some brew with my fake ID. A few of my nonschool friends would be waiting for me when I got home.

I was able to keep my reputation and positions at school because no one there knew about my drinking. I never partied with people from school. At the time I thought I did so because they were superficial and their mere presence annoyed me, inhibited me. In retrospect I see that I was successful in the various spheres of my sober life, and in order to maintain that success while continuing to drink I had to preserve certain barriers.

About halfway through the fall of my senior year I started getting thoroughly bored by my drinking routine. It had lost the excitement. I felt old and tired; I could almost feel myself getting numb. I decided I wanted to clean up my act—to start a real relationship. I planned to build up a relationship slowly, at the same time cutting down on drinking and partying. Eventually we would spend all of our time together and I'd have no need to drink at all. It was a good plan.

I picked out a sweet, innocent underclassman, Ted. Within a week we were passing notes between classes. Already I felt like a normal teenager again, excited at the idea of being someone's girlfriend. I could almost feel the spiritual calluses softening up.

And then came the big football game that Friday. I hadn't gone to a game sober in ages. At first I tried to make plans with some of my old non-drinking friends. But I hadn't called them in months; they couldn't just drop their new friends and welcome me back with open arms. Friday came and I couldn't resist. My drinking buddies got a bottle of tequila and we drank a good portion of it before walking over to the field.

Before I got very far I ran into Ted, as I was hoping to. What terrific luck! We saw each other from a few yards away and both burst into smiles. I ran into his open arms. He picked me up and swung me around. This was the way it should be, I thought to myself. I stood with him for a bit until I spotted my friends, looking impatient as ever. I gave Ted one last hug.

The night was still young when the halftime show ended. I was beginning to tire of putting on fake smiles for my old school friends. Luckily I ran into an old acquaintance—Rick Marciano, who had graduated two years earlier and was still a legend among the lady folk. I greeted him with an extra close hug and barely stepped away after the embrace. We talked for a few minutes about nothing; then he told me about a party after the game. I already had plans, so he gave me his number to meet up later. "You'd better not forget my number!" he said as we parted.

Don't forget his number? Who was he kidding? Did he really think he was the pursuant here? Or that any girl in her right mind would give up such a golden opportunity? I walked away feeling even happier than the eight drinks had made me feel.

And what about Ted? I did think about him for a moment as I walked away from Rick. But this was such a once-in-a-lifetime opportunity that I couldn't pass it up. By then I was so good at making excuses for myself that I hardly had to think twice to defend my actions. Ted and I hardly had anything going, I told myself. It wasn't like we were going out or anything. Plus, I thought, maybe it was a bad idea to try to have a normal relationship. Maybe I wasn't ready for it yet. And that was that.

That night one of my only true friends from school was throwing his first big party. When I arrived, all the popular kids from his grade were already there. After a few drinks, I called Rick to invite him over.

The next thing I remember, Rick and I were making out in the bushes in front of the house. Someone persuaded me to at least find somewhere more discreet to do whatever I wanted to do; so Rick and I hopped in his car and drove away. That was all people needed for the rumors to start.

Before long Ted heard the story. He called me Sunday night. It was horrible. He told me I was the first person to ever make him feel like a real man. Why did I do this to *him*? Was he not fast enough for me? He was crying. There was nothing I could do to make amends—not just to Ted, but to myself, my family, my church, God. In that moment the gates opened up. Feelings of worthlessness, guilt, shame—all the emotions that I had been refusing to feel, that I had intentionally dammed up inside me by drinking alcohol, alcohol, and more alcohol—all came rushing out in a torrent.

It was a shock to my system to feel so many emotions all at once, after feeling nothing for months on end. It was paralyzing. Ted was sobbing. But what could I do? I was bawling inside, but I had forgotten—or perhaps unlearned—how to express those kinds of emotions.

As the weekend passed I dreaded Monday. I considered staying home but thought that would be a cowardly public statement. I went to school and could feel the stares, hear the whispers as I walked by. By the end of the day I could feel heavy darkness blanketing my soul. It was too much to bear. I had to shut myself off or else I would have a nervous breakdown. I was sure of it.

Eventually things at school died down. I didn't regain my ability to feel, but I didn't really expect to either. I had undergone emotional trauma. I would never be the same. Sometimes I pitied myself. I'm only eighteen, I would say to myself. I'm not supposed to have to grow up this fast. But I knew I had only myself to blame.

It took this harrowing experience for me to realize I had become obsessed with the powerful feeling I obtained from controlling men. I began the arduous process of changing my promiscuous behavior. Through it all, though, I never thought to quit my drinking. I knew that my self-control was weakest when I was drunk, but quitting drinking would disrupt my whole life. And I just wasn't ready for that. At that point, I needed all the comfort I could get.

In many ways, college proved just like high school. I ended up far from my Sunshine State at a liberal arts college in the Northeast. I quickly earned a reputation as a fun partier, and everyone had a funny "One time Sarah was so drunk . . ." story to tell. But something was missing. I was making friends at parties, but not real friends. Back home I was accustomed to the security of having a tightly knit inner circle of friends who knew me and my family and loved and adored me. They were people whom I loved and adored, too. Getting drunk with strangers just wasn't the same. Feeling desperately homesick, I searched for anything that felt familiar in this land of bitter winds and gray skies.

That was how I found La Alianza, the college's Latino student organization. I had never called myself a Latina, or even a Hispanic, but attending La Alianza meetings and events made me feel closer to home. At first it was the little things—hearing English spoken with a heavy accent, just like my mom, or eating *platanos maduros*. But I quickly realized that I felt a true kinship with the other Latinos. It wasn't just the prospect of eating *yuca con mojo*—my favorite Cuban dish—or greeting someone with, "¿Cómo estás?" For the first time in my life, people were talking about living in poverty and were using those memories (for some they were more recent than for others) to bond, to come together. It was like someone turned the light on in the closet and claimed that all my old junk was worth something after all—that I could take out all my old boots and outdated coats and wear them proudly. I could brag that I too had made a game of collecting those little green food stamps and pasting them on cards.

Additionally, I had a rich cultural heritage of which I had been unaware. Having grown up in the South, my Hispanic background hadn't been a real factor in my self-identity. Compared to my sisters I had the lightest skin and hair, and in school I wasn't singled out as a "minority." People assumed I was white, and for all practical purposes that's how I thought of myself. But I was quickly discovering my Latinohood. I could compare methods for cooking *tamales*, or call my grandpa for his *arroz con pollo* recipe, and all these little details that I had lived out could earn me membership—*compañerismo, confraternidad*.

Elsewhere, I was still doing plenty of drinking—sometimes at fraternities, sometimes alone in my room. Even though I didn't love going to frat parties, I think that environment was part of my comfort zone. While the Latino social scene was a lot of fun, I rarely let go of my inhibitions completely. At times I felt like an eighth grader hanging out at a high school party: watching everyone else to figure out how to act cool. Most of the other Latinos had been immersed in the culture and community to a much greater degree than I had been, and I was still learning as I went along. On the other hand, I knew exactly what to expect and what was expected of me at a frat party.

I was also scoping out the male population. And I had found someone quite remarkable: Dan.

I had met him my second day on campus. The moment I saw him my heart started racing. Dan wasn't just good-looking, he was strikingly so— he was *gorgeous*. As we began to talk, I saw that his beauty was not just skin deep. Our friendship was like love at first sight. From that first night and every day after, my amazement, delight, and admiration of Dan just grew and grew.

We spent almost all our free time together. We could be found lying side-by-side on the Green doing homework, meandering through town, and eating breakfast, lunch, and dinner together. Not only did we have a terrific time, but I was constantly in wonder of how alike we seemed, despite our apparent differences. He was from the Northeast, I was from the South; he was from the big city of Boston, I was from a midsized tourist town; he was the oldest of his siblings, I was the youngest; he was Chinese American, I was Cuban American. But we seemed to find common ground in everything: we had comparable experiences, held similar values, and approached life from very much the same perspective. We were like two puzzle pieces made of different materials, by the hands of different craftsmen, who had spent their lives adjusting to the fact that they would never quite fit in with the rest. Then all of a sudden, by a twist of fate, we discovered that we fit each other—together, perfectly. The fact that we were both involved in cultural student groups brought us even closer. We could participate in each other's organizations more easily because we were seen as active members of the broader ethnic student community, rather than as white outsiders.

It was three months into our friendship before we confessed our romantic love for each other. The ensuing months were heavenly. We were so in love and happy about it that the most frequent comment we received from friends was, "You guys make me sick."

The only thing we didn't have in common was drinking. Dan wasn't a big drinker. His social scene in high school had never included drinking as a regular activity. Our freshmen year he went to the frats because that was the main social activity, but he didn't derive his pleasure from drinking, like I did. Once we started dating, it wasn't long before my partying became a problem for us. Dan tired of staying at frats until midmorning when he wasn't even having a good time. But I wasn't willing to give up my fun just to go home with him. I don't think it was a matter of being addicted to alcohol at that point. I just enjoyed the scene—the people, the noise, the drunk intellectual conversations, and, yes, the drinking. But maybe that lifestyle is part of the addiction.

Dan and I never discussed these issues. One night at a frat, after he had left, I kissed another guy. It wasn't a long, passionate kiss—just a quick peck. But the guilt was overwhelming. I confessed to Dan the next morning. We talked about why it had happened, and finally about how I needed to control myself when I drank, but we only scraped the surface. The real conversation started when I confessed to a much greater transgression. Dan and I had started dating just two weeks before winter break. On my trip back home I had slept with a recent ex-boyfriend. Dan almost couldn't handle it when I told him. We nearly broke up. But my begging and pleading finally convinced him that *he* was the one I wanted to be with, and that I would never let it happen again.

Other than those incidents, our relationship was wonderful. It was the happiest, healthiest relationship I had ever been in. We never came out of the "in love" stage. We were affectionate and snuggly and passionate, but we also had stimulating intellectual discussions and challenged each other's perspectives.

At the end of our freshmen year, we were faced with a summer apart. I had an internship in Miami, about five hours from my hometown, and he had one in Boston. I knew I'd be spending several weekends at home, and a part of me wanted the freedom to be able to hook up with people at parties, if the opportunity arose. I explained to him that it wasn't because I didn't want to be with him. In fact, I wanted to marry him, eventually. But I felt that I needed this last chance to be free and irresponsible before I grew up and settled down. He, on the other hand, couldn't understand how we could be anything but monogamous and still stay together. In the end, he put his foot down. Either we stayed exclusive or we broke up. I agreed. We would stay exclusive.

All summer we talked every day. We talked on the phone at night, we e-mailed each other from work during the day. All was going well. I had visited home a few times and was confident in my ability to stay true to my promise.

The Fourth of July was always a big celebration in my town, and it was especially a huge drinking affair. My mother's family had planned a big barbecue on the beach. When that side of the family got together, there was always some wine or beer involved, although usually no one got drunk—they just got happy. By the time the fireworks ended, I was very happily drunk. I had invited a few of my old drinking buddies over, for old times' sake. While we were all hanging out on the front porch, I began to notice how attracted I was to one of my old friends. When everyone else had left, we started kissing. One thing led to another and we ended up in bed. I didn't really want to have sex with him; that wasn't at all what I had in mind. But that's what happened. I was so drunk that I didn't really care. All I could muster was a questioning, "Um, Jim?" as if to say, what are you doing? But I didn't feel strongly enough about it, at the time, to put up much of an argument. The experience proved terribly unenjoyable.

The next morning came and I felt like shit. I knew I had to tell Dan. That had been his one request: "Sarah, if you care about me in the slightest, you'll give me the respect of telling me, if anything happens over the summer." I boarded the bus back to Miami and thought about how I was going to tell him. How I was going to explain that it wasn't passionate, it wasn't meaningful, it had just happened. Most of all, how was I going to keep him from dumping me?

I called that night. I cried. He was silent. It was almost as if he had expected it. He broke up with me. I sobbed, I pleaded, I tried everything I could, but nothing would change his mind. Finally I told him I would quit drinking.

"Good. You need to. But that's not going to make what you did any better. And it won't solve the problem, either. I want you to want *me*. No one else. Whether you're drunk or sober. I need to be the object of your love *and* your lust. You need me, but you don't want me." Maybe he was right. But I had to do something.

I called AA that night and found out where the meetings were held. Making a strategy for how I could put an end to this self-destructive cycle at least gave me something to think about.

For twenty-four hours Dan and I were in our separate hells. I called him the next night. I could hear the distaste in his voice. I didn't deserve him. We both knew it. I had caused him so much pain. But we were even more miserable apart. So he took me back. It was going to take a long time to mend his broken heart and regain his trust. All I could do was hope—hope that we weren't over for good.

Quitting drinking was the only thing I could actively work on to improve things with Dan. Every effort of mine to quit was bolstered by the thought that it might make things better between us. It was easy while I was in Miami. I barely had a social life there, so I rarely had the opportunity to drink. My visits home were the true test. My family had become so accustomed to my drinking habits that they questioned my sudden abstinence. Over the next few months my sisters and parents each took their turn explaining that I need not be so extreme. Drinking moderately should be the goal. But I knew myself. I knew I couldn't drink without getting drunk. I never had experienced that mentality. My mind only worked a certain way. From the very first sip, the only goal was to get wasted. I knew that my craving wouldn't be quenched by one drink. It would only whet my thirst. It wasn't the taste that I desired, it was the feeling: that euphoric buzz that leads to a numb semiconsciousness. No, I couldn't even have a sip.

When I first quit drinking, I felt like I was missing out on the best parts of life. Who can go back to a normal lifestyle once they've experienced the passion and extreme highs of living for the moment, completely rid of the inhibitions of societal norms and personal conscience? The memory of my fast-paced, extravagant lifestyle was not enough. I wanted to experience more. Being at a college where drinking made up the bulk of social interaction did not help. When I saw crowds of drunk people meandering through frat row I felt so much hostility. I wanted to be there, I wanted to join them. I didn't want to grow up yet. And, damn it, I shouldn't have to. What I knew had been fun and exciting. How could something else be anything but dull and mediocre?

To Dan, my decision to quit drinking on that July day, was a statement that I had recognized, at last, all the pain and injury that my alcohol use had inflicted on myself and those around me. But that's not what it was to me. To me, it was admitting that I couldn't be faithful when I drank, and that keeping Dan was more important to me than continuing to drink. Realizing the myriad ways that alcohol had affected my life would be a long process.

Before I could see that my alcohol use was the cause of many problems, I had to admit that I had problems. I needed to admit that *by my own standards* my life had gone to hell. In all my escapades, I thought I was defying society's standards, but in the process I forgot about my own. I had to admit that I had slipped so far from where I wanted to be. Instead of living life by fighting against the norms, I had to explore my own dreams, and then work toward my ideal.

I feel like I did a lot of harm in my days, to myself and to others. I broke the hearts of guys who were foolish enough to invest feelings in me during my alcohol and sex binges. Until now, I never thought about what I had done to them. I saw sides of myself that I had previously never believed I was capable of. God gave me the ability to influence people, to captivate them. I desecrated those gifts by using them for sexual conquests and to further myself politically. This is not religious guilt, put on me by someone else. It's the way I feel inside.

It took me two years to gain enough distance to be able to talk about drinking without wanting to be engaged in it, deep inside. I'm finally secure enough in my identity as a nondrinker to be able to look objectively at my experiences. I have just started this process. It seems like I'm rather late—two years and I haven't made much progress. But the way I look at it, at least the process has started.

The prospect of losing Dan that summer two years ago made me realize that the pleasure of drinking was not worth the cost. That autumn when I returned to school as a sober person, Dan and I were able to develop an even deeper relationship and commitment to each other. A year later we conceived our daughter; another year passed and we were married on the sandy beaches where I grew up. Today my desire to love and care for my family gives me a whole new appreciation for the sober life.

The events recounted here have very little to do with the life I live from day to day. I am tempted to put them away in a dusty corner of my mind and leave them there to be forgotten. But I also know that remembering is vital. The person I am today is a result of all my experiences, positive and negative. My empathy, my humility, my willingness to give others the benefit of the doubt—much of this comes from knowing the fragility of my own integrity. We are all imperfect souls; wisdom is found in remembering our imperfections.

At twenty-seven years of age, Sarah Fox finds herself happy and fulfilled—as a woman, a wife, and a mother. She and her family have relocated to her hometown where she is a teacher and her daughter attends second grade.

BICULTURALISM

ON BOTH SIDES OF THE BORDER

José García   The Hatred Within

We were always horrible to the poor old man, Mr. Connors. He was the stereotypical high school substitute teacher—scolding us in a voice that echoed off the back wall and putting us to work with boring written exercises. We would respond by acting up, throwing papers, talking back, and pulling practical jokes, tormenting him in any way we could.

"Poor old guy," I thought. No more than five feet tall, he was bald except for the fringe of white hair that circled his bare dome. He wore rectangular eyeglasses and always came decked out in a full gray suit. I think it was the only suit he owned because he seemed to wear it whenever he substituted.

One morning, only a few minutes into the tormenting, the national anthem began over the PA system. As always, we stood up while the music played. Usually we did a good job of being quiet, but one time my friend Andrew and I kept joking and chatting as the music played.

When the song was over, Mr. Connors did exactly what I expected the typical "old-timer" would do. He began to yell at us for showing disrespect to the nation, but instead of focusing his obvious anger at both of us, he looked dead at me.

"Why don't you try that in your own country?" he barked.

Silence. I was in absolute shock. Did he really just say that? Without a second's pause I responded, "Why don't you try that in yours?" I took a step forward. There was no mirror there, so I have no sure idea what I looked like. But knowing how I get, I'm sure my face turned a bright red, my eyes became narrow and angry, my eyebrows crouched down. When I'm enraged, I make it very obvious. And it usually has the desired effect of intimidation because it's such a contrast to my usual jovial expression.

"This *is* my country," he answered back without a pause. I took a few more steps forward, not rushing at him, but with a slow threatening pace. "Well, this is *my* country, too."

"Well, how about your parents' country?" he asked, seeming not to realize that he was pushing me more and more, and that with every comment he uttered he was becoming more and more offensive.

"How about *your* parents' country?" I snapped back in the same mocking tone.

"My parents are indigenous," he said smugly.

The word at the time was unfamiliar to me. Although I was mad at myself for not knowing it (I wanted to step above this man as his intellectual and physical superior), I shot back, "What the fuck does that mean?" I didn't know what had come over me. I didn't swear at teachers, even substitute teachers. I joked, I kidded around, but I was always as respectful as my sense of humor allowed me to be.

He answered back by saying that the word meant his family had always lived here. Since he didn't look Native American, I had to assume he meant his ancestors came aboard the *Mayflower* or a similar absurdity. At that point I was at the foot of his desk, an arm's length away from his gleaming dome. I had no idea what I was doing. How can you ever be prepared for a confrontation like that? What did I hope to do when I reached him? Hit him? Spit in his face? I stood there barely a second before Andrew and my other pal Dave came from behind me and pulled me away, yelling, "Come on, José, back off! He's not worth it." And I knew he wasn't worth it. But what was it? What had happened to me? What did I think I was going to do? Why was I so enraged?

I wasn't the kind of student who turned violent so quickly—not with students and especially not with teachers. But something had come over me. My shock and disbelief at his words had drawn me magnetically toward him. Did he really say that? To this day, it remains the first situation that comes to mind whenever someone asks me if I have ever encountered outright racism. It was a slap in the face. But in hindsight the incident reveals more about me than it does about Mr. Connors.

Why did he look at me and not see a student like any other, or even an annoying teenager who had little respect for his country? Why did he appear to view me as a brown-skinned foreigner who didn't belong and deserved to have his identity questioned by a high school substitute teacher? That day in my sophomore year I felt like a minority. I felt like a Latino student. I felt like I didn't belong. Every other day, however, I took pride when my friends told me, "José, you're so white."

I'm surprised that it isn't harder to admit. As I see it now, I was a sell-out in high school. I was a "box checker" (someone who takes advantage of minority status). I was "a coconut" (brown on the outside, white on the inside). Name the insult and I was the epitome of it. In college, a friend referred to Latino students who didn't recognize their background or culture as "those who didn't associate." That was me. I didn't associate.

My high school was pretty diverse. The students in the honors and Advanced Placement courses I took, however, were almost all white. I was lost, along with a handful of other students of color, in a sea of white faces. Given the fact that my classes were full of white students, it's no surprise that my friends were all white as well. I occasionally hung out with the one other Latino student whom I had known since kindergarten, but he, too, didn't "associate." He dressed in khakis and corduroys, polo shirts, and button-ups, clothes that most people considered "preppie." And in my high school, preppie was synonymous with smart, and smart was, with a few exceptions, white.

Daniel, my good friend from the fourth grade on, was white with blond hair and blue eyes. My two best friends at the time, Nelson and Sara, both had dirty blond hair and piercing blue eyes. The pack of a dozen or so girls I hung out with my junior and senior year were, with few exceptions, white. All of them were upper middle class. Most of them owned cars when they turned sixteen. These were my friends and I was proud of them.

But it was more than just the fact that they were white. I don't think there's a problem with having a lot of white friends, and I don't think I sought them out because of their skin color. They were just the people I saw every day. But what *did* matter was the attitude and thoughts that grew from this valuing of whiteness. Why did Mr. Connors's comments hit me so hard? Precisely because I was in denial of the fact that I was any different from my friends. I was like them. They were like me. It hurt me to be singled out as a Latino because, deep down, I really did believe that I was better then most Latinos. I was smart. I was a hard worker. I was ambitious. I was successful. I was funny. These traits, I thought, were uncharacteristic of most Latinos. Mr. Connors brought me down, and I'm sad to say that that was the biggest reason he upset me so much all those years ago. He tore me away from my misconception that I was accepted and belonged in the white world, which I saw as the embodiment of the good, happy, and successful life. He forced me to confront my own racism.

I talked to my mom about this late in my senior year of high school. I actually complimented her on her parenting skills. I pondered how she had managed to raise us in a way that made us better than most Latinos. It never occurred to me how wrong this thinking was. I would never have dared to repeat my racist thoughts out loud. But at the time, I thought them. I saw other Latinos and would often assume the worst. It was easy to convince me that someone was a drug dealer or a criminal, as I was already biased against them. And I always made that distinction clear: I, and for the most part my nuclear family, was not a part of "them." But these were all thoughts I kept buried deep down inside. I continued to check off "Hispanic" whenever forms asked for the optional race/ethnicity classification. I took pride in it then. With so few Latinos who aren't wastes, I figured I was helping myself. They would see me as an anomaly, I told myself. I was unique and that made me very happy.

So, besides the little box that I would check off from time to time, my culture and background meant nothing. In fact, I would treat it as a joke:

"Quit stealing my money, spic."

"Hey, don't look at me, I'm just a spic."

"Ahh, those spics just don't get it."

"You're such a grubby, grubby spic."

These were words I spoke, phrases that sprung out of my mouth and the mouths of my closest friends. They were always said in jest, and I always approved. I found it funny, because I thought being called a spic was pretty damned ironic. I recall a white friend telling me I was more white than he: I acted white, I dressed white, I talked white. In essence, to him I was normal, and normal was white. You're not part of a gang? You must be normal, you must be white. You don't shoot up every morning or carry a gun? You must be normal, you must be white. You don't speak Spanish in school, you don't know how to Latin dance? You must be normal, you must be white. And I laughed when he said I was a spic. How funny, I told myself, me . . . a spic? I thought I was anything and everything but that.

Besides these occasional insults, which I then thought were perfectly fine, my days at school had nothing to do with being Latino. I was normal, I told myself, therefore my ethnicity couldn't be my prime characteristic. I considered it a contradiction. This kind of thinking—this utter disdain for who I was—is something most people will never be able to understand. I think it's natural for adolescents to question their identity, but I did more than just question: I denied everything that was natural to me.

I would avoid the sun as much as possible late in high school. Why? Because I tan pretty easily and I didn't want to get too much darker than other students. A slight tan was okay, but I didn't want to get carried away. I didn't want to stick out. Sometimes I would actually fret over my darkening summer tan. How can I remain as white as possible? I would look in the mirror each morning and wish not just that my skin and features were different, but that my whole ethnicity could be washed away. My self-hatred lay at the core of my being. And that's where I kept it.

When I brought my friends home, I would be ashamed when my mom and dad, whose English was so bad, spoke to them. I would cringe when my dad tried to crack jokes, because his thick accent made him sound like some teenager in a man's body. I would be embarrassed when my dad swore without pause and told them some anecdote. I would never bring my parents to school as other children did for events or programs. Worst of all, the superiority I felt over Latinos I also felt over my parents. They were older, and more experienced, but because they couldn't communicate on the phone with their mortgage bank as well as I could, or because I understood the seven o'clock news better than they did, I felt like I stood on a higher plane. I used to look at my best qualities as traits that were somehow incompatible with the language I spoke at home, the color of my skin, and the values my parents taught me.

My story, my struggle as a Latino student in a white community, is also the story of my parents. The two cannot be separated. I now realize that much of my journey is a continuation of what they began so many years ago. They emigrated illegally from Honduras to the United States several years before I was born. In Honduras my father was on his way to becoming an engineer; my mother was a schoolteacher. When they came here, they lost everything and were forced to take menial jobs in a country where the language confused them. Within months they were caught and sent back by *la Migra*. When they came to the United States a second time, they struggled constantly but they also thrived. My oldest brother, Luis, who is nine years older than me, immigrated with my parents. My other brother, Steve, five years older than I am, was their first child born in the United States and therefore was given the most American name they could think of.

Until I was seven we lived in the "poor" section of our city. Surrounded by black and Latino kids, the feeling I can most recall is fear. I was scared of riding the bus to school. I was scared of the other kids. I was much like the scared white boy in a black neighborhood. I was scared of the others because I saw myself as inherently different. Even in elementary school, I had begun to develop the self-hatred and racism I would carry with me throughout my adolescence. All I knew was that while I was home, I had to cover my head with my pillow to drown out the police sirens and gunshots. But when I went to school and sat with the "smart kids" in the reading and math courses, I was nestled in a peaceful, white community. When my parents were finally able to save enough money, we moved out of the poor section and into the white community I held so dear.

My father was, and still is, a drunk. Drinking was more than just something he did; through the years it had become a part of the man. I cannot imagine him without a beer in his hand, just as I cannot separate the man from the violence he inflicted. I respected and looked up to my father when I was young, but perhaps most of that came from my fear of him—fear of what he would do if I misbehaved. He was a pretty intimidating man, with a big round beer belly and huge biceps and calves. Some of my earliest memories are of me hanging off his extended arms, like a skillful monkey swinging along the trees. He had a loud, booming voice. His Spanish was always rough and convoluted. It wasn't that he spoke poorly, it was just the slang or expressions he picked up and used as if they were Standard English: "So I told him, 'Hey guy, fuck you, okay? Fuck you.'" He seemed to always be telling a story, always swearing, and, of course, always drinking. He was in his forties, but to me he sounded like a teenager trying to be cool. But as I grew up, I came to see him as a meaner, darker character. He wasn't just big anymore, he was scary. His resonant voice, which sounded like he was yelling even when he was in a good mood, often brought me to tears.

The last time my father hit me is still vivid in my mind. I was in seventh grade. I had a paper route all through middle school, and I usually delivered the papers right after school. One weekday after school I went to a friend's house instead of delivering my papers. We hung out the whole afternoon, playing cards and telling stories. I didn't get home until a little after five. I froze when I saw my dad standing on our front steps as I rode my bike into the driveway. He stared at me, clearly angry. My dad didn't even wait until I was inside the house to start yelling: "¿Qué hora es esta para llegar?" He asked why I was late. Living in front of the high school, I was aware of the crowd of students staring at me as my father scolded me. I went inside, angry that my father would embarrass me like that. As soon as I was inside he slammed the door and continued his abuse: "¿Dónde estabas, babosada?" In Spanish he called me a little shit, irresponsible, no good, for not calling and telling him where I was. His face was bright red as his words tore through me.

As he stormed upstairs, I knew where he was going and what he was getting. The door to my brother Steve's room, which is down the hall from the kitchen, opened up and I saw his face pop out. I clung to him as little brothers tend to do. "If he hits me, I'm running away." I whispered, "If he hits me, I swear, I don't care, I'm running away." Tears were already streaming down my face and I braced myself for what I knew was coming. I heard my father pound down the stairs. He swung a belt and I foolishly tried to block the blows with my hands as he screamed to me to put my hands down. Again and again he brought the belt down across my thighs. The pain spurted in quick stings. There's no pain worse to me, at least in my memory, than the feel of a belt against my skin. I just wanted him to stop. I screamed louder, begging him to stop.

Eventually he stopped, probably tired of my screaming and tears; he turned abruptly and went upstairs. I remained crying, curled up in a little ball on the kitchen floor. I wished that I had the guts to actually stand up, grab my things, and leave the house forever. I had imagined and planned it so many times before—what things I would take with me, where I would go. But it was never meant to be anything more than a product of my imagination. Instead of making my plan a reality, I cried, just as I had done so many times before.

I'm not sure if he had been drinking that day or if it was just a bad mood. I mean, why hit your son for being late? My father, and the way he made me feel that day, became the personification of Honduras and my cultural roots. He was exactly what I wanted to avoid becoming. When he drank, I saw him as a stupid, pitiful fool. And it didn't take long for me to project those feelings onto all minorities around me—except my mother. I saw her as different.

My mother is the sweetest woman in the world. She would do anything for me, including staying married to my father. She did it for me because she knew a divorce would hurt me. She did it for me because she didn't want us to have to move out of our nice home in front of my high school. She did it for me because she needed my father to help pay for college. I guess I take it for granted that it really was all for *me*. But there's no doubt in my mind that it was.

I was born with a heart murmur, which made me vulnerable as a child. My family took extra care of me, but more than anyone my mother was anxious for my safety. It was partially because of her personality, but also due to the circumstances. The combination of my sickness at a very young age and the fact that I was her last child—forever her baby—meant I was bound to be treated differently. She poured the last of her motherly instincts and care into me. Well into high school she would tuck me in at night and wake me up in the morning. Some nights I asked her to rub my back, and though she jokingly complained, she always did it. My closeness with my mother was a contrast to my father, whom I saw as the enemy.

As I grew up, my importance in the family and in her eyes grew. Luis never finished high school and failed my parents' dream of being the first son to graduate college in America. Steve failed similarly after only two terms away at the state university. I became their last chance. Out of thirty-two cousins on my father's side, I am the fourth youngest yet only the second to go to college. When Luis got into trouble, my dad unloaded on him in the only way he knew how. My father's mother had supposedly whipped my father into submission many years ago. A rope would have been a welcome change to some of the instruments he was beaten with as a boy in Honduras. Yet somehow he grew up loving and thanking his mother for every bit of punishment she handed to him. Similarly, my brother Luis has consistently defended my father for the pain he has inflicted on us. He, out of all of us, has stood by as my father's sole defender. For that reason, among others, my brother Luis and I did not often get along. Even though he knew my dad beat me, Luis felt he had gotten it much worse and viewed me as a spoiled brat.

My mother did not defend my father for most of their marriage, nor did she fight back. She quietly withstood his verbal abuse whenever he drank too much. Over time, however, whether it was the freedom she felt now that she was in the United States or her own personal growth, she began to speak up and assert herself. When he yelled, she would yell back. Usually, though, she was the voice of reason to his temper tantrums. Most of the time he didn't listen and kept on shouting, stalking off in anger and sleeping for the next few weeks in the basement, where he had a bed. Eventually, when I was in high school, my father moved most of his clothes down there and for months at a time would not sleep in his own bed with my mother. Through it all they stayed together . . . although "together" is a strange word to use for two people who never spoke, never stayed in the same room together for more than a moment, and were married, it seemed to me, in name only.

When they argued, my dad would say anything to interrupt her, to keep her quiet, to regain the peaceful life he remembered from Honduras. Her spirit took him by surprise. This wasn't the way it was in Honduras, he must have thought to himself. This wasn't the way it should be. The wife, he felt, was supposed to cook his food, serve him his drinks and meals, clean the house, stand by him always, and never talk back. But my mom, the wonderful woman that she is, would not stand for that. She knew that she was an American woman now and that things would have to change. Sometimes, crying to myself, I would hope that my mom would just give up and stop arguing back. I respect her now for being strong, but as a little boy I just wanted the shouting to stop. But no matter what, I always blamed my father. He was exactly what I didn't want to become, and yet he was also the biggest male presence in my life. In my mind he represented Latino males, therefore I had no desire to grow up and become one.

As easy as it is to blame my father, another side of him, a gentler one, surfaces in my memory. He isn't always the man who beat me and yelled at my mother; sometimes he's the man who sacrificed so much for his family. During my sophomore year in college I was profiled in the college newspaper as a campus activist. The article described everything I was involved in and all of my accomplishments. I referred to my mother as the "force in my life." A few days after it was published, I sent the clipping home. I was worried how my father would take it. When I finally spoke to my mom about it, she said they had read it together and they both had cried. He was not angry or jealous, as I would have expected him to be. She told me that my family had had a barbecue and invited all my family members. Sometime during the party, my father pulled out the article, which he had already taken to work to show his friends, and translated the article into Spanish for my relatives. My mom told me that everyone was so proud of me, but my thoughts were with my father. This is the man I call my dad, this is the man, who, along with my mother, I strive to prove myself to each day in spite of his harshness to me. When I look back on my life, I won't see it as a success unless both of my parents see it that way as well. In the back of my mind is the knowledge that if things had gone differently twenty-odd years ago—if my parents had made just a slightly different decision, or if my father hadn't worked half as hard—my life would be completely different. I owe something to them, whether I like it or not, and that knowledge drives me to achieve, even when I feel that "I have too much to do."

That's why my narrative can't be separated from my parents' story. Their journey to the United States didn't end when they arrived for good, or even when they finally became citizens. The two stories continue in tandem, and just as important is the extended family they left in Honduras and the extended family that traveled with them. Growing up, I was often surrounded by my many aunts and uncles, cousins and second cousins. Just as my father became the embodiment of the Latino man—everything I didn't want to grow to be—my extended family also represented my ethnicity, my culture, and the target of my racism.

I saw my nuclear family as different from their little clans, and as I grew up "different" also meant "better." We Garcías were somehow special. My aunts were either single, divorced, or remarried. My cousins were constantly being arrested, having children out of wedlock, causing their parents grief. My cousins were the only Latinos I had any close connection to, so to me their behavior exemplified all Latinos. They got into trouble, broke the law, stole, cheated, lied, and were disobedient. Although my brothers and I occasionally exhibited some of these behaviors, I nevertheless saw us as above it all. My female cousins got pregnant, moved in with boyfriends, married and divorced early—all the kind of behavior that I considered "subwhite." To do the wrong thing, then, as I saw my cousins do the wrong things, was to be less than white, to be *not* succeeding in the United States.

It is true that my brothers and I were generally better behaved, and better educated, and better mannered than many of my cousins. But instead of leaving the comparison there, I took it a step further and said that this was because they were Latino and were acting it, while we were Latino but we had somehow overcome our heritage. Overcome our heritage! This idea disgusts me now, and yet there was a time I didn't even question it. I didn't think of my family as successful because we were Latino or in addition to being Latino, but *in spite of* that fact.

The notion of overcoming my heritage recalls a poignant incident that occurred during a family vacation to Honduras. On the road, a small child around my age came up to our van and asked for a ride. We told him we didn't have any room, but as we started to drive we noticed that he had climbed on the back of the van and was prepared to ride with us, at fifty or sixty miles per hour, holding on to a ladder. At the time I disliked the little brat; I couldn't believe he had the nerve to try and hitch a ride from us. A dozen years later I think of that kid and can't help but see myself. If circumstances had been different, I could have been him. That notion would occur to me again and again, but at the time, and even as I packed my bags for college, I still looked at that boy—at so much of my identity—with disdain.

My parents didn't pressure me much to succeed; I put the pressure on myself: I was the one who had to bring respect to my family after Luis dropped out of high school and Steve dropped out of college. Luis and I constantly argued, and he refused to come to my high school graduation. I think my success only highlighted his failure. My parents' pride in me was a sharp stab at him. He had been expected to be the first one to do so many things that I was now doing. Steve was more complacent, always assuming he would return to school and catch up with me. And that's how I left for college—angry with most of my family, convinced that I was better than my family and my heritage, and bearing the burden of bringing home what my parents wanted to see: a good report card and a college diploma.

For the most part, college was everything it was supposed to be: I was having the time of my life and meeting so many amazing people. It wasn't until my first meeting of La Unidad, the Latino student organization, that I had my first confrontation with the hate inside me. I had gone to the meeting because I felt an obligation to go. Despite my belief that I was better than my background, I was also confronted by the feeling that my status as a "box checking" Latino was what got me into college. Why else would I have identified myself as such? "Associate," "identify"—words like these meant the difference between being seen as an outsider to the Latino community or a link within it. If you identified, that basically meant you acknowledged your heritage, you went beyond your box-checking status.

I went to that first Unidad meeting because I felt an obligation, not because I felt I would gain anything from it. I didn't want to be seen as a Latino student by the mainstream, but I also didn't want to be seen as a sellout by the Latino students. My self-hatred and hatred of my ethnicity was deeply buried, and I had no intention of making it known. I barely thought about it, and that's the way I liked it. But my first weeks at college were characterized by a sense of exclusion, a sense that I didn't fit in anymore. Dressed in attire from Abercrombie and Fitch, attending their parents' alma mater—the average student seemed so different from me. I was afraid someone would suddenly discover that I didn't really belong. I had an overwhelming feeling that I had to start my life over again, build myself back up, yet I didn't know who I was or how to go about it.

That first Unidad meeting we all sat in a stuffy room, the Latino students on display for one another. I was immediately hit by the feeling that I was very un-Latino. The others somehow exuded more Latinoness. It was in their accents, the speed of their speech, the Spanish words they mixed into their English. They all talked about home cooking and dishes that they loved, and although I loved my mom's home cooking, I didn't know the correct names of the foods she prepared. But most importantly, they all seemed to know more about their individual cultures. They were more culturally, socially, and politically aware then I ever thought I could be. What did I know about Honduras? I couldn't even tell you what kind of government they have there, let alone how "my people" were doing. What did I know about Latino culture, besides what I learned in school, which was nothing? My cultural ignorance had never even occurred to me as a problem; suddenly it became a very big one.

The worst moment was when we went around the room and introduced ourselves. One by one they spoke, pronouncing their names with a full Spanish accent. Some people I knew always did so, but a few caught me off guard. "Drew" became "Andrés," "John" became "Juan"; the speed at which people said their names increased, and as we quickly went around the circle, I didn't know what to do. Of course I could easily have used an accent, but I never did and I didn't want to do so just to fit in. I even had a fear about doing that. What if it came out badly? What if I couldn't even say my own name right? I didn't want their eyes on me, didn't want them to snicker and know that I was only a fake. I just wanted to come to the meeting, sit back, and feel like I had made up for the fact that I checked "Hispanic/Latino" instead of "White," which is what I wished I were, or "Other," which is what I felt like.

When the introductions finally came around to me, I blurted out my name, José García, with a full accent. I felt like a sellout, not because I didn't want to be Latino, but because I was willing to hide my true self in order to be accepted as Latino. I was more confused than ever. Inside I knew that I thought poorly of Latinos and that my racism was deeply rooted, yet I was willing to act unlike myself in order to be accepted by my Latino peers. I didn't know who I was or what I wanted. I only knew that I wanted to be accepted. I wanted to please everyone, and was finding I couldn't please anyone.

My confusion got worse before it got better. I had gotten involved early in my freshman year in my college's student government. Representing the student body, the organization constantly worried about whether or not they were truly being representative. So they would literally take a count based on gender and race/ethnicity. I wasn't just a normal involved student, I was the token Latino, or so it seemed to me.

The word "token" was one that I would get to know well as time went on. Token Latino, token minority, people of color vs. minority, ignorance vs. racism, the relationship of power in racism, prejudice, institutional racism . . . these were all terms and phrases that I had never been acquainted with before my first year at college. I had a crash course in being nonwhite. I'm convinced that if you asked a white person, half of those terms would draw a blank response. It's not simply because they're white but because they have had no contact with these issues. I'm a great example. I had never considered any of these issues, yet I was that person of color, I was that token minority. I was *supposed* to know. That lesson came to me during a student government meeting when I was asked to give my opinion as a Latino. I wasn't asked to give it as a student who happens to be Latino, but to give the official Latino opinion, as if all we Latinos got together one day and took a straw poll on a number of issues, all of which came out unanimous. There is diversity among races, but there is also diversity within races. I wanted my friends to be color blind. I didn't want to be seen as Latino or ethnic or "Other." In a short time I went from hating my ethnicity to not minding it, but still being grateful when people could ignore it. The inner hatred I had grown up with was gone, but something rotten remained. I still had a ways to go before I could embrace and actually be proud of my culture, rather than just tolerating it.

I continued going to Unidad meetings, continued struggling through my ignorance. I heard other students of color talk about the racial issues they had confronted growing up. I began to find more and more aspects of my childhood that related to their childhoods—similarities in being the children of immigrants. Most of all, I was surrounded for the first time by students who shared my skin color and also shared my academic success. I was no longer the exception in a sea of white faces. The wall I had built up between myself and my ethnicity began to break down. Despite being 70 percent white, my college introduced me to diversity. So before I realized it was happening, that lifelong correlation between "white" and "successful" stopped making sense to me.

I recall a late night conversation with my friend Jake, who is half Latino and half white. He casually mentioned that he was against affirmative action, that he saw it as reverse discrimination against white students and felt that it only served to emphasize racial lines more. As he put it, "Why should white people today have to suffer for what white people in the past have done?" This comment led to a passionate debate. I argued that, despite what he believed, there was a racial divide in this country. It was social—as evidenced by my high school substitute's behavior years before. It was economic—as evidenced by the poor section of my hometown that bused me in and out when I was younger. It was educational—as shown by all the white faces in my upper-level classes from elementary school through high school. It was cultural—as witnessed by the isolation I felt at my first Unidad meeting. "You're right," I argued. "Most white people of today have nothing to do with what happened years before. But that doesn't erase the problem. That doesn't change the fact that minorities are still suffering because of what happened years before. Furthermore, whether whites are directly at fault or not, it doesn't change the fact that whites have benefited. Because others have lost, whites have gained. It's not a question of right or wrong—it's just the way things are. But that doesn't mean we shouldn't try to change things." Jake kept arguing that minorities just needed to "stop feeling sorry for themselves."

That night I developed my own theory on this subject: "Look Jake, it's like life is this one big long-distance race. Ever since the race began, the minority runners have been oppressed, kept back, slowed by slavery, by conquest, and so on. And all this time the white runners have been getting ahead. Suddenly, all restrictions are dropped. No more slavery. No more segregation. Everything is made equal. But is it really equal, Jake? All that equalization under the law doesn't change the fact that all these white runners have had a centuries-long head start. How does that translate to real life? In economics, in education, in social attitudes? These are all big problems, and they call for big solutions. I don't think affirmative action is the best long-term solution, but it is a temporary one until people are willing to make the bigger commitment."

Jake said that he used his Latino background to get in to college, just as he used his running talent (he was recruited by the college for cross-country)—that was all his identity as a Latino meant to him. With my mind entrenched in issues of race and ethnicity, I was outraged at him for saying something like that. And yet just a few months before I could have said the same thing.

At college, once I began to deal with the long-suppressed issues of my ethnic identity, the flood gates opened. Sometimes I got in serious arguments and found myself saying things I couldn't believe I was saying. In those moments I claimed all white people were racists or the U.S. border should be completely open all the time. But that was part of my learning process, of pushing forward. I was in the process of testing, trying things out, seeing where thoughts would go and then evaluating whether I still believed them or not. I was trying to find myself under years of buried ignorance, self-hate, and prejudice toward my own culture.

In another late-night conversation with friends, I recalled that small boy who had wanted to hitch a ride with us in Honduras, who I had disliked so much. "What's so different between me and so many of the naked kids I see running around in Honduras, begging on the streets? Sure, I think my drive and my work ethic have been important, but I think the key difference has been the opportunities I have had—attending schools that are leaps and bounds above anything in Honduras and pursuing so many things that my parents never had the chance to. And yet it might have been completely different. It could be another kid sitting here today and me in Honduras. That's why I don't think I'll be happy in life unless I'm helping them realize their own potential. I want to give others all the opportunities that I had." And the minute I said it, I knew I believed it with all my being—I knew I would never look at my role or purpose in life in the same light again. I was never religious, and yet I felt I had found my calling. I knew then I could never be an investment banker or businessman. My place was in service, in education, in any field where I could use my skills to improve the lives of others and help them open doors.

In spite of my new insights, the same demons remained inside of me. When you look at yourself in the mirror for years and see someone who is unattractive because of his skin color, hair color, speech, and other characteristics, those negative feelings don't go away easily. I felt I had a big nose, that it was too round and not slim enough. I hated the fact that I would always be a good four inches below average height. I even came to dislike my boring brown eyes and black hair. My own insecurities about how I looked and fit in remained. Even though I was growing intellectually and emotionally, I had not yet purged many of the old thoughts that haunted me.

My self-hatred was also hatred of my background and my relatives. My perception of myself and others had been altered by all the new people I met at college. Generalizations I had held to—that all Latinos are lazy, all students of color are inferior to whites—were shattered while I was at school. My relationships with members of my family and their relationships with each other had also been forced to change as a result of my absence. My leaving home was exactly what my family needed.

Just how far the healing had progressed is evident in a radiant photo taken at Luis's new apartment, which he shared with his fiancée, Sandra. In the photo, we're embracing each other tightly. My father has one arm extending far to his right to reach my brother and the other hand is tightly grasping my mother's shoulder. My mother is smiling beautifully, it's a genuine smile. She seems truly happy—happy to have her family all around her. You can almost read her thoughts: she has her family together again, different from before, but together. Caught in that photo is me kissing my brother. For no other reason than because I was feeling happy and wanted a funny picture, I embraced Luis's face and kissed him on his right cheek. He remained smiling while looking at the camera, his arm tightly around me. After the photo was taken, Luis wrapped his arms around me and pulled me in for a full hug. Steve came over as well. And right there, in the kitchen of my brother's new house, with my parents and his fiancée watching, Luis began to apologize to me for mistreating me for years and years. As we embraced, Luis sobbed, "I'm so sorry, José, I'm so sorry for everything I put you through. But you know I did it because I loved you and wanted only the best from you. You're my little brother, there's nothing I wouldn't do for you." He then opened his arms to Steve, and with the three of us wrapped in each other's arms, forming a little circle, Luis continued, with tears in his eyes, "You guys are my brothers, my little men. I love you two so much. So fucking much! I'm always going to be there for you guys, whatever you might need. You fucking come to me, all right? There's nothing I won't do for my brothers." The tears were coming down my cheeks now, and Steve, usually calm and reserved, also began to cry. Our coming together in love and reconciliation was the climax to what I had slowly been developing the whole year—my acceptance by and of my brothers after years of alienation. While we hugged, I remember hearing my mother tell my father to look over at us. I sensed her deep inner happiness. She was so proud to see her sons finally come together.

Several months later I took another step forward in my journey. I interned in Washington, D.C., working as a research assistant for a nonprofit organization focused on strengthening the Latino community. I found myself surrounded by people who had centered their lives around making a difference in the Latino community. Two men in particular, leaders in the organization, further altered my views on Latinos. Both had gone to Ivy League schools and their résumés were packed with incredible experiences. They could have done anything they wanted to in life, but they chose to give back to their respective communities. I met many prominent Latinos through them, and my perceptions of Latinos, which had expanded exponentially since high school, was further improved. Any significant prejudices I had were eliminated by the success of these two men. I admired them *and* they were Latino. In the past, I would have joined these two facts by thinking, *in spite of* their being Latino. It's such a small detail and yet reveals so much about how I thought.

I was still working in D.C. when I flew home for the weekend to see the production of a musical in my high school. I saw the show with Dan, my friend since the fourth grade. I told him about my involvement in student government, my increased activism, and life in general at my small liberal arts college. But since I was in D.C. at the time, I also mentioned my internship and the great time I was having. With pride, I pulled out my business card. "Empowering the Latino community?" He read off the card, smiling at me and waving the card to a mutual friend from high school. "Look Chris, José is Latino now. Look at the card. Our little brown friend's creating community!" His tone was mocking and they both began to laugh as they gazed at the card. "This is the biggest load of PC bullshit. I can't believe you're a part of this crap!" He laughed louder, staring at the card in disbelief.

I felt crushed. This had been my childhood friend? This had been the life that I had enjoyed so much? I was ashamed of who I had been and what I had believed, but I didn't think the shame ran so deep. Was there anything I could turn back to? Was there anything that didn't stink of my racism? It had been a while since I felt so uncomfortable, fidgeting in place, wanting to be anywhere but there. And right then I was struck with a realization that came just before I would have begun feeling sorry for myself. "Hey Dan, fuck you," I said. His mouth opened in disbelief, his laugh stopped in midbreath. I continued, "Just because you haven't grown up in the last two years, doesn't mean that I haven't."

"Hey, Mr. Latino, don't take it personally. I just think that doing this sort of thing is very unlike the José I knew in high school," Dan said, handing the card back to me.

"A lot about me is unlike the José you once knew. People change, Dan, and ya know what? I'm happy with the changes I've made." I gave both of them one last look in the eye and then returned to my seat in the theater. I don't think I was particularly articulate or eloquent, but I got across what I wanted. I didn't back off.

As the show continued, I recalled that late-night conversation with Jake and the passion with which I spoke of privilege and racism. An image of that boy from Honduras came to mind and I again imagined myself living his life. I then remembered Mr. Connors, the substitute teacher, and the anger he had made me feel. I reflected on the dozens of conversations in which I called myself a spic and spat on my culture. Finally, I thought of my mother and father and all they had given me and continue to give me. Dan, who silently took his seat next to me, had accused me of being "very unlike the José he knew in school." I smiled, happy that he was right, proud that I didn't joke along with him and deny what I had spent two years forming, what is still forming, what I hope never stops forming.

After graduating from college with a major in history, José García began teaching in a public school in a large urban school system in the Northeast. He continues to teach mathematics at a small alternative school in the same system. He works primarily with low-income African American and Latino students and believes that a rigorous education is the key to opening doors and changing the paths of his students' lives. He is happily married to his college girlfriend.

Marissa Saldivar   Was It Worth It?

Antonio stood behind me, leaning in as if to smell the sweet perfume I had strategically placed on my body. His black guayabera was unbuttoned at the top, revealing his soft black chest hair. The look of passion on his face overwhelmed me, and all I could do was stand with my back to his chest and tilt my head ever so slightly so that Antonio could lean his head against my neck. My hair had been pulled away from my face in a tight, high bun, accentuating my high cheekbones and almond-shaped eyes. I wore a black fitted top that hung off the shoulders; my neck was bare. Antonio was my only accessory. I had a slight smile on my face and expressed a sense of mischievous pleasure. As the photographer snapped away, I held on to Antonio's hands, not for the expression of the moment, but for reassurance that such intimate photos were not wrong to take. And as I repeated to myself that this was for a class project and did not reflect the type of woman I was, I could not help but wonder how my mother would react if she ever saw these pictures. I almost felt guilty for posing in such risqué photos, and yet I never realized how much this experience would change my life.

Antonio was from New York City and extremely different from any other guy I had met. The child of an upper-class Cuban father and a Colombian mother, Antonio plucked his eyebrows, manicured his nails, dyed his hair, and wore belts with rhinestone Gucci emblems. He had sung on Broadway, loved sushi, and swore by the music of Whitney Houston. At first I didn't know what to make of him: Was he gay, or was it just his New York City culture that made him different from the boys back home in Los Angeles? I eventually decided it didn't matter; he was a great friend and made me feel good about myself.

Because of his background in theater, Antonio knew a lot about makeup. I, on the other hand, had never worn much of it, mostly out of fear of looking like some cheap Mexican prostitute or *chola*. Besides, I never considered myself beautiful and didn't think makeup was going to solve my problems. Growing up I was the studious one, and my cousin Yvette was the beautiful cheerleader. In an effort to make us closer, my grandmother used to sit us down on her couch and say, "Yvette, you talk to Marissa about your boyfriends and dates, and Marissa, well, you talk to Yvette about what you study in school." My family presumed I had no other life but that which revolved around my education. While no one called me ugly, I grew up feeling that way.

Miraculously, Antonio saw a raw beauty in me that not even my grandmother had seen, and he realized that with a little help I too would recognize my own inner and outer beauty. One day in the middle of the winter term of my sophomore year in college, Antonio got the nerve to take me on my first trip to the makeup counter. There I learned not only about the best products for my skin but also about the beauty my ethnic features had afforded me. I was shocked and amazed to hear the New England make-up artists praise me for my large eyelids, high cheekbones, and almond-shaped eyes. They were happy to apply my makeup and thought it a privilege to work with what they considered a great face. I had never considered anything about my looks "ethnic" until I came to New England. As more and more people complimented me for my features, I started to feel like those beautiful women in the *telenovelas*.

At the time of our first photo shoot, Antonio and I had only known each other for a month, but our photos were to become a prelude to our future relationship and a vehicle from which I moved from an isolated, plain caterpillar to a confident and beautiful butterfly. However, this transformation was not an easy process. Not only did I have to come to terms with the woman within but so did my family. As my experiences at college both physically and mentally changed me, I grew distant from my family; they questioned my college learning and associated my physical transformation with "evil" New York influences. The more I struggled to balance my educational experiences at Dartmouth with my cultural upbringing in Los Angeles, the more challenges life then threw my way. But it is through these challenges that I have molded myself into the strong and determined Latina that I am today, and the woman and mother I will soon become. I am pregnant.

Although I grew up in Los Angeles in a predominantly Latino community, my schooling and residential environment did not reflect that culture. As a result, most of my early friendships were established in my predominately white Catholic elementary school, which was a thirty-minute drive from my home in a small, isolated cul-de-sac. At St. Brendan's Elementary School I joined the Girl Scouts, where I made friends; not one was a Latina. Growing up, race had never been an issue and was rarely even referred to. However, there was one time when race and my own identity made me feel out of place.

We were on a Girl Scout outing to the El Capitan movie theater in Hollywood. It was already dark by the time the Disney movie was over, but the lights from the marquee and surrounding stores kept the gated parking lot relatively well lit. We were walking to the van when two men—one Latino and the other black, both dressed in baggy jeans and sweatshirts with hoods that practically covered their faces—appeared on the opposite side of the gate walking toward each other. My friends immediately got frightened and ran to the van. When I asked why they were so scared, one replied, "Didn't you see the two gangsters? I thought there was going to be a shootout." I was confused and wanted to know why, since I hadn't been scared by the two suspected "gangsters," so I probed further. They responded, "They're dark, look mean, and are probably in gangs. Don't they look like thugs to you?" Hurt by their racist assumptions, I replied, "But I'm Mexican, are you scared of me too?" They laughed, saying, "But you're not really Mexican, you're different, not like them." Back then I wasn't exactly sure what they meant by their comments, but I do remember feeling, for the first time in my life, that I was different.

While at the time I didn't associate their reactions with racism and socially constructed biases, their actions did cause me to start questioning my ethnicity and identity. As a third-generation Mexican, did I have any claim to a cultural and ethnic identity? I didn't speak Spanish, but I sure didn't look white. From an early age my ethnic identity confused me, and seeking answers from those closest to me, I turned to my father. In response to my questions, he told me I was not Mexican American, but rather American Mexican.

I wasn't quite sure why it was so important for me to identify as American first, but my dad was very adamant about it. I now realize that for my dad, his Mexican heritage was not always a positive attribute, and while he was proud of his ethnicity, he feared what repercussions it might hold for me. Growing up in East Los Angeles in the '60s, my father was ridiculed and sometimes reprimanded by his teachers for speaking Spanish in the classroom. When he was a teenager, gangs ruled the streets of East Los Angeles. Luckily for my dad, he avoided the pressures of being forced into the local Mexican street gang by being the drummer for a local band that was always on call for the gang's parties. Although he was not affiliated with the gang, he was affiliated with the street and would get into fights with blacks and members of surrounding gangs, fighting for his own pride and the pride of his Mexican community. Later in life, as a dark-skinned Mexican truck driver, he was automatically stereotyped as a "spic" and "wetback."

In the 1980s Mexican immigrants in Los Angeles were being paid extremely low wages to drive shipments from the L.A. harbor into the industrial districts. Throughout the truck-driving industry, Mexican immigrants were blamed for taking white people's jobs and for causing salaries to decrease. As a result, my dad worked hard to distinguish himself from the newly arrived Mexicans. "These damn illegals, driving trucks without proper licenses and causing accidents that kill innocent people," he would say every time he saw a harbor truck driving dangerously. Growing up, I always wondered how my dad could hate Mexicans so much—after all, he was a Mexican, or rather an American Mexican.

Equally influential to my conception of identity was my grandmother, who helped to frame my involvement within the Latino community. In the 1960s and 1970s she was involved in the Chicano movement and worked with the Brown Berets, a Chicano activist organization. By the time I was born, my grandmother was heavily engaged in city politics, working to get her friends elected to office. She hosted fund-raising events and election-night parties in her home. My grandmother was also involved with organizations such as LULAC (League of United Latin American Citizens) and worked in the guidance office of a local public school for more than thirty years. As soon as I could walk, my grandmother had me marching in parades shouting, "¡Sí, se puede!" (Yes, we can!). As I got older, I helped with the set up at voting stations, cooked for fund-raising dinners, and stood in front of public schools passing out political flyers to parents. I was never aware of the politics involved with any of the campaigns I participated in, but wherever my grandmother took me, I helped out. As a result, I grew up heavily steeped in community service and in the politics that directly affected Los Angeles's Mexican community.

With my grandmother's support, during the summer before my senior year of high school I attended my first Chicano/Latino Youth Leadership Conference at the University of California—Davis. The conference consisted of about one hundred college-bound high school students from throughout California. They promoted cultural pride and community involvement. A major focus of the conference was reminding the participants that education and success were important, but that they meant nothing if you didn't give back to the community, a theme my grandmother had also consistently instilled in me while growing up.

It was at this conference that I learned of a new identity, a Chicano identity, one in which I didn't have to chose between being American or Mexican. I learned that while "Chicano" originally had negative connotations, the members of the Chicano movement had reclaimed the term and associated it with empowerment. I also learned that the term Chicano embraces one's Mexican heritage while acknowledging American influences. Chicano doesn't mean you speak Spanish or know how to cook *menudo*, but it does mean that you live the life of a dual culture; one that is American and one that is Mexican. It is the duality of culture and identity that defines the Chicano/Chicana, and I embraced that. Finally, I had an identity that described my cultural heritage and upbringing. I was no longer a hyphenated individual, was neither Mexican nor American but a Chicana, and I was proud. With this new identity I could feel comfortable in both the *carnecería* (meat market) in East Los Angeles and the supermarket near my high school. It didn't matter anymore; I knew who I was and I was proud and relieved to have identified my cultural heritage. With this new identity and mentality, I embarked on a quest to attend an institution of higher learning that would challenge me to share my cultural heritage and grow into a strong and empowering Chicana leader.

I had initially decided to attend the University of California at Irvine, which made my father happy because the university's proximity to our home would have allowed him to visit me frequently. In fact, he had already begun planning his visits. So when I told him I had been accepted to a top Eastern college, and they were going to pay my way to visit the campus, I heard the fear in his voice. I knew he was proud, but I recognized that he wasn't ready to let me leave. He immediately reiterated his concern regarding the high cost of tuition, especially since my parents were beginning a divorce and UC Irvine had already given me what seemed like a great financial aid package. I assured him that I didn't really want to go to college in the East (I was fearful of the snobbish, rich students I was sure I would encounter there) but that I might as well take advantage of the free trip. So off I went. It was my first time on an airplane, and when my dad dropped me off we were both afraid. For my father it was a fear of having to let go of his daughter. For me, it was a double-sided fear. What if I didn't fit in and hated the school? But my bigger fear was just the opposite: What if I fell in love with it? It would mean a profound separation from my family and Chicano culture. As it turned out, I really did like the college and decided to go there, especially when their financial aid package was far better than UC Irvine's, so I really had no reason *not* to go. Well, maybe two reasons.

At the time, my parents were just beginning what turned out to be a very long and nasty divorce. My two younger siblings and I are extremely close, so when I moved out of my mother's house and in with my father they resented my decision and felt that I was abandoning them. They soon understood my decision, however, and were happy to know that at least someone was taking care of our father. But my decision to attend college in the East meant that once again I was leaving my siblings behind, this time moving completely across the country. As much as it hurt me, I knew that this was the best decision for me. I also knew that it was time to start thinking about myself and to consider my emotional health, which at that point was shaky because my parents' divorce had put me in the middle of a bitter battle that had worn me out emotionally.

Freshman year at college was rather difficult. Not only did I have to cope with my first-year studies and leaving home, but my most difficult transition was dealing with the Latinos of the East Coast. In Los Angeles, I used the term Latino synonymously with Mexican; for me they were one and the same. But on the East Coast, Mexicans were few and far between. At college I encountered Colombians, Cubans, Dominicans, Puerto Ricans, and other Caribbean Latinos with whom I had nothing in common. Not only did they not understand the dynamics of the Chicano culture, but many of the Latinos I encountered denied my own Latinidad for the simple fact that I did not speak Spanish. I felt alienated from the pan-Latino organizations, but I did find my own space within the Chicano organization, where I met a lot of Chicanos from the Southwest. I felt comfortable with these friends and started getting involved in the Mexican American community. However, by the end of freshman year, just as I was beginning to find my place within the college, I was confronted with a challenge that has affected my life dramatically.

In April of my freshman year I was found guilty of violating my college's honor code. My friend and biology lab partner, José, and I had been working on our reports on the computers in the library. The night before the report was due, José and I were just beginning the ten-page assignment.

We finished relatively quickly, and by 2:30 a.m. José went downstairs to pick up our lab reports from the printout window. He had printed some extra graphs and on the way up the stairs had mixed up our graphs. We were lab partners and our graphs looked so similar that it was hard to immediately tell them apart, especially at 3 a.m. when we were both exhausted. In my chemistry class and in José's physics class, lab partners were allowed to submit the same graphs but were required to submit individual reports. Assuming that the same applied for this biology class, we grabbed the graphs, slipped them into our lab report, and went home.

Two weeks later I received a thick manila envelope in my mailbox. Inside was a very formal letter from the Judicial Affairs administrator informing us that we had been accused of violating the honor code. Included in the packet was a list of procedures we had to follow, contacts that might be helpful, and the detailed research our professor had conducted to *prove* our fault. I was immediately appalled that two weeks of investigation and debate had occurred without my knowing that my academic integrity was being questioned. How come no one ever asked José or me what happened? Why did my professor take such extreme measures without consulting me? It all seemed like one big misunderstanding, and yet my standing with the college was being threatened. I was scared, mad, frustrated, and embarrassed. Our hearing lasted for an hour and a half. Interestingly, our professor admitted that she hadn't reviewed the honor code with the class, but rather assumed that we would know what was allowed. Despite the fact that we had been unaware of our violation, the college suspended us.

My dad took the news of my suspension rather well. He remained calm and supportive throughout the whole ordeal. I, on the other hand, felt as if I had slapped him across the face. After all, he was living in his motor home in his parents' driveway in East Los Angeles just so he could afford my tuition. My dad used to have a saying, "A real man isn't a man unless he is living under his own roof." But because of my college expenses, my dad was eating his own words and living with his parents.

When I returned to Los Angeles, I cried a lot at night and kept myself locked up inside the motor home. Realizing I was depressed, my dad confronted me. "Hey," he said, "you can't let this get the best of you." It was only later that I realized he was right. I was depressed and I was allowing my suspension to tear me apart. It was at that moment, sitting in the dark, cramped motor home, when I vowed I would use this experience to my benefit. I told myself that I was better than this and that no one was going to dictate my life. I was going to take charge of my circumstances and prove to my college that they had made a mistake. More important, I needed to prove to my father that he hadn't made all of those sacrifices in vain. I promised myself that I would again make him and myself proud.

I came back to college the following term with a vengeance; I was no longer a naive little girl. I had shed my innocence and ignorance and vowed never to let this experience get the best of me. I got involved in every single Latino organization on campus and even founded organizations that I felt the Latino community lacked. In a community where I once felt alienated, I now thrived and eventually became president of three organizations. My motivation for involvement in these organizations was threefold: I wanted to make the Latino community stronger, I wanted to prove to the college that they had misjudged me, and I wanted to make my father proud.

It was through this intense organizational involvement that I got to know Antonio. He was also extremely active in the Latino community and, like me, sought to create stronger foundations for Latinos at the college. We both lived in the Latino house and spent so much time together that we quickly became best friends. Antonio helped to complete the transformation that had begun with my suspension. He introduced me to the New York world of beauty and glamour. Through the photo shoots and shopping trips to New York City, my own outer beauty and self-esteem were blossoming. I was moving out of my childhood into becoming a beautiful woman, and I could not wait to share my transformation with my family.

That summer Antonio came home to Los Angeles with me. The first time my family saw my new look was at my cousin Laura's *quinceañera*, the traditional celebration of a young woman's fifteenth birthday, which in Mexican culture symbolizes the transformation from childhood into womanhood. Earlier that day I went to the salon where they layered and straightened my hair just for the occasion. My makeup included dramatic eyes, with eyeliner that extended well past the normal boundary of my large oval eyes. I wore a lipstick that mixed purple and red under a thick coat of clear gloss. My black halter-top dress had been purchased in New York City, along with the skinny, black five-inch Bebe slip-on heels that Antonio had given me for my birthday. I wore rhinestones on my ears and neck and an air of confidence that no one had seen me with before.

Antonio was another story. Dressed in a black long sleeve shirt with the sleeves rolled up to his elbows and the top three buttons undone, and black slacks, he clearly stood out. His white skin was emphasized by the dark colors of his outfit and the bright lights near the DJ. But it was his accessories rather than the color of his skin that stood out the most. Although it was already 9 p.m., he wore black Gucci sunglasses, a Gucci belt with a rhinestone *G*, and pair of black Jimmy Choo fur shoes. As we walked into the crowded, festive dance hall hand in hand, we clearly looked out of place. After my family realized who I was, the compliments poured in. I looked fabulous, and my aunts at least were happy to see the change. My father and my uncles, on the other hand, would have liked me to hold on to my childhood a little longer. They immediately blamed Antonio and his New York influence for my transformation. Grabbing him by the neck, my cousin Hector felt the need to explain to Antonio that I was still a young woman and if he were to hurt me, my family would hurt him. And while my father did not make a big deal about it at the time, I knew he no longer saw his little girl in me. I was a grown woman and sooner or later he knew I would be married and on my own.

In order to combat his sorrow, my father immediately began his long process of letting me go—a process that was finally completed when I announced my pregnancy. At first he didn't know how to go about the letting go. I had changed so much and so quickly that he was conflicted. In front of him he saw a confident woman whom he could be proud of, but he was not yet ready to let go of the little-girl image he had associated with me. So, his immediate reaction was to cut me off completely. He continuously reiterated how I was no longer his little girl, and every time he saw me putting on my makeup or on the phone with Antonio, I could see the pain in his eyes. I am the oldest and his first baby to move away, and while my dad understood that it was bound to happen, he wasn't ready to deal with it. He didn't call as often, and he became distant with me. His tone of voice changed from that of a best friend to a distant relative. I knew he was scared to talk to me, scared to watch me grow up, and scared of what I'd tell him next: namely, that I would not return to live in L.A.

Antonio was a romantic and seduced me with his smooth words, classical elegance, private and exotic dinners and wines, and his New York charm. He was sophisticated, smart, witty, and could cook, which made him desired by just about every minority woman on campus. Once a week he would take me out for two-hundred-dollar candlelit dinners at a small, upscale Italian restaurant. After these luxurious dinners, we would walk hand in hand back to our dorms and student life, but during those dinners Antonio made me feel like I was in another world, a world full of things that even my dreams weren't made of, and though it frightened me, I liked it.

I was initially scared of Antonio. Why was he so interested in me? It didn't seem that I would be his type, and yet he was so persistent. He gave me a new image and helped me to come out of a shell that had always kept me behind the scenes. Here in front of me was this perfect man who was in love with me. But how could he tell so quickly? We were just dating; it sounded too crazy to be true, and I wasn't ready to believe him. In fact, I was too scared to believe him. What would falling in love with a New Yorker mean for my future? Aside from that, Antonio was just so very different, the complete opposite of what I had envisioned for my future husband.

As we began our senior year in college, Antonio began the investment banking recruitment process. He had numerous interviews, all for positions in New York. It was no surprise to me that after graduation he planned to move to New York. As his dream became a reality, I began to withdraw from the relationship, fearing the dramatic change my life would take in allowing myself to love this man. What did he expect me to do? Leave my family forever? Yes, I loved him, but living the rest of my life in New York, a city that stigmatizes Mexicans as short, poverty-stricken Indians, was not my idea of the perfect place to spend the rest of my life, apart from my entire family. Antonio loved the city and we both knew that the investment banking industry offered more opportunities in New York than it did in L.A., but my thoughts were only of myself and my family.

For a time our relationship grew unstable. Antonio sensed me withdrawing and in an attempt to lessen the pain of a breakup, he also began to distance himself from the relationship. My love for Antonio was unlike anything I had ever experienced, and yet I was ready to walk away from it out of fear and a belief that I needed to live in Los Angeles with my family. Around this time my father and I began having a lot of discussions about his relationship with my mother. Their bitter four-year divorce was almost at an end, and the more my dad and I spoke the more I realized that I was destroying my own relationship with Antonio and becoming more like my mother.

When you ask my mother to name her family, the first three people she names are her two parents and her brother. In her words, "Those three people come first and should always come first." In my mother's framework, her husband and children were not included in her immediate family. I, too, had been putting the love of my life on hold for fear of leaving my family. But by loving Antonio he was becoming my family, my future husband, and learning from the lessons of my own parents' failed marriage I knew I had to put both Antonio and myself first.

Aside from my initial reservations about our relationship, fall term of senior year started off great. Antonio and I had spent most of the summer together in New York City and then a week in Kauai, Hawaii, and a week in Las Vegas and Los Angeles to see Celine Dion and Mariah Carey, two of Antonio's favorites. We came back rested, ready to finish our senior year, and extremely low on birth control pills.

Antonio and I had talked about having children early on in our relationship. We loved each other and wanted a big family. In fact, one reason why I chose to end my studies in biology and my early aspirations to become a doctor was that I didn't want to be married to my career. I wanted to be devoted to my family. The doctors I had shadowed at the hospital never seemed to spend enough time at home, and I realized that such a profession was not worth the costs. However, while the idea of getting pregnant and beginning our family was tempting, Antonio and I knew that we both needed to graduate before we could even begin to think about starting our family. So when my birth control ran out and we decided to have unprotected sex, we did the math. If I were to get pregnant, the baby would be due after graduation and therefore would not drastically interfere with our education. I wasn't planning on attending graduate school until two years after graduating, and I didn't want to wait until I was twenty-seven to have my first child. So we risked it and decided to put our future in the hands of God. Deep down we both wanted me to get pregnant, but there was no desperate need for us to do so now. We played roulette with my reproductive system for a week, and when my next period was due, I was late.

It was a Thursday, November 6, to be exact. At around 4:30 in the afternoon Antonio and I were in the car on our way to purchase our first home pregnancy test. I was embarrassed to be seen making the purchase, so I made Antonio go into the pharmacy alone while I went into the clothing store next door to wait for him. He carried the little white paper bag very delicately into the store, and I knew it was time for us to meet our fate.

As I walked to the bathroom in my dorm, my muscles tightened and I felt doomed. I made Antonio go into the women's restroom with me for support and out of fear that I wouldn't have the strength to take the exam alone. I started feeling guilty. What had I been thinking? Was I really ready to have a baby? What would people say to a pregnant student walking around campus? Had I been selfish and unrealistic to think that as a college student I could actually support and raise this potential child? Only time would tell, and delaying the test was not going to stop anything.

As I watched the two purplish pink lines appear, I couldn't help but cry.

While the thought of getting pregnant had been enticing, the reality was almost too much to handle. I longed to share the joy Antonio was expressing, but the fear of my family's reaction to the news kept me from doing so. Feeling more comfortable telling people other than my own family, we called Antonio's parents first. While we had always gotten along well, I was nowhere near prepared for their reaction to our news. "Oh, gracias a Dios, a baby!" Antonio's mom congratulated me, crying tears of joy. "I know you're scared, but whatever you do, don't kill it. Antonio's father and I will help you with everything." While Antonio's dad didn't cry, I knew he was beyond happy. They reacted as if Antonio and I had been married for ten years and they had been waiting for a baby from us. I couldn't believe their joy and I wondered if they had heard us right. . . . we were having a baby and they couldn't have been happier.

Against Antonio's advice, I waited until the next morning to call my father. As I began crying, I told my dad where I was in the decision process, and throughout the conversation he was supportive and encouraged me to keep the baby. While it was a shock for him, he was excited to know that he was going to be a grandpa. I felt I had to let him know that termination was an option, so as to ease his shock and to let him know there was a way out, just in case he flipped out. But I knew he wouldn't. My dad has always been there for me, no matter what. His response was, "You're old enough to make your own decisions and deal with the consequences. You created a baby, and now you have to take care of it. How's Antonio doing?" I told my father about Antonio and his family's reaction and it seemed to put him at ease. He was glad to know that I wouldn't be alone.

After my conversation with my father I tore up the abortion papers that I had taken from the college clinic. I had been reserving the option as a possible response to my parents' reactions. But I came to realize that this was my life and my family, and hence my decision to make. Antonio and this baby from this point on needed to come first. There was no more anxiety about living in New York City and no more questions about leaving my parents behind. At the same time, dealing with my mother and what everyone else would say, particularly at college, was clearly on my mind, but I thought it selfish to destroy a life over such petty concerns. Terminating my child's life would also have destroyed my own.

Antonio, my dad, my brother, my sister, and I decided that waiting until Christmas vacation to tell my mother in person would be best. We took my mother out to breakfast and broke the news to her. My mother couldn't speak, and as her mouth fell open in shock, her eyes teared up. All she could do was order a Bloody Mary and excuse herself to the bathroom. For the next four days my mother cried each time I announced my news to a new family member. But once I told her about the baby, I wasn't scared anymore, and I knew that with time she'd get used to being a grandma.

Both sides of my family, although initially shocked, took the news rather well. After all, what could they say? Antonio was a good man and the baby would not interfere with my graduation plans. However, the most difficult thing for everyone to accept was not the news of a baby, but rather my permanent move to the East Coast. As I look at things now, I can understand my family's concern and sorrow when they learned of my decision to live in New York with Antonio. With the baby and wedding plans on the way, I know my father knows that the move is for the best, but I still sense that in some way I have betrayed him, as if I had forgotten all of the sacrifices he has made to ensure my future success.

I am the first person in my family to live outside Southern California. After three generations, I am the first to attend college and leave the family. While my aunts and uncles have always used me as a role model for their own children, they now fear their words. They know it is important for their children to attend college, but at what costs? I will probably never come back to live in Los Angeles, and while I will always keep in close contact with my family, things will never be the same. I will almost never be around for Sunday barbecues and family parties. And with a baby on the way, will my family ever really have a close relationship with my daughter?

As a soon-to-be mother who was a sociology major, I have many new anxieties as the birth of my baby girl approaches. She will be raised in New York City; her father, a consultant for an investment banking firm, will make more money than my two parents combined. Already my daughter will grow up in a higher social class than I ever did. Manhattan will frame her world in a perspective I can't even begin to imagine. She will probably attend her father's high school alma mater, an elite institution of learning where CEOs pay a tuition of $25,000 to teach their children how to make the best use of their white privilege and maintain ignorant views on issues of race and inequality. While I may not want my child to be exposed to such an elite white culture, isn't this what will ensure her own future success in life? Getting the best education possible, establishing the most important social networks, and meeting all of the right people is bound to make her struggles in life less challenging. Yet I worry about her future and how her world will be framed by her privilege.

I have struggled in my life, and my parents even more so. It makes sense that we should hope that the next generation will not have to work and struggle as hard to reach success as the previous generation did. After all, isn't that the American dream? My grandparents emigrated to this country from Mexico to give their children a better chance and more opportunities in life. My parents worked hard to ensure that their children would obtain an education that would provide them with financial stability without having to break their backs to earn it. And as the birth of my daughter nears, isn't this what I should wish for her? Shouldn't she have the best? Shouldn't she want for nothing? And if I can give it to her, shouldn't she have just as much as the next privileged girl? My fear is are the social and financial privileges that my education has given me worth the deeper costs and losses of family and culture. So I can't help but ask myself, "Was it worth it?"

One month after graduating from Dartmouth College with a major in sociology, Marissa Saldivar gave birth to her daughter. She works at a professional services firm as a recruiter in New York City. Marissa and her husband are expecting their second child in November.

Abiel Acosta   The Double Life

I am in today's edition of my college's daily newspaper. There is a whole page devoted to an interview I gave and a picture of me sprawled out on a couch with my arms covering my face. I am passed out from losing too many games of pong and drinking too much beer. On the lower left-hand corner of the page is another picture of me—this time wearing a coconut bra in a fraternity basement. I am smirking at the camera trying to act serious, even though I look ridiculous. There is a guy next to me with his right arm around me and his left hand cupping the left coconut shell of the bra. His head is bent toward my chest and he is sticking out his tongue as if ready to lick my nipple.

Throughout the interview, I talk about sleeping with a friend's mother, drinking a lot of alcohol, playing beer pong, making "noises with my armpits," avoiding Mexican "homies" and "hood rats," and wearing a coconut bra. The whole interview is supposed to be funny and witty. Since the newspaper came out, I have been getting a lot of compliments from friends and strangers. "You're the big man on campus now!" "That interview was hilarious. I loved it!" "You are funny as hell. You're gonna get a lot of lady action this weekend." "You just became a campus celebrity from that article. Enjoy your fifteen minutes."

Being the "campus character" in my college newspaper proves that I am fully assimilated into the college, that I am not one of those Latinos who self-segregates with other Hispanics and joins the Latino fraternity, but one who took advantage of college—its remarkable academic and extracurricular opportunities—like any other white person. I joined a predominantly white fraternity and am one of five Latinos in the house. I get along with almost everyone I meet because I like entertaining people and making a fool of myself. I am a wild, extroverted, funny drunk.

Although I am pretty happy about the article and the response I have been getting from people at school, I would never show my parents the interview. My parents do not know the "partying" side of me and would be shocked to hear me be so vulgar and see pictures of me looking so stupid. My parents learned that I drink not that long ago, and they still think I have never been drunk. They do not know anything about my sex life and the ridiculous things I do or say in college. I am naturally a quiet, well-mannered introvert, but when I am at school, I tend to be outgoing and wild. My personality does a complete 180, and I force myself to be extroverted to entertain people and get along with others. I live a double life.

Although I am American and have visited Mexico only a few times in my life, I deeply value my Mexican culture and heritage. I grew up learning legends and myths of a distant homeland I hardly ever saw. I learned of people hearing the ghost of La Llorona, the "weeping woman," crying for her dead children near rivers, how the earth used to open up to swallow disobedient children, how a local dance hall my uncle used to go to closed down because people once saw the devil dancing there, or how my great-grandfather once offered a ride to a beautiful woman and, upon trying to kiss her, saw that she had a horse's face. My mother told me these Mexican stories in English and occasionally used Spanish words when she couldn't find a better word in English to fit the story. They are the same stories she heard growing up and the same stories her mother heard growing up.

Whenever I ask my mom what it was like growing up in Mexico, she talks about how tough life was for everyone, especially for her mother. My grandmother raised six children alone after her husband died, and because she could not financially support the family on her own, she expected the older children to get jobs. Even with the older children working, there were days when she forfeited her meals to the children because there was not enough food for everyone. While living in Zacatecas, Mexico, my widowed grandmother was courted by a wealthy *ranchero*. Although he was already married, his wife was a paraplegic and he wanted another woman to sexually gratify him. My grandmother initially rejected any propositions and advancements the ranchero made, but she was eventually pressured into becoming his mistress. She had three children with this man (my mother being the youngest), and after my mother was born, my grandmother fled north to Juarez, which borders El Paso in Texas.

My mother never met her father and was closely guarded by my grandmother, due to fear that the ranchero would kidnap her. My mother went to school in Juarez and immediately after finishing sixth grade was expected to find work. At eleven, my mother became a housekeeper and babysitter for other families. She was required to clean, sew, wash, and cook all the meals. She had to make *tortillas* from scratch every day and was punished by her employers if she did not roll them into perfect circles.

On the other side of the border, my dad had a tough life growing up as a Mexican American. His parents did not speak English and his father barely made enough money to provide for the whole family. My dad grew up in El Paso and was the third oldest of eight children. His older brother Manuel, as the oldest male in the house, was supposed to help provide for the family and take care of the younger siblings. However, Manuel was a troublemaker and street fighter. He became a *pachuco*, or a Chicano gang member, and was feared by many in the neighborhood. Since my dad was the next oldest male, the responsibility fell on him to take care of the family. He remembers having to walk five miles every day to the grocery store to buy bread and bologna for his siblings, mowing lawns every summer and giving over half of his paycheck to his parents. However, even though he helped support his family, he was ridiculed by his siblings and mother for having the darkest coloring in the house. (Irony at its finest: Mexicans have great pride in their Aztec heritage and frown on the rape of their land by the Spanish conquistadors, yet it is far more desirable to be a light-skinned Spanish-looking Mexican than a dark-skinned Aztec-looking one.) During his teenage years, his mother told him to leave the dinner table because his acne disgusted her. He was the first of three of his siblings to graduate from high school and the only one to get a college degree; however, he did not receive any affection or support from his parents. Immediately after his high school graduation, he hitchhiked to California with a couple of his friends without letting anyone in his family know, and he did not return for six months.

My parents met while working together in a Levi Strauss sewing factory in El Paso. My mom was seventeen and my dad was twenty-one years old. They dated for less than a year before getting married. Since my mom was expecting a child at this time, my dad needed to quickly find a better paying job. He enlisted in the navy and the two moved to San Diego, California. My mother had my sister Monica while my dad was away at boot camp. He was not home that often for the first three years of Monica's life, and his paycheck was just large enough to buy diapers, baby food, and other essentials needed for an infant. My parents remember the days when all they could afford to eat was Taco Bell—they could not even buy groceries to make *real* Mexican food. When my father finished his contract with the navy, my parents decided to move up north to Ventura, California, where two of my mother's sisters lived. El Paso was out of the question for my dad; he did not want to raise his daughter in the same *barrio* he grew up in. Ventura offered the better choice since it was cleaner and safer, and there was *familia* there to support them. I was born in Ventura where they still live.

Today my parents own a Mexican restaurant. Actually, it is closer to a taco stand. Maria's Mexican Food on the Avenue is adjacent to a liquor store and a tiny ugly house and across the street from a trailer park. There is a small parking lot that all three buildings share and some benches in front of the restaurant. My aunt and uncle first opened it in the 1970s, and the restaurant did so well they opened two more in Ventura. Eventually, they couldn't handle taking care of all three so they sold the first one to my parents about eleven years ago. To this day, it is still well known for its *carne asada burritos*, but during Christmas time, everyone always orders the *tamales*. There is one small window where customers order and receive their food. The inside of the restaurant is cramped, stuffy, and hot. The employees, mostly uneducated immigrants from Mexico, prepare the order in the kitchen while others are chopping jalapeños and onions, shredding beef and chicken, or rolling corn burritos. Ever since my dad left his job as a drug rehabilitation counselor eight years ago, he has been helping my mom with the restaurant. He gets up every morning at 4 to make the *frijoles* and *arroz*, while my mom arrives at 8 to open the restaurant and take orders. The restaurant closes at 7 p.m. and is open every day of the week. Although the restaurant is very successful, my dad hates working there. He feels as if he is losing his intelligence because he only interacts with uneducated immigrants and rude customers. There is nobody around to talk politics and history with and nobody to share the new "word of the day" he learned that morning.

My sister Monica and I were raised very differently. My parents were strict with Monica but relatively lenient with me due to our Mexican culture's notion of *machismo*. While the female is supposed to be obedient, innocent, and virginal, the male is supposed to be hardworking, strong, virile, and masculine—he must have *machismo*. My parents unintentionally ingrained in me this notion. They went out of their way to make sure Monica kept her innocence by giving her early curfews and not allowing her to stay overnight at friends' homes. I, on the other hand, was allowed to stay out late at night and leave to go on dates at the time Monica was supposed to be home for curfew. My dad always offered advice on how to act as a man. He'd say, "Do the opposite of a woman. It is more appropriate for a man to mow the lawn and throw out the trash than stay indoors crocheting, washing dishes, and knitting." Other times, he'd describe machismo: "*Machismo* comes from the root *macho*, which used to mean a male mule. The *macho* is strong, virtuous, and loyal; it can pull the carriage better than the donkey and horse. The female mule is called a *mula*. They can be very stubborn like donkeys or jackasses. That's why women are sometimes called *mulas*."

Machismo requires men to be masculine; men should be hardworking, tough, unemotional, callused, and hairy. The notion of *machismo* can be misogynistic and very homophobic since there are specific gender roles that people must adhere to. A man's place is outside the house working to put food on the table, while a woman's place is indoors keeping the house and raising the children. If a man is inside the home doing a woman's job, he is considered a sissy and a faggot, or a *maricón* and *joto*. He does not show pride in being a male and is therefore looked down upon.

Aside from being taught the tenets of Mexican *machismo*, I grew up only speaking Spanish. I learned most of my Spanish from my mother's mother, Tita, when she would take care of me the first five years of my life. My relationship with my grandmother was different than the ones she had with her other grandchildren. To her, I was her son. According to my mom, this all originated from a dream she had a week after I was born. Supposedly, she dreamt that she was in the hospital giving birth to me; the dream was so vivid, she could feel the birth pangs and the joy of holding me after the birth. Ever since her dream, she treated me differently than the rest of her grandchildren. I remember her cooking every meal for me, walking to the nearby Mexican grocery store, and watching only Spanish television shows. She tolerated "Sesame Street" in English, but I was not allowed to watch "Mister Rogers' Neighborhood" and "I Love Lucy." The few times she could not take care of me, she was upset at my mom for hiring a babysitter who made me Campbell's soup instead of the homemade kind.

My grandmother made it known to everyone in the family that I was one of her favorites among her thirty grandchildren. During family gatherings, she told my aunts to take their children away from her whenever they cried and bugged her, but I was able to stay with her as long as I liked, no matter how fussy I was. If I did something mischievous, she denied that

I did something wrong. My cousins, on the other hand, were reprimanded and considered greedy brats who should learn to be more like me. I could never do wrong in her eyes. I was the good kid who never erred and who showed promise in school. Because of this, my parents decided to send me to private school. They thought it would be a better environment to foster my education and keep me away from any Mexican gang subculture that could ruin my "good boy" image.

Just the fact that I was male gave me a special status in my family. While my sister went to public school all her life, I was sent to private Christian schools. Money was not an issue when it came to my education—my parents found it more important to keep me away from public schools. My mom wanted to send me to private schools because she found promise in me, even as a young child. She always told me, "You learned your ABCs when you were only one year old. Although you couldn't say the letters all the way, we knew that you understood. We saw that you were a fast learner and thought that a public school would not challenge you enough." My dad feared that I would grow up becoming a *cholo*, or Mexican American gang member, which was prevalent in public schools in the area. He wanted to send me to private schools to get me away from the Mexican gangster culture and succeed in life as a respectable American.

My parents got what they wanted. I went to private schools where there were hardly any Mexican gang members present. In fact, there were hardly any Mexicans present at all. I was not exposed to the Mexican culture of *vatos* (dudes), homies (homeboys), and cholos, but instead to the surfer, skater, and preppy culture of the whites. Before starting school, my initiation into American culture, I spoke very little English. I was basically a Mexican with U.S. citizenship. I remember feeling out of place as a child because most of my classmates had a good handle on the English language. For example, I remember having to bring in a recipe of our favorite food for an assignment in kindergarten. I brought in the recipe for tacos, although half of it was in Spanish since I did not know the English words: "First you need to heat the *manteca* [oil] until it is hot. Then you put in the *tortillas* to cook it. I like *tortillas de maíz* [corn tortillas] for my *tacos*, not *tortillas de harina* [flour tortillas]."

As my schooling progressed, I gradually lost my native tongue (my grandmother had died when I was about six years old) and felt more comfortable speaking English at home; I became more American and less Mexican. I was never a surfer or skater, but I was able to fit in because I did not act like other Mexicans my age. I did not shave my head, crease my jeans and shirts, speak in Spanish slang, or get bad grades. In fact, I was never allowed to. My dad never let me cut my hair short as a child, even though all of my white friends did. He was afraid people would think I was a *cholo* and look down on me. My father always wanted me to present myself respectably and show that I was not the stereotypical Mexican thug that is always causing trouble. I essentially became a white kid with brown skin, a Spanish last name, and a Mexican family.

In middle school, I started considering myself as an anomaly. I was a Mexican going to predominantly white schools getting the best grades in class. I was considered a goody-two-shoed popular dork, an image that came from the fact that I always got straight As, received high honors awards, and at one point received the "Good Christian" trophy at an award ceremony. I had no idea how to talk to girls and flirt with them like the rest of my guy friends; I was the innocent Christian geek whom all the teachers loved. However, I was also part of the "popular" kids group since I was best friends with the other Mexican kid in my class who was the star of the basketball team.

By the time I started high school, I was unable to speak any Spanish. I had incorrect grammar and a terrible vocabulary. I knew certain phrases and words that I occasionally used when speaking "Spanglish," but for the most part my ability to communicate was nonexistent. I went to a small Catholic high school of about five hundred students and took classes where I relearned some of my native language, although I didn't practice enough to become fluent again.

Since it was "cool" to be a football or basketball player at my high school rather than an innocent Christian geek, like I was in elementary and middle school, I decided to join the football team my sophomore year. I became friends with teammates and cheerleaders. Even though I was still pretty innocent and did not go to parties and drink like the rest of the "popular" kids on weekends, I was still able to hang out with them. I was in a marginal position in our social sphere. I was never fully enveloped into a particular clique at school, but I was able to move in and out of different groups with ease. I was a part of the innocent, Christian kids group, part of the smart kids group, and part of the cool, popular white preppy kids group. There was even a group of Mexicans who pretended to be thuggish that I was accepted in, just because I was Mexican. I felt as if I was just enough Mexican to be different from the whites and fit in with the other Mexicans, but just enough American to still fit in with the surfers, skaters, and preppies and be somewhat different from the other Chicanos. I was ethnic and cultured, but Anglicized enough to not alienate myself from any particular group. I was assimilated. Since I was never fully inside any of these cliques, I was never expected to hang out after school or on weekends with them and party. I wasn't even looked down on for hanging out with other groups. I was just everyone's friendly acquaintance. I wasn't satisfied with that, but I accepted it.

When senior year came up and it was time to start picking colleges, I only applied to the top institutions America offered: Stanford, Harvard, Yale, Dartmouth, MIT, UC Berkeley, and UC San Diego. I really do not know why I applied to only the "good" colleges. I was never pushed by my parents or teachers. I just did it. My dad wanted me to go to the Ventura County Community College because he didn't want me to leave home. I think I applied because I was being heavily recruited by many schools. All the Ivy Leagues sent me flyers, USC always sent me junk to apply to their honors program, and Tulane even sent me a pen to fill out the application with. I assumed that if so many schools were recruiting me, I must be a good enough candidate to be accepted into an Ivy League school. I remember filling out every application, writing every personal statement, and even paying for every $60 application fee. Although I had my parents read over the applications and personal statements, I did not really accept their critiques. I did not trust my mom because of her limited education, and I usually felt as if my grammar was better than my dad's.

Unfortunately, I was not accepted into all the colleges I thought I could get into. Even though I went through rejection after rejection, I never lost hope. I think what kept me going was my mother. After I sent my application to Stanford, my first choice, she told me God spoke to her in a dream telling her that I would go there. Consequently, I became very confident that I would be accepted. Once that didn't happen, she again dreamed God spoke to her telling her that there is a better school for me down the road that I would get in to. Throughout her life she's had the idea that God is going to use me for something special. I have always been brought up thinking that God has a plan for everyone, but according to my mom, since my birth, she has felt that there's something God has specifically planned for me. While I was applying to colleges, her best friend also told me she had similar feelings about me since I was a child. I applied to these top schools on the belief that my life is in God's hands and that He'll lead me where I need to go.

I did get into a good college, but I have always felt insecure about whether I was only accepted to increase their diversity. Looking back, I feel

as if my identity has changed very much since I came to college. It all
started my senior year in high school when a friend of mine since middle
school, and one of my first crushes, passed away. Within a couple months
of knowing each other, Charlene and I became friends. The only thing we
had in common was our Mexican heritage, but even then, she was more
Anglicized than me. She never learned Spanish and could barely tell the
difference between a *burrito* and *gordita*. However, we still made jokes
about Mexicans having to stick together and not betray each other's trust
whenever secrets about crushes or other junior high gossip arose. By the
time we graduated from junior high, Charlene and I were best friends. We
went to separate high schools but called each other occasionally during my
freshman year, and we usually hung out on the weekends when she visited
her grandparents' home down the street from me. Eventually I stopped
calling Charlene as much, and we hardly ever saw each other. By my junior year, everything about middle school was pretty much out of my mind
and life. I had my driver's license, my own car, my first job, and I was getting closer to entering the popular clique in high school. I even had a small
enterprise of selling food my parents brought from the restaurant to classmates. Everybody knew me as the "burrito man," and people gave me their
money and their respect.

In February of my junior year Charlene called as I was headed out the
door to a Bible study. She said she had good news to tell me, but I rushed
the conversation to make it to Bible study on time. The next time I heard
Charlene's name was to learn that she had died in a car accident. At her
wake I learned that the good news she had wanted to tell me was that
she had become engaged. I think I cried more than all my other friends
throughout the entire wake, including her cousin Josh, whom she was very
close to. I felt this deep pain within me and I was unable to get rid of it. I
soon realized that it was guilt. I had taken a good friend for granted and I
learned the hard way that relationships are not here forever.

I felt like I changed a lot after Charlene's death. I vowed to never take
friends for granted and to make the most out of any relationships I have.
To this day, I put a lot of effort to maintain my high school friendships,
and, as a result, I have built strong friendships with people I was just acquaintances with before. Some of those friends say I'm one of the few who
still keeps in contact with them. After Charlene's death, I also vowed to
make the most of life and live each day as if it could be the last. However,
in doing so, I feel like I lost a lot of the innocence I once had. I drank my
first beer two weeks after her death, and I was not afraid to do things I

swore I would never do. I started going to high school parties and hung out with the popular people I never used to see outside of school. I drank and drove home twice, I lost my virginity in a drunken hook-up, and I went to a strip club a couple times after I turned eighteen. I also changed my relationships in high school. I went through a complete metamorphosis. Though I am an introvert by nature, I forced myself to become very extroverted in order to meet new people. I finally learned how to pick up girls and go on dates with those I rarely met outside of school. Toward the end of my senior year, I finally ascended the social ranks and became part of the popular group made up of all the good-looking girls and jocks.

Most of the changes I went through my senior year in high school carried on through my years at college. I again did not shy away from meeting new people and I put my best effort into maintaining relationships. I knew that our time together would be short in these four years, but I would attempt to make the relationships meaningful and memorable. So far, I think I have succeeded. I lived each day as if it were my last and made the most out of each experience, even if it was a bad one. It's funny how some of my friends are barely realizing the fact that we might not see one another again after graduation. Whenever they come to this realization and seem upset, I reply, "That's been in my mind since freshman year. You just gotta live these last days as if it's your last and make the most of them." I've only told a few friends about Charlene and how her death changed my outlook on life. They are usually surprised when I tell them I am truly an introvert who forces himself to be outgoing—some believe that I am joking with them. They do not know how much I enjoy being by myself, and how I sometimes escape from them by going to a secluded area to pray, write poetry, or play piano.

My family expects me to become a lawyer or a broker—basically any "respectable" occupation that allows me to be rich. Although Maria's Mexican Food on the Avenue is the family-owned business, my parents do not want me to work there after graduation. The family has aspirations for me to put my education to use and become rich and successful outside of the Mexican food industry. When I started college, my mom wanted me to be premed because I once showed interest in the occupation and dressed up as a doctor for Halloween when I was six years old. When I told my parents I wanted to major in religion, they were shocked and upset: "What are you going to do with a religion major? Do you want to teach high school or something? If that's what you wanted to do, you could have gone to a different school!" I eventually acquiesced and changed my major to economics—a major that has some "value" in the real world. It was the perfect choice since I've always been business oriented. After all, I was the "burrito man" in high school.

My fraternity is predominantly white. There are about six Asians, five Latinos, two blacks, two Indians, and one Native American in a house with 108 brothers. I've never felt the need to socialize only with Latinos, but I feel as if my identity changes, depending on whom I am interacting with. When I am with my white friends, I feel very Mexican. I have accents on certain Spanish words, I am very critical of the Mexican food that my college or local restaurants try cooking, I talk about the "Mexican barbecues" we have back home, and I listen to Spanish music. Although I feel as if my ethnicity and heritage are irrelevant when meeting people, I make it a point to tell them I am Mexican: "Look at me, I am not white. I am different from you." I am proud of being Mexican. However, I am also self-conscious of the stereotypes, such as being an illegal immigrant, being lazy, or being in a gang. I sometimes make jokes about these stereotypes with my white friends: "Whatchu talkin' 'bout, foo? You don't wanna mess with me, ese, cuz I know Mexican judo. Ju don't know if I gotta knife. Ju don't know if I gotta gun."

When I am around other Latinos, I feel more stiff and serious around them. I do not speak Spanish and I am usually studying and working while they are hanging out and having fun. At home, I feel "white" because I go to college, get good grades, play piano, and do not party as often as my other friends. Ray, my best friend from home, thinks that I am only attracted to white girls and find Mexican girls unattractive. I like all girls. I just don't like the cholas with black lipstick and painted-on eyebrows. I can hear my dad's voice telling me, "You better stay away from those Santa Paula and Oxnard girls who only wear black lipstick. I'd rather have you marry a nice quiet *gabacha* [white girl] than a Mexican *chola*." I always try to explain to Ray that I like Mexican girls too, just not the ones in our city; the Mexican girls around our city seem as if they are immigrants or from the ghetto. I guess they are not white enough.

College has taught me a lot. I learned everything from chugging beers quickly and throwing good room parties to researching, thinking critically, and problem solving. During my time at college, I feel as if I also grew out of the *machismo* way of thinking that I was taught as a child. I came to college using the words "fag" and "gay" freely. I made fun of friends if they dressed too "gay," and I sometimes employed the phrase "Stop sucking dick, you homo" when friends seemed too obsequious. My dad's number-one fear is definitely me becoming homosexual. He is very homophobic and never ceases from making offensive remarks or jokes. He always tells me, "If I ever find out that you are a *joto*, I'll knock your teeth out and kick you out of the house." I always laughed at the threat and took no offense to it because I knew it would never come to that. However, much to my dad's chagrin, I now defend homosexuals whenever he makes a bad comment. Since coming to college, I have become more open-minded and tolerant of homosexuals. Some of my friends and fraternity brothers are gay, and I really can care less about their sexual orientation. I am the most tolerant one in my family, and for that reason I probably do not hold the image of having *machismo* anymore. Men are supposed to be masculine, not sissies, and the fact that I defend homosexuals means that I am on their side, not the *macho* side.

I sometimes wonder what my grandmother would say if she were still alive. She would probably be proud of me for doing so well in life and going to a good college, even though I have lost all the Spanish she taught me. She would make a big fuss to all her friends about my success and continue to compare me favorably with her other grandchildren. To some degree I feel as though I have lived up to her image of me. Although I am not a perfect angel, as she believed me to be, I have worked hard throughout my life. Every good grade I get and anything I accomplish, I feel as if I am doing it for her and the family. And I always remind myself that my accomplishments are less important as stepping-stones for my future success than as tokens of gratitude to make the family proud. Whenever I drink, smoke, curse, sin, or do whatever else at school that would shock my family, I always feel guilty, as if my grandmother is looking down on me from above and is unhappy at what I've done and what I've become. Once again I feel the burden of not living up to her standards, which motivates me to straighten up and work harder. And though it has been over fifteen years since she passed away, she continues to be an integral part of my life. I miss her a lot. The funny thing is that even though my memories of her are few and weak, she still has this amazing power to motivate me to live at least one half of my double life in a manner to make her and the family proud.

After graduating with a BA in economics, Abiel Acosta started working as a financial advisor/investment broker for a small company in Los Angeles. After two years there, he decided to move back home to Ventura and build his practice near the rest of his family.

Miguel Ramírez   The Unknown Want

When people think of Mexico they think of Aztec pyramids, the chok-
ing smog of Mexico City, or perhaps the savage heat of its copper-hued
deserts. I can't see any of that from where I live, but I can see the slums of
Tijuana—shacks built of plywood and cardboard that cling to the face of
a hill.

"That's Mexico," I told my friend Liz while we were picking apples in
my backyard. She was visiting from Boston and was still slightly jet-lagged.

"What?" she said, turning her head to the south.

"Yeah," I said, casually. "Down by the ocean, between the spot where
the neighbor's row of pine trees ends and the cemetery cross stands."

"Wow, I see it! Do you go all the time?" she asked.

She rinsed a green apple with the hose and climbed my neighbor's
wooden fence to get a better view of Mexico.

"Not really," I said, joining her on the fence. "We don't have family
there; my parents are from the interior of Mexico. Anyway, it's not going
anywhere, so we've never had a need to go. It's always just kind of there."

"In case anything went wrong," she teased.

"Yeah," I said.

From my earliest memory of Mexico—that place over there—I knew it
was where I belonged, though we didn't live there. The United States was
my home, but it wasn't mine. When you cross the international border
into the United States you are asked to declare your citizenship; I always
thought that they only asked Mexicans. I have never felt at home in the
United States, partly because of my parents. Although my mother has lived
in the United States for most of her life, she has never learned English. We

speak Spanish at home, and my parents have always said my sister and I are Mexican. We refer to Caucasians as "Americans."

From my travels in Mexico as a child, I knew I liked life in the United States better than life in Mexico, but I have nevertheless always felt like a guest here. In elementary school I was in bilingual education, and I didn't know any white people personally until I met my fourth-grade teacher. For most of my childhood all I knew was that the president was white, my father's boss was white, and, from television, I knew that there was an entire place populated by only white people. I was not white and I did not have access to that world.

In elementary school I was the ESL (English as a Second Language) learner, in high school I was the college-bound Mexican, and even now I don't feel like a Dartmouth student but rather a Latino Dartmouth student. I never found a place where I fit in, where my identity wasn't qualified by my race—and later by my sexual orientation. Nevertheless, I was always well liked and accepted, and so I never questioned my feelings of detachment. It wasn't until college that I realized my efforts to succeed in school were fueled by a need, an undefined want to find a place where I could simply *be*.

My family's history begins in the United States. My father is originally from the south of Mexico, but he grew up near the Mexican-American border, crossing back and forth. His immediate family lives in San Diego, and only my grandmother keeps in touch with her family back in Mexico. My mother left the northern city of Obregon, Sonora, at twenty-two and traveled to the United States alone. Her family is still in Mexico. We keep in contact with them and we often visit, but we are not particularly close— there was a distinct break when my mother came to the United States.

On one of my trips to visit my mother's family, I learned that I wasn't Mexican. I was at a candy store with an older cousin and overheard her conversation with a store clerk.

"My aunt has been in the States for twenty years," she said, "but he [indicating me] was born there."

"Really," the clerk said, handing me a bag of candy. "He speaks Spanish very well."

"Even though he's American, they speak Spanish at home."

American?

"No," I said. "I'm Mexican."

"Honey," my cousin said, "your parents are Mexican, but you were born in the United States. Like your sister."

Later that night my father confirmed the news. "You are Mexican," he said, "but you were born in the United Sates. You are Mexican American."

I was only seven years old, but even at that age I knew that being Mexican American meant I wasn't really either one. I was not upset by learning this, especially since the location of our home implied I was somewhere in the middle—we were Mexicans living in the United States and we could see Mexico from our backyard. More than anything, this knowledge confirmed a sense of difference that my parents and my teachers had instilled in me.

I was always well behaved and frequently was compared favorably to others by my family and teachers. I was good while my cousins were bad. I helped at church when most of the other children were distracting and unruly. My mother likes recalling the time I impressed an old white man at a restaurant. He understood Spanish and was impressed by my behavior as I spoke with my family. He wanted to give me money, saying there were few children like me "these days." My parents thanked him but refused the money.

Some months after this encounter, my mother walked me to my first day of kindergarten, my very first day of school. I was excited because I was wearing brand-new clothes and brown dress shoes that hurt my feet, though I was too afraid to complain.

"Kindergarten," she said, as I looked down at my aching feet, "is the first rung on a ladder that leads up to college. In college you learn to be a doctor or a lawyer or whatever you want to be. Your father and I weren't able to go to college, but you will. Your sister will go first and then a few years later, when you're old enough, you will go too."

Later that day, my kindergarten teacher asked the class why they were in school.

"Because my friend is here," Julio said. By the time we were in high school Julio had a child. And since our high school graduation I've heard that he's had trouble with the law.

"My mom made me come," Jessica said. She was a very pretty girl who, it turned out, watched sleazy Mexican soap operas with her mother every night. Jessica came to school every day as a different character from one of the shows.

Then my teacher asked me. I told her, "Kindergarten is the first step on a ladder to college." Her face froze, and I thought I had done something wrong. Then she smiled and said, "Very good." From that day on I was her favorite and the one the other students were told to emulate.

As I progressed in school, I liked getting attention and praise but didn't like being singled out for the academic success I was having. I'd fidget and play with my fingers when my parents told me to talk about my last exam or the books I was reading during church picnics or family reunions. Even though I was given special attention, other students never picked on me. I learned that if I was modest about my success and helped my classmates, especially my popular classmates, I would be fine. I was surprisingly well liked. When other students were savagely teased or physically attacked, I always wish I had done something to stop it, but then I was nine years old and just wanted to fit in.

I was always the ESL student—no matter what I did, my identity was mediated by that fact that English was my second language. In fifth grade I entered a speech contest sponsored by the local Rotary club. I was very nervous in the days leading up to the competition. I didn't like to speak in public because people occasionally teased me for my accent—especially when I did well on exams. Nevertheless, I won second place.

The day after the competition I took my medal to school and showed it to my teacher during recess. After school I walked down the hall to Ms. Wheatley's room. She was my fourth-grade teacher and truly one of the best teachers I've ever had. She was essential in helping me make the move to English-language instruction, making me read out loud in front of the class on a regular basis.

"Ms. Wheatley!" I called, running into her classroom. The chairs were stacked on top of the desks and she was hanging up spelling tests in the back of the room. She turned and saw the medal and her face lit up. "What's that?"

"I won second place in a speech competition."

"Honey, that's great!" She gave me a hug as her husband walked in. "Miguel, this is my husband."

"Hello, Miguel," he said, giving me his massive hand to shake. "Miguel was my student last year and he just won second place in a speech contest," Ms. Wheatley explained. "He came in from the ESL program and you would be amazed by his progress. He was one of my top students by the end of the year."

ESL? I just smiled, gripping my medal in my hands. That acronym was stigmatized at my school. Most of the ESL students were Mexican and we teased each other about our immigration status. "I'll call the Border Patrol on your mom," the kids would yell at each other. "You're ESL!" they cried.

On the playground, ESL was the equivalent to "Special Ed"—being mentally retarded.

In junior high I was no longer ESL, but I still had my accent. Once, in my seventh-grade history class, I was reading out loud from a textbook. I was a good reader, consistently scoring at the top of my class. I was reading about Egypt; I remember seeing the topography of the land in my head as I read.

"The Egyptian desert," I read out loud, "is in some ways a typical desert. It has intense heat, dry winds, sparse vegetation, et cetera."

"Ec zetera," I said, and everyone giggled.

"It's fine," Ms. Bell said. "Keep going."

I finished reading the section and she called on someone else. Later in that class period Ms. Bell returned our last tests. "I'm not very happy with your exams," she said. She paced around the room, looking each one of us in the eye as she handed back the paper.

Andrew, the boy next to me, had failed his exam. He was as smart as the rest of us, but he never did his work. I had earned an A. I didn't show anyone my exam; I just placed it on my desk and looked down at it, smiling. The perfect white sheet was beautiful, and my score, 100/100, written so delicately in blue ink, looked painfully elegant.

When I looked up, smiling, Andrew was glaring at me.

"Ex sssseterra," he said, and looked away.

It seemed that no matter how well I did in school, I would always be an ESL student; I would always be different. Two things happened in junior high that confirmed that difference. I experienced my first blatant instance of racism, and I realized I was gay.

For as long as I can remember, I have had erotic feelings toward other boys. In junior high I realized this meant I was gay. I liked watching professional wrestling and I liked wrestling with other boys. It was a game we all played, but even then I knew that the pleasure I experienced was different.

There was a boy I spent a lot of time with in third grade. I guess I had a crush on him. During recess one day, we wrestled. I was taller and much stronger, but instead of pouncing and pinning him to the ground, I grabbed his shoulders. He pressed his shoulders into my chest and we became locked, each trying to push the other back. I grabbed his waist with my left hand and I could feel him struggling to get leverage in order to knock me over. I knew he was trying to win, to end the match as fast as possible, but I was trying to prolong it, only countering his moves. Finally, he lost his balance and fell on his back. I sat on his stomach and pinned his arms to his chest. The fact that we were touching exhilarated me. I didn't understand the nature of my feelings, but I knew to keep quiet about them. Still, I was never ashamed of them.

My parents never warned me about homosexuals—they never talked about sex at all. However, the pastor at my Catholic church was very liberal, and he organized a support group for gay, lesbian, bisexual, and transgender parishioners. When I was twelve, he hung a section of the AIDS quilt inside the church and spoke about the quilt, AIDS, and tolerance for homosexuality during his sermon. The only time I heard comments about homosexuality with a negative connotation was from boys at school.

My classmate Michael was a short, effeminate boy who could only play with girls because the boys would beat him up. "He's a faggot," another classmate informed me. I was in seventh grade and I knew by then that the word *faggot* meant boys like me, but it didn't bother me. I knew that there was a relationship between the words *faggot* and *gay* that was similar to the relationship between the words *spic* and *Mexican*. I knew that I was Mexican, but not a spic. By then I also knew I was gay, but not a faggot.

All my life, I had been told I was different. By seventh grade I knew that included being a homosexual. I never felt ashamed. I figured there were more of us out there and I just had to find them.

During that school year, my sister came home from her first year at college and told my parents she was Chicana.

"What's wrong with being Mexican?" my mother asked.

"Nothing," my sister said. "Chicana acknowledges my Mexican heritage, but also my American heritage. There have been Mexicans in California since before there was a California and we have a culture here that isn't completely Mexican or completely American. This culture is called Chicano."

My sister's announcement made me think; if Chicanos were just now finding an identity, then there must be more gay people out there who were also searching—I just had to find them.

When I was in eighth grade, my parents bought me a computer and a subscription to America Online. They made the wonderful mistake of putting the computer in my bedroom, and within days I knew I was not alone in my feeling toward men.

In tenth grade I came out to my parents. By then, I was absolutely sure about my feeling toward men; it was my feelings toward women that I still had to sort out. Although I preferred men, I believed I could still be with a woman. That later turned out to be false.

"I'm bisexual," I said.

My mother was visibly shocked. The image on the silenced television reflected blue off her glazed-over eyes. She asked me, "Is it that you like to wear women's clothes?"

"No," I said, "I don't like dressing like a girl."

"Well, what?" my mother asked.

"I am attracted to men." I was slouching and sitting on my hands. I could see into my room behind my mother's shoulder and I wanted to crawl into my bed.

"This is big news," my mother said. "I think you should think about this more."

"OK," I said.

"Don't tell your cousins," she pleaded.

"Fine," I said.

I returned to my room and phoned my best friend Iriz. She had recently come out as bisexual also and had urged me not to tell my parents.

"No way!" she said when I called her. "You told them! You're dumb! They didn't get pissed?"

"No," I said, surprised. I knew my parents wouldn't disown me or do anything drastic, but I had expected some kind of drama. In fact, I was a little disappointed when I didn't get it.

When my mother came in an hour later and told me she and my dad would support me in whatever I did, but they wanted me to see a psychiatrist, I was a little relieved and excited. The shrink turned out to be incompetent. During our three sessions, he made a half-hearted attempt to convince me that my homosexual feelings were a phase, and we spent the rest of the time talking about movies. Not films with gay themes or questionable characters, just movies he wanted to watch, good reviews he'd heard.

My parents and I never talked about my homosexuality again and I let them believe what they wanted. I figured I would one day enlighten them further, and until then it would be a known secret. I never considered coming out at school either, although my urban, multiethnic public high school was a truly open and inclusive place. Groups of friends were diverse and they included honor students, athletes, and kids in marching band. There was no racial tension or division by class. I am sure that if I had come out as gay in high school I would have been accepted by the student body and supported by administrators. But I kept my sexuality a secret to all but one friend. I already didn't fit in because I was one of the few going to college, and the last thing I wanted was to be the gay, college-bound Mexican—the Other. (I feared my "gayness" would isolate me more from the general population.)

My feelings of otherness were fueled by an act of racism I faced in junior high during the time I was confronting my sexuality. My sister had come home for Thanksgiving during her freshman year at UC Santa Cruz. We were at the airport waiting for the plane that would take her back, when two INS officers, dressed in civilian clothes, walked up to us and asked to see our papers.

"Our papers?" my dad asked. He looked around at the travelers surrounding us.

I was sitting next to my mother, who was looking through her bag to find her green card and our birth certificates. When crossing the border into the United States, INS officers at the border would ask our citizenship. Karina and I would say, "American citizen." Now, confronted at the airport, I kept repeating that in my head, "American citizen, American citizen."

"Yes," the first officer said, "proof that you can be here."

They were standing above us drawing suspicious glances and curious looks. They were both wearing jeans. The first officer was wearing a blazer over a golf shirt. The second officer wore a green windbreaker and didn't bother to look at us and hid behind dark aviator sunglasses.

I watched as my father, smiling and still sitting, took out his wallet and removed his green card. He took the papers my mother handed him and passed them to the first officer. I kept thinking, "American citizen, American citizen." I wanted to be ready in case they asked, to answer correctly the first time. I was too afraid to smile, and I tensed up when my sister stood to face the officers.

"Wait," Karina said. Pencil thin and barely five feet four, she looked the first officer in the eye. "Who are you? Where are your badges?"

"Excuse me?" the second officer said, suddenly annoyed.

"Your badges," my sister said again. She turned to look at him.

"How old are you?" the second officer asked.

She hesitated. "Seventeen."

"Then you don't know our policies," he said.

The officers exchanged glances and then flashed their badges, but too quickly for us to get a good look. Then the first officer thrust the papers at my father and cleared his throat.

"Very good," he said. "Have a nice day."

They turned and walked away, quickly leaving the terminal.

"They can't do that," my sister said.

"It's all right," my father assured her, trying to quiet her down. "They're gone."

"That's not right. They can't just make us identify ourselves. We weren't doing anything wrong."

"At least they picked us," my mother said. "When they asked for our papers, I saw some people rush to the bathroom."

That was a time of anti-immigrant sentiment in California. Bands of men roamed the hills of San Diego trying to catch illegal immigrants. There were also racist groups who would impersonate INS officers and question people they thought might be illegal immigrants. My sister believes that the men at the airport were impersonators.

We sat around for another half hour, trying to return to our conversation and ignore the glances from the people around us. My sister was upset, but my parents were only embarrassed. I didn't understand why we were made to identify ourselves, why we were singled out. Even though we were dressed well and "knew how to act," our right to be in this country was tentative.

I didn't fit in at school because I was college bound and because I was gay, and I also wasn't "American." There didn't seem to be a place for me. While still in high school I looked forward to attending college, which I thought would be a place where my differences would be accepted, where being smart, or gay, or Mexican wouldn't be a big deal. I was fiercely independent in applying to schools, filling out forms, and signing my parents' names, even paying for my AP exams from money I earned at work.

I just wanted to find a place where I would finally fit in. I picked Dartmouth because it was literally the Ivy League school farthest from home in terms of miles and hours of travel. I knew most people there would be wealthy and white, but I thought my difference would be accepted nonetheless. I arrived at Dartmouth, found I wasn't "gay enough" for the gay students and that I was noticed by others for being Hispanic before I was Miguel. So much for fitting in.

During my sophomore year I began to tell more people I was gay. I never talked about it freshman year because I wasn't sure how people would react. I wanted to get a better feel for the gay community at Dartmouth before throwing myself into it. By sophomore summer, all of my friends knew and I was attending Dartmouth Rainbow Alliance meetings, but I wasn't completely comfortable with my homosexuality, partly because of the other guys who were coming out.

I tried to find a community of like-minded men, but I found only a network for random hook-ups. Because I didn't like to hook up, most of the gay men assumed I wasn't out. I didn't get much help from my gay friends. Most of the gay men I've met have had some kind of eating disorder or complex due to the way they viewed their body. They showed it with gossip and backhanded comments directed at friends. I'm a senior now, and I have been in a monogamous relationship with one of the few emotionally stable gay men on campus for a year. Yet, the same people still ask me if I'm out. I haven't fared better with the larger Dartmouth community, where, after asking my name, people ask my race.

"So where are you from?" Peter asked. White and wealthy, he is a typical Dartmouth student.

"San Diego," I said.

"No," he said, smiling at my confusion. "Where are you *from*?" And after a short pause, "Where are your parents from?"

"What does it matter?" I often want to ask.

"Well, I'm from San Diego," I said. "My parents are from Mexico."

"Oh, so you're Mexican," he said, smiling.

I often get that response, and I always want to respond, "If that were the case I would have said so."

Minority students wait until they know me better before they ask my race. But it's usually the second question white students ask, and I don't understand why. Is it information they need in order to know how to talk to me or how to treat me? Would they ask someone, "Are you gay?" or, "What does your father do and how much money does he make?" Not only do they ask, they have the audacity to then label me: "Oh, so you're Mexican."

I have always had to deal with outsider status and I have accepted the benefits that come from it, although I've always felt tension around it too. It has allowed me to deal with my homosexuality without feelings of solitude or shame, and I have never felt pressure to conform. Many Latinos on campus feel they are not Latino enough, so they take steps to enhance their Latinoness. Unfortunately, they often confuse the ghetto with authenticity. I have never fit in with anyone, yet I've never felt my identity was uncertain.

Still I love to say I am not Mexican in the usual ways. I dress like an American, I walk like an American, I see the world like an American, and when I visit Mexico I do not fool anyone—before I say a word, people know that I am American. Even my Spanish isn't Mexican. I speak Spanish at home, but my formal education was in Castilian Spanish. I don't know Mexican idioms or slang. I am, in fact, American, but in America, my home, I feel like an expatriate. My place in this country is often questioned, and my access to the culture and language has always been tentative.

I have always tried to make my race superfluous—to make it just another fact, like the color of my eyes or my preference in music. All of my early efforts in school were to show my teachers that I wasn't just another ESL student, and later to show my peers that I wasn't just the "Mexican student." I believe I failed to do that.

I will be living at home after graduation from Dartmouth out of a sense of obligation and not because I want to. I'll have to talk to my parents about my homosexuality, and have to deal with bringing gay friends home and introducing my parents to my boyfriend, who is moving to San Diego. I am confident that they will eventually accept me, but they will need time. Until then, I'll have to be careful with my actions and my behavior.

My homosexuality only compounds the problems I face as the child of immigrants. My parents sacrificed their happiness for my sister and me; they made our dreams their dreams. My father has never complained, but I know he hates his tedious job as a ship welder. When I enrolled at Dartmouth he took out loans. My mother told me that once his financial obligations have been paid in full, he will retire. We hope that it will be in five years.

I also know that my mother would like to be closer to her family in Mexico, but she stays in the United States because of my sister and me. She came to the United States alone when she was a young woman, and although she was here legally, immigrants like her were victims of harassment and abuse. On the news we once saw a group of white teenage boys who were on trial for savagely beating several elderly Mexican migrant workers. "It never gets better," my mother said. "I had my papers and I followed the law, but that doesn't mean anything to some of those people." I sensed the violence and resentment in her words, and I'm sure she often wanted to go back to Mexico. But, as she once told me, "I'd never seen your face, but I stayed here for you."

I love my parents dearly and often feel the need to bow my head in tribute to them, but there is now a break between us. They support me and they love me, but they don't understand what I did here at Dartmouth and they will not understand my life—not even that I am entering a higher economic class.

I also feel a paralyzing sense of obligation. When I could have earned an A but settled on an A-minus, it felt like I slapped my parents in the face. No matter how successful I am, it will never make up for the fact that my parents put themselves, their personal dreams and goals aside so I could succeed. I don't know how to make up for what they've done for me.

Even though I plan to live at home, I will only be visiting; I can't reconcile the schism with my parents, and I feel a similar distance from my community in San Diego. I went to college, to Dartmouth no less, and some of my neighbors think I am "uppity." Some of my high school friends don't understand why I "wasted" my time with college—they are driving brand-new cars and wearing fancy sneakers, while I still have my clothes from high school. They just don't see the long-term effects of our different decisions. Like most first-generation college students, I face the issue of class. I moved up, and I can't go back. I love my home community, but I know that I'll only be an expatriate there, too.

Despite—or perhaps because of—the heartache it has caused me, being an outsider has motivated me to succeed. I spent twenty-one years doing my best in school in order to fit in. Without that incentive, I don't know what would have happened to me. I am thankful I came to Dartmouth, because here I learned the brutal truth that I will never find a place where I will feel at home. I expect the same in the professional world—I'm sure I'll be accepted, but I don't think I will fit in.

I can't say I feel at home at Dartmouth, because my values are too different and the college campus isn't religious. Some of my peers find it odd that I plan to return home in order to make my parents happy. They tell me to strike out on my own, to be my own person. At Dartmouth individuality is privileged, but even so I have never really felt lonely. I have wonderful memories of my four years here and I met my closest friends here. I felt the same way in high school—I had my very close friends, and then there was everybody else.

When it comes down to it, I really can't complain. I have opportunities that my parents never had and more options than most of my high school classmates put together. The dilemma I face is choosing what I'm going to do with my charmed life. That's a wonderful dilemma, and it's what my parents worked so hard for. The terms of my success haven't been easy; I will always be an outsider and I can't ever go back home. I accept these truths, but sometimes, when my parents ask me about school and they smile politely as I recount my triumphs and express my concerns, I wonder if the terms have been too high.

At Dartmouth Miguel Ramírez majored in creative writing, and he continues to improve his prose in San Diego. He currently works with students with physical and developmental disabilities. He wants to be a filmmaker and plans to move to New York City to take classes in film production, work in the industry, and eventually enroll in film school.

MENTORING

THE SOMEONE IN MY LIFE

Angelita Urena   Orgullo Dominicana

It was 6 o'clock in the morning, and instead of being in a content slumber I was stomping to the window to see who was outside making a ruckus. I wanted to yell, "Shut the fuck up!" But instead what came out was an unexpected rush of emotion. I thrust my dorm room window open and found myself surrounded by loud Spanish chatter and music. I knew they were coming, but they caught me by surprise. My mom looked up at my window and screamed, "La trulla llego, pero no podemos entrar" (The troops have arrived, but we can't get in). Any normal family would have called to wake me up, but not mine; they decided to wake me up with a symphony of voices in Spanish, English, Spanglish and a blast of *merengue* from the car stereo. They were all wearing T-shirts with my graduation picture on the front, Dominican flag on the back, and a green logo that read:

> *Congratulations Angelita*
> *Your Dreams Came True*
> *I am so proud of you!*

The flag bore the inscription:

> *Angelita*
> *Orgullo Dominicano*

I opened the door and welcomed my family to our Ivy League graduation day. When they suddenly grew quiet, I knew they had something up their sleeve. Natanael, my uncle, who could never keep a secret, said, "We got baseball caps and Dominican flags too!"

I cringed knowing they were going to be loud as hell throughout graduation day. I've often felt embarrassed about how loud my family is, especially when we get dirty looks from people around us. But being loud is part of my family, part of my culture, and today I was proud of my fifty family members outfitted in Angelita "graduation gear."

My family could not afford a hotel stay, so they all woke up at midnight, and within the hour were on the way from Brooklyn to Dartmouth to watch me graduate. I simply did not know how to thank them, and I still don't. I was happy they were wearing my name on their T-shirts so *everyone* would know that this was *my* family. I was proud of all of them, from "El Negro," who had just gotten out of jail, to cousin Yuyi, who is an attorney for the New York City Department of Education. I looked at my mother, knowing this was all her doing. I kissed her and gave her my heartfelt thanks.

As I shook the college president's hand and received my diploma, I heard my family roar with pride. I turned to watch them wave their Dominican flags as the mostly Caucasian crowd looked on in awe. As I left the podium I spread the enormous Dominican flag my family had draped over my graduation gown. I was proud to be one of a known handful of Dominicans to graduate from Dartmouth. I closed my eyes and savored the moment.

Also in the crowd, but apart from my family, were my biological father and my half-sister Ariasi. I had not heard from my dad in months, and the unexpected sight of him was jarring. Did he know or care that I made it without him? My half-sister's presence sent a chill up my spine. I shook off the bad feelings they evoked and looked back to my support group: my mom and her family—*my* family. As I walked back to my seat, I thought about my life, where it started, and how I ended up on the stage of an Ivy League college with a diploma in hand. My mind drifted back to my childhood.

After singing a song over and over, I fell to the floor, exhausted. I lay watching a cloud cross and slip behind the roof of my house. The aquamarine bungalow was built by my mother's father out of spare wood from a construction site. I loved this small palace, especially the tin roof, which made a wonderful symphony when it rained. I really did not mind that rain also meant water would pour in to our house through the holes in the rusted roof. Thirteen family members were crammed in to this one-room bungalow, with rooms defined by carefully patched curtains. I slept on an old mattress with five other people. We had no running water and had to use a latrine, but I had no complaints: I had plenty to eat and tons of space to play.

My mom usually called me every night. My grandmother would always tell me my mother was in America working very hard to send me money for food, clothing, school, and that one day I would live with her in America. "Be nice," my grandmother would whisper as I picked up the phone, "Dile te quiero" (Tell her that you love her).

One day my mother did call to say she was ready to bring me to the States. The INS process had delayed this for almost five years. This kind of cruel separation occurs in many families; the process of reuniting loved ones can take years. My mother considered herself lucky that she only had to wait five years to reunite with her only child—a child whose first steps and first words she had missed. My mom vowed to never miss another special moment in my life.

My grandmother raised me, she witnessed my important moments, and she was not ready to let me go. But soon my mother was at our door with new shoes and a new dress for me and, most important, a one-way plane ticket to JFK airport. My father was by her side, and we left my childhood palace hand in hand, ready for a new beginning.

The next period of my life, though it offered its share of challenges, was one of the happiest times I've known. I was not only part of a family but of a team whose goal was to live the American dream. My parents were living a very hard life. My mother had two full-time jobs and was a part-time student. My dad worked as a cab driver for sixteen to eighteen hours a day. But we were happy. Their discipline and determination were contagious, and my family asked nothing of me other than to do my best in school. That was my job, they told me, but the weight of being a good student did not fall solely on my shoulders. My mom made a schedule to maximize the time we could spend together and to make sure she could help me with my homework. My dad would wake me at 6:30 in the morning and get me ready for school. As hard as he tried to make me look my best, my pigtails were always lopsided. I would then give my half-asleep mom a kiss and was off to school.

My father picked me up from school, took me home for dinner, and then dropped me off at the babysitter's. I would do my homework and be asleep by seven. At about that time my mom would be punching out of her second job and rushing to make it to class on time. She would pick me up around midnight, and we'd ride home singing a silly song to keep ourselves awake. Once home, my mom would cook and help me with my homework. Some nights we got so frustrated trying to learn English we would cry in despair. After our work was done, we would sit down with a warm cup of milk and talk about our day. At about four a.m. my mom would put me to bed again and go to sleep herself. After about two hours the cycle would start again, lopsided pigtails and all.

My father, the black sheep of his family, was working hard in an attempt to achieve the economic status his family had in the Dominican Republic. He was an Abreu "gente de dinero, piel clara, y pelo bueno" (people of money, light skin, and straight hair). The family name had its roots in the Spanish word for "Hebrew," a testament of a Sephardic Jewish ancestry they could no longer trace. My mother belonged to "los pobres de la republica" (the poor of the republic). Yet it was in the poorer class that my father struck gold: my mother. She had curly red hair and *sangre morena* (black blood).

Race and class divisions are never openly spoken about in the Dominican Republic; it's simply interwoven with the threads of daily life. It's something you grow up breathing, living, and eventually internalizing. For example, men and women try to marry people lighter than themselves so that they can "improve" their bloodline. Black skin is associated with everything negative: poverty, crudeness, failure, the uneducated, the ugly, the unwanted. White skin is considered an antonym to all of that. Marrying someone darker than you, or perhaps with nappier hair, bigger lips, or a nose with a small bridge is considered "dañando la raza," spoiling your race, spoiling your descendents.

I myself am a mulatto, a mutt, a mix of the "good" and "bad." While growing up, I internalized the idea that I was not as pretty as my cousins on my father's side. They were all whiter, taller, skinnier, had straighter hair and light-colored eyes—a stark contrast to my charcoal eyes and hair. I remember holding on to my dad when he introduced me to his family. For such occasions I would have my hair straightened before I went to see them so that I could look "pretty." To this day I straighten my hair for interviews, picture days at school, or for any other important event.

My mom, on the other hand, thought my hair was beautiful. However, the fact that she relaxed her own hair reinforced my idea that curly hair was "pelo malo" (bad hair) and straight hair was "pelo bueno" (good hair). It took time, but as I matured I grew to love the fact that I was an ethnic and cultural mix. I embraced the contradictions within me and became empowered by them; the process was actually quite fast because I had more important things than looks to worry about.

My life in the United States was very different from my life in the Dominican Republic. Afternoons spent playing with my friends under the warm Caribbean sun were replaced with afternoons in a babysitter's apartment crammed with eleven other kids. I would try to do my homework, but the little kids hungered for my attention and the babysitter depended on me to help her with them.

"Angelita, can you change the baby's diapers, he's crying but I am cooking and I can't leave the hot stove alone with you kids running around," Lina yelled from the kitchen. "Lina, I have homework to do," I told her as politely as I could. She replied, "I know, honey, but you are the oldest in the house right now and as you can see my hands are tied." I couldn't change him until he stopped crying, and I needed to get back to my homework. By the time I finished changing him, he was hungry. I knew Lina would tell me to feed him, so I sat on the bed and recited the lines I had to memorize as the baby drank its milk. He finally fell asleep, looking peaceful and happy. I would have loved to join him, to take a nap before my mom came to pick me up, but I still had homework to do.

I must have fallen asleep doing my homework at the table, because I woke up to my mother demanding to know why I was asleep at the table with a bowl of cold rice and fried eggs and a page of math homework still left to do. My mother was very upset. "Lina, the only two things I ask you to do is to feed her the food I prepare for her and sit her down at the table and make sure she doesn't get up to play until she is done with her homework. You somehow can't do either; you've given her food to your kids instead and she is still not done with her homework!" Lina had no excuse.

My mom was picking up my things as she scolded Lina. She gave me a kiss on the forehead, put my jacket on, put my book bag on her back, grabbed my hand, and we walked toward the apartment door. At the door, my mom turned around and knelt down. She looked at me straight in the eye and asked, "Why didn't you finish your homework today?" I never lied to my mom, so I told her what I was doing, that I had to change the baby, feed him, and put him to sleep. My mom got up and glared at my babysitter. "Lina, my daughter is eight years old; she shouldn't be feeding a baby, much less changing him. She's not the babysitter, *you* are! I am sorry; we won't need your services anymore." My mom tugged at my hand and we walked out. Once outside, my mother let out a heavy sigh. She did not know what to do. Lina was the fifth babysitter in the past year. She couldn't find anyone who would just do the two things she asked: feed me and make sure I did my homework.

My mom called in sick the next morning and tried to find me another babysitter, but there was no one we could afford. Finally, she called her sister and asked her to take care of me. For the rest of my childhood, I bounced from house to house. Sometimes I would stay at my aunt's, other times at my uncle's, sometimes even at my uncle's hardware store. My mom felt better when I was with family. She at least knew that they would make sure that I was safe.

As I was often left alone, I invented ways to entertain myself. I sang rhymes to myself and carried on conversations in different voices. "¿Mija, con quién hablas?" (My daughter, who are you talking to?), my mother asked one day in a worried tone. She knew that I was alone in my bedroom, yet she heard me singing and talking. I was by myself, yet I was running my mouth as if I had a whole group of friends with me.

The next morning, my mother told me to hurry up because I had a doctor's appointment. She was taking me to a child psychologist to be evaluated. I don't remember what happened during my checkup, but I do remember the diagnosis. I remember it because it triggered an idea in my mom that changed our lives forever, and not for the better.

"Your daughter," the doctor paused for a second while my mom held her breath, "is a very intelligent young lady. Please do not be concerned about her talking and singing by herself. She is simply using her imagination to adapt to a familial environment where she is the only child."

My mother walked out of there, relieved about my mental health but worried about me growing up without siblings. I often mentioned that I wanted siblings and my mom didn't like me growing up without my older half-sisters. She was one of twelve children and knew how wonderful and fun growing up with brothers and sisters could be. She decided that she would bring my father's daughters over from the Dominican Republic. They were the daughters of my father's ex-wife, but my mom had been sending them money since she married my father. She bought them clothing and helped pay for their food, school supplies, and medical bills. "If I brought them to the U.S., they could have a better life and Angelita could get to know her sisters better": my mom smiled at the thought. She would raise us all as her own children.

"Angelita, how would you like it if I brought your sisters to live with us?" my mother asked at the dining room table that night.

"I'd like that."

"Honey, don't get ahead of yourself. We don't know if we can afford to bring them here, nor know if we can make things work out," added my father in a serious tone. Little did we know how his warning would become reality.

A couple of months later, my mother, father, and I were waiting for the plane that carried my three sisters. Their mother had given up her parental rights without hesitation. The paperwork was expensive and hard to get approved, but my mom had overcome those hurdles. I looked at the birthday card in my mom's hand. It was for Rosemary. She was turning twelve that day and my mother had prepared a welcome home and happy birthday party to celebrate these special occasions in one event. Mom had stayed up all night decorating the house and baking a birthday cake for Rosemary, and making other welcome gifts for my other two sisters, Ariasi and Yaniris. We were eager to embrace the girls and welcome them to our family. As soon as their plane landed, a whirlwind of excitement took us over. It lasted too short a time.

At the age of nine, all I wanted was for my new sisters to love me and accept me, but they never gave me a chance. They treated me like an outsider. They pushed me away. Were they upset because I had lived with our father most of my life while they had not? Did I represent the life my father had chosen when he left them behind in the Dominican Republic years ago?

I sometimes felt my father exacerbated the animosity my sisters felt for me. He wouldn't stop using me as an example: "Why can't your grades be as good as Angelita's? Why can't you learn English as fast as Angelita?" I can still see their angry faces and the way they shot their eyes in my direction whenever my father made these comments. In the years that we lived together I can never recall them looking at me with love, only with disdain and hatred. It took me a long time to understand that I didn't deserve to be treated that way.

My mother took great care of all of us. Every Friday evening she spent hours doing our hair. She would put rollers in, blow it dry, and then wrap it so that we looked pretty for church. One morning in church, my sister and I were sitting in front of a boy she liked. At the end of the service he gently grabbed my hair and commented on how beautiful it was. My sister looked at me with anger; she had the same hairdo, but his flattery didn't fall on her. I didn't think anything of the incident until something horrible happened.

The next day I was in the shower washing my hair. My long black hair seemed impossible to detangle. My arms were too short to reach and I had to call for backup. "Mami," I yelled over the loud shower. I waited and listened for a response. "Mami, I need help detangling my hair," I tried once again. Still no response. I was about to turn the shower off when my eldest sister, Ariasi, walked in. She and I had the same kind of *pelo malo* (bad hair), so she knew what a call from the shower meant. "Where's Mami?" I asked. "She's cooking, so I offered to come help you."

Come and help me? I thought. She offered to come and help *me*? My sisters go out of their way to *not* help me. I was a little doubtful of her sincerity but didn't show it. I knew she was mad at me for the compliment the boy had given me, so I was simply glad she was talking to me. Maybe the sermon had made her want to be nice, I thought. She grabbed my hair and began pulling at the tangled curls.

"OooooOOouuuuuuch!" I yelped. "Stop, it hurts!" "Hold on," she said. "I need to give you one more washing and then put in more conditioner. Close your eyes so the shampoo doesn't get into your eyes." I trusted her, and I closed my eyes. I felt my sister rub something very carefully all over my scalp and hair, and I figured she was spreading the detangling conditioner. As the minutes passed I began to feel an intense heat on my head. Was the water getting hotter? No, it still felt cool on my skin, but why did it feel hot on my head? I wiped my eyes and opened them. I couldn't talk, I was gasping for air in the middle of my sobs. My locks were all over the bathtub. Over the next few days 80 percent of my hair fell out. Ariasi had put chemicals on my scalp and hair that burned it all to a crisp. I was inconsolable.

Over the years my mother tried her best to spread her love and affection equally among us and show as little favoritism as possible, but this time she had to defend me. She held me close and tried to calm me down. "Ariasi, you'll have to explain to your father why you did what you did," she said. When my father heard of the incident he just kept on reading the newspaper. I was shocked at his apathy.

The next weeks were bad for everyone. My parents had to pick me up from school because I couldn't stop crying when I saw my long locks fall off onto the chairs and desks. How did things get so bad? Since my sisters arrived, I had lost my hair, and I had bruises from them beating up on me. If I got into an argument with one of them, they would all jump on me, three against one. Of course, I always ended up getting hurt. My mother begged me to explain where I was getting the bruises. I told her it was from playing around in school, and since I was something of a tomboy, she believed me.

I was afraid to tell her the truth. My fear stemmed from a moment that still haunts me. My parents were out and I had gotten into an argument with my oldest sister. She hit me, and I said I was going to tell Dad. She grabbed me by the collar and then let me go without saying anything. I began to walk down the hallway to my bedroom, when I heard footsteps behind me. I quickly turned around, thinking that if she was coming to hit me again, I was going to fight back. But when I turned around I stopped cold. My sister was holding a knife and looking at me with a blank expression. I walked backward, trying not to make any sudden movements. She grabbed me by the collar and held the knife to my neck. She had a really strong grip. She was clenching her big white teeth, her nose was only a few centimeters from mine. "If you ever tattle tale on me, I'll kill you," she said calmly. I looked at her in disbelief. I could see my other two sisters looking on. They did nothing to stop that moment of insanity. She let me go and walked away, calmly, toward the kitchen, I assume to put the knife away. I stood there gasping for air, my eyes still crossed from focusing on the tip of the shiny blade.

A few weeks later I heard that my grandmother, my mother's mother who raised me when I was young, was coming for the first time from the Dominican Republic. The night she arrived I told her everything my sisters had done to me, everything they had done to my mother. My sisters and father had caused so much pain, both physical and emotional. I told her about the knife. I told her my mom treated all of us equally and was trying to earn their love but to no avail. I also told her my dad didn't discipline the girls or try to mend things in the house. And I told her why. I had recently figured out what my sisters had known for over two years— my dad had a mistress. He wouldn't discipline my sisters because he was planning to leave my mother and he feared they would out him before he was prepared to go.

I felt so relieved after getting it all off my chest that night. After years of holding things in, of following the rule that what happens at home stays at home. After all those years of not showing emotion for fear my sisters would hurt me, I was finally able to let it out with tears and sobs on my grandmother's lap.

Soon after, things exploded in our house and my parents had the worst divorce imaginable. After years of working in the United States and creating a successful construction company in the Dominican Republic, as well as a car service in the States, my father left my mother and me in the street. He had put all the assets he shared with my mother under his brother's name in the Dominican Republic. By the time my mother petitioned for divorce, there was nothing on record of any of their shared wealth. My father had always taken care of finances, so my mom had nothing that proved she owned anything; the businesses they owned were now under someone else's name and our bank account was near zero.

I was torn apart by my parents' feud. I couldn't talk to either of them about what I was feeling and I became a very angry person. As I got older, I learned of other things my father had done to my mother, things she did not tell me in order to preserve my illusions about him. After the divorce my relationship with my father deteriorated in a matter of weeks. He did not even give my mother child support. The only good thing that came out of the divorce was that my half-sisters left with my father. He set them up in an apartment and he moved into another home with his mistress. For the rest of my adolescence my mom struggled to raise me and I hated my father for putting us through that. Then he got ill.

I hadn't spoken to my dad much since my parents' divorce. He hurt me too many times, and although our lack of communication was due to a lack of effort on his part, I was relieved because I didn't want to see much of him. Then one day, out of the blue, he called to say that he had been diagnosed with precancerous polyps in his colon. I began going to the hospital with him to translate and to make sure he knew what the doctors were saying. I think my dad could have asked someone else to do this for him but he needed support. His entire family was in the Dominican Republic, and his mistress was too uneducated to be of help. The only blood relatives he had in the United States were my half-sisters and me. He could have asked them to skip their college classes and go with him, but he decided to ask me to skip my high school classes instead. Not because he loved me more, or anything of that sort, but because I was the one who had done the translating in the household since I was seven.

I entered my father's car and closed the door. I had a calculus exam in two days and was missing the review lesson. I cleared my thoughts and looked at my dad. "Sion, Papi" (Bless me, Dad). "Que Dios te bendiga, mija" (May God bless you, my daughter). He gave me a kiss on the forehead and one on each cheek. It is tradition in our family to do this with your parents when you meet them or leave them. Some people do it out of habit, but I still do it because I feel naked without my parents' blessing. The car smelled of strawberries. "The car smells good," I said as I looked at my dad. "Yup, I just came from the carwash and bought these." He grabbed the strawberry-scented cartons hanging from his rearview mirror. "They match the color of the car and I bought them 'cause they are red, your favorite color." My favorite color was blue, but I didn't tell him that.

"So, how are you feeling dad?" "Bad, real bad. I couldn't sleep from the pain last night." He didn't have to tell me. The dark bags under his eyes were enough to let me know that he was not well. We finally got to the hospital. "OK, then let's begin," the doctor said, opening a folder that was at least three inches thick, my dad's medical record. My eyes were glued to the doctor and every move he made. He pulled out a set of X-rays and pictures. I had no clue what I was looking at, but it wasn't pretty, and whatever part of the body it was it did not look normal.

"What are polyps? Are they cancerous?" I asked the doctor. My hand was resting on my father's leg and I could feel him tapping his foot on the floor. The smell of the hospital was beginning to churn my stomach. I knew what polyps were; I had researched the word in the school library the other day, but I wanted to hear it again, just to make sure I had not misunderstood anything. My dad looked at me blankly, waiting for me to translate. "Well, they could be," the doctor began. "The biopsies taken show that he is in a precancerous stage. The good thing is that we have caught this early enough and can operate, but we must do it as soon as possible." He continued to explain the logistics, papers to be signed, who was liable for what, and all the other details of my father's health and the implications and dangers involved in the operation. I turned to my dad and held both his hands. He knew this was not going to be good. "Papi, primero no te asustes" (Dad, first of all don't be scared.) I had translated many things in my life. I knew the translation to every sentence the doctor had uttered. I took a deep breath, feeling my heart pound. I swallowed my fear, my need to cry at that moment, and translated.

That night I got home and realized that I had my weekly bio quiz the same day as my father's surgery. I hoped the teacher would let me take it early. I cried myself to sleep; the tears were of fear, desperation, and anger. I was angry at a lot of things, and I was angry at my father for a lot of things. He had not been a good father for the last two years and he destroyed our family by being unfaithful. When he divorced my mother, he divorced me, just like he had done with my sisters until my mother brought them back into his life, our lives.

His actions had caused my mother to have a nervous breakdown right after the divorce. I still get pangs when I remember her lying there in a hospital bed, failing to respond to my words and caresses. It took her a month to come around. I spent days by Mom's side, talking to her, although she did not know who I was. The doctors suggested that my father visit, to see if he could get her to snap out of it. He refused to do it, coldheartedly saying that her condition was none of his business. "It would be giving false hopes," he said. He wouldn't do it even though I was asking him through tears. A couple of days before my mother was to be committed to a mental institution, I went to her room. I picked her up by her hospital robe, made her sit up, and I yelled in her face: "You can't leave me by myself, come on get up! God damn it, if you love me you'll get out of this! . . . Fine, stay here, leave me alone. I thought you loved me. . . . Mom, don't let him do this to you!" I had little hope this would work, my aunt Tatao tried something similar a few days before without success.

She wasn't responding. I let her go and she slumped back into the hospital bed. I buried my face in her chest and cried my soul out. After a few minutes, I saw her eyes begin to tear up; she was trembling. Any other time this would have been a scary thing for me, but at that moment it was the best thing that could have happened in the world. My mother was reacting.

Before I left, I held my mother and told her I loved her and that we could get through this together. She didn't say anything back that night, but I knew she was going to be OK. Outside, my aunt Tatao was waiting in the car. I told her what happened in the hospital room and her eyes lit up. The next day when we went to visit my mom, she was in her street clothes and was signing herself out of the hospital. The doctors were really nervous; they said they did not know how long she would last, whether this convalescence was permanent. My aunt Tatao told them to leave my mom alone and that she would be fine. After that, Tatao took us in and took care of my mother until she could stand on her own two feet. Throughout this time my dad never showed a bit of concern for us.

Had my father not behaved the way he did, we could still be a family. I don't mean my parents would still be married, but if my dad had not been so vile, they could have come to terms with the fact that they had fallen out of love, gotten a divorce, and they could have been civilized to each other. Unfortunately, my father fell into the stereotype of Latino men who divorce their children when they divorce their wives. And my mother became the stereotypical single Latina mother, forced to become a mother and father at once. Now that my father was sick, I couldn't ask my mother to help me. The family divisions were deep and permanent. My father had to go through this alone; I had to go through this alone with him. It was up to me to go to the doctor with him and stay by his bedside while he recovered in the hospital after his surgery.

School became an escape from the things that were going on at home. I couldn't change things at home, but I could control what happened in school—so I did. I dove deeper into my studies to numb the sting of being discarded once again by my father after he regained his health. His phone calls stopped just a few days after he was out of the hospital. He no longer needed me to translate and take care of logistics. I was determined to show him that I did not need him to have a happy and successful life. But I was wrong; I did need him in a sense, for it was my anger toward him and my desire to show him that my mom and I could make it on our own that motivated me to get ahead in life. All so that one day I can walk up to him and say, "I've made it, and I only needed my mom to do it. You were not there during the tough times, so don't you even think of walking into my life during the good times."

I tell myself I no longer feel anything for my father, but the truth is that the thought of him always brings me to tears. At some point I stopped knowing whether they are tears of sadness about my loss or of anger for all the pain he has caused in my life. What I do know is that after he used me and threw me away, I made a decision to no longer consider him a part of my life. Through the years I thought of him as little as possible and concentrated on trying to make it for Mom and me. The years went by, and one day in the spring of 2000 I opened an envelope that sealed my fate for the next four years. It was an acceptance letter to Dartmouth College.

My entrance into the Ivies was less than glamorous. The van my mom's boyfriend was driving started smoking two hours into the five-hour trip from New York City to Hanover, New Hampshire. The old red Chevy van finally broke down right in front of the Exit 13 sign, Dartmouth's exit ramp. I looked to my left and saw gridlock. I scanned the long row of cars to see if anyone looked like they might be willing to help us. Most of the cars were full of anxious parents and nervous freshmen. Suddenly, something struck me. The cars were all very new and expensive—BMWs, Audis, every brand of new 2000 minivans and 4×4s on the market.

What struck me even more was that everyone within sight was Caucasian. Everyone in the passing traffic would slow down and look at us as if we were aliens. I felt like rolling down a window and screaming at the top of my lungs, "Yes, we're aliens, but we have our green cards!" Despite the fact that I knew I had every right to be there in a broken car and had done nothing to warrant the looks of pity from blue-eyed strangers, I felt a growing sense of fury. I felt as if I were naked and on display. My mother was not bothered by everything that seemed so embarrassing to me. She has always been oblivious to the judgmental looks of other people. Eventually, a state trooper and a tow truck came to our rescue, and a few hours later I was officially registered as a Dartmouth College freshman.

While we were organizing my things in my new dorm room, my mother realized that other kids were bringing in lounge chairs, TVs, small refrigerators, and other things I did not have. She immediately left me to organize my room and came back with tons of nice things we couldn't afford. "Ma, I would have been fine without those things." My mother's reply was simply, "I do not want you to feel like you are any less than these kids while you are here studying." As I look back at my time in college, I can honestly say that I never felt that I was worth any less or was any less intelligent than anyone else. What I did feel was that I was different.

During the first week of orientation I spent my time being directed through a maze of activities designed to make minority groups feel welcome. I had not thought about being a "minority" at Dartmouth and was slightly taken aback when I began to realize that my individual identity of "Angelita" now had an addition tacked on to it: I was now "Angelita, a Latina at Dartmouth." I do not know why, but the more people tried to put an ethnic or racial label on me the less I felt they understood who I was, where I came from, and where I wanted to go. I began desperately to search for someone who might be able to see the real me.

During a Latino reception I felt someone tap me on the shoulder. I turned around to face a petite, dark-skinned girl. She did not have to open her mouth. We embraced and did not have to say a word; we knew everything about each other as soon as our glances met; most of all, we knew we needed each other. We were two immigrant Dominican girls who almost two decades earlier had been born in the Caribbean and had somehow ended up at an Ivy League college as a result of hard work, luck, and some serious financial aid. As we chatted, we spotted another girl who wore a deer-in-headlights expression that resembled ours. It turns out that Mildred and I were right: the girl we spotted, Lydia, was half African American and half Dominican. That night we promised to take care of one another during the next four years. By the end of our freshmen year we realized that we were the only "visible" Dominicans in the 2004 class.

The reason why I say "visible" is because many people tried to hide their ethnicities for certain reasons. First, it is no secret that there are not very many Latinos at Dartmouth, and of those few, even fewer who have anything more than superficial contact with their culture. Second, the pressure to fit into mainstream college culture is powerful and affects everyone. Due to some European ancestry stemming from the days of "conquistas and colonizations," a good percentage of Latinos have features that make them look white, and many of this kind of Latino pass themselves off as white. It's not that they deny their culture or lie about it; it is more that they just go along with the assumptions people make from their physical features.

Anyway, the fact was, there were few visible Latinos at Dartmouth. I remember that throughout my undergrad career we would joke that we were "reducing the Dartmouth Latino population by half this weekend" when going away on road trips. We would say such things in jest, but we were all aware that it was probably true. What was no laughing matter were the expectations that came from other students and some professors who saw us as token Latinos in the classroom. Not only were we supposed to be overly eager to share our knowledge about our culture, but we were also expected to stand up and "clarify" things when ignorant comments were made about our Latino culture and about minority communities in general.

By senior year, I was still hearing things like "I am against racism, in fact I try to make one brown friend a week." It is unfortunate that someone who would make that kind of comment is in an Ivy League institution, but what is truly sad is that these people are not an anomaly on campus. What is even more distressing is that Latino students like myself are struggling with too many other things (financial, physical, and emotional) to speak up every time we are expected to. There are simply too many ignorant comments and too few students to "set the record straight." As a result, I learned how to pick and choose my battles.

The pressures at college definitely made it hard to go on, especially every time we lost a fellow Latino on our path toward earning our diplomas. By junior year, Mildred and Lydia, the other two Dominicans in my class, were gone. Mildred left sophomore year to get married. I know that her decision was based greatly on how little support she received in her academic endeavors. She had a baby last year and graduated from a community college. Lydia was suspended for nine terms for something she did not do. With such a large percentage of students who are suspended being minorities, I often question whether the system is fair.

Fortunately, I survived the Ivy League minority experience. I don't mean to imply that I am not grateful for all that has been given me. My college experience exposed me to a whole world of new possibilities and gave me the monetary and institutional support that I needed for all of my academic pursuits; nonetheless, my success often came with great difficulty. It was a rough ride, but one that I needed to take.

And now I found myself at the end of that long ride. On graduation day, I sat in a corner of the college's common area, overwhelmed by the occasion. The room was filled by my family and the scents and sounds they carried with them. Everyone was dancing, laughing, eating, and chatting. I glanced over at my college dean through the glass wall of his office. I was grateful for his presence. After such a dramatic ride, I was glad that there was at least one outside person to witness my exit from college, Dominican style. My mom sat next to me and asked, "Are we embarrassing you?" I gave her a reassuring smile. I have to admit, there was a time about four years ago when I was insecure about who I was and where I came from, but thanks to my experiences at college, that was no longer the case. Looking for further reassurance, she asked me, "Then why are you sitting in this corner by yourself?"

"Because I can see everyone from here," I explained. I felt blessed and lucky that so many people were rooting for me all those years. My mom took my hand and closed her eyes. "I am so full of pride. I hope you know that everything I have done in my life has been to bring you to this moment," she said in almost a whisper. I was speechless. All I had done was stay sane, get good grades, and get a college degree. My mother had moved to a foreign land, gone through a divorce, and worked her behind off to finish raising me on my own—all to give me a chance for a better life. I was so swollen with emotion that all I could manage to say was an all too simple "Thank you, Mami."

In the other corner of the common room I spotted my dad and sister; they looked absurdly out of place. Then my gaze involuntarily moved toward an opening door where an alum I had met earlier that day was walking in. That morning we had met in the hallway of my dorm building. She had handed me her daughter's garbage bag, thinking that I was a janitor. I handed her garbage back and stated what to me was more than obvious: "I am not a janitor, I am a graduating senior." Now I saw the same lady give me a quick smile and wave. I closed my eyes for a second, then exhaled and relaxed.

Let me try to put what I was feeling and continue to feel into words. I was finally comfortable in my own skin. I was a confident Dominican American young woman who was proud of my origins, grateful for my past, and fearless about my future. I got up from the corner, took my mother's hand, and took center stage in what had been turned into a dance and party floor by my family. As my mom and I danced we hugged each other tightly, knowing for the first time that we were going to be OK, knowing for the first time that we had no regrets, because on graduation day we finally felt that all of our sacrifices were worth it.

After graduating from Dartmouth Angelita Urena participated in the Japanese Exchange and Teaching Programme (JET) and taught English at three high schools in Japan. Subsequently, she started law school at Cornell University and has just finished the first year of the JD/LLM in international law.

Robert Cotto   The Coquí's Call

"Are you really American?" Nikola, a young Bosnian Serb man, asked me this on a research trip to the former Yugoslavia in the middle of my senior year in college. I answered quickly, "Why don't you think I am American?" Pausing for a while, Nikola replied, "Because you look black but have light skin, not like your friends." I am American, but in Bosnia the people stared at me as if I were from another planet. Many of the Bosnian students that I met looked at me, awestruck. Through a translator, I asked a Bosnian Muslim girl if she had ever seen anybody who looked like me. I will remember her reply for the rest of my life: "Only on MTV."

In this far corner of the world, I found myself having to answer a question I have heard all of my life—"Robert, What are you?"—and its variant, "Who are you?" Since my childhood I have had to answer this question to people of all colors—even Puerto Ricans. Today I can answer the question more comfortably, as I have found the words to describe my journey. It is an adventure to look Afro-indigenous, to be from a working-class Latin American immigrant family, to be the first graduate from college after three generations in the United States, and to fulfill the responsibilities of a Latino male that come with having a privileged education. All of these aspects of my life brought me to Bosnia and have been instrumental in driving me forward.

To Nikola I replied, "Yes, I am American, but my family is Puerto Rican. I am also Puerto Rican." Maybe that answer will change ten years from now, but that is the best I can give now. I am American and Puerto Rican and I am successful in many ways. But embracing these identities was difficult because of deep family crises that I survived by detaching myself emotionally, which sometimes made it hard to understand myself as a Puerto Rican kid. I now view my tendency toward emotional withdrawal and my determination to succeed in school as intimately connected to my search for a stable identity.

All four generations of my father's family are Puerto Rican. My bilingual, working-class world was so much more vibrant than the monolingual, white, sterile life of my school. I can remember my uncles playing spades or dominoes when I was a kid. They would bicker about a sports game, but a new box of Newport cigarettes calmed everybody down. An ambulance would sing down the street while salsa music would be blasting from the stereo system in the basement. A new rhythm was added to the mix when everybody started slapping their bodies to smash the mosquitoes during our weekend summer parties. After a long week, my family escaped through these parties together. We sat atop the stone porch on white plastic chairs and upside-down buckets. Budweiser cans lined the side of the porch; the few pale lights attracted moths. Every person looked different in terms of skin color, body shape, and hair type.

We often roasted a small pig on an open fire, which was complemented by white and orange rice, beans and pigs' feet, meat stews, multiple salads, fried and boiled plantains, and *pasteles*, which are a pumpkin or yuca and meat pie cooked in a banana leaf. Of course, after the food there would be dancing. Everybody who could walk without a cane danced merengue or salsa. Yelling in both Spanish and English, the elder members of the family sat watching everybody and reminisced about Puerto Rico. My aunts would tell me about life on the island. Although our lives were humble and often difficult, Puerto Ricans enjoy life this way.

My family has continued this tradition of coming together to celebrate our good fortunes. Like many immigrants, my family was able to do better for themselves in the United States because of the economic difficulties darker-skinned people have in Puerto Rico. It was most important that the family stay together, so we re-created our home traditions in Connecticut, sharing a humble happiness on holidays and weekends through our small parties and family gatherings.

No one was more central to these gatherings or to my life than my mother, Esperanza. She read to me as a child and she made a small library for me as soon as I could read. Language was never a problem at school in the United States because I always knew English. In fact, I learned English and Spanish at the same time, so I have two first languages. Unfortunately, in school I had to speak only English, and I almost completely forgot Spanish. Because I knew English very well, attended class every day, and did not get in trouble, I went through my elementary school years without much conflict. My mother made sure of my attendance, good behavior, and always asked me, "What did you do today in school?" She helped me with whatever homework she could, even after she divorced my father and worked full time.

My mother was born in Hartford to Peruvian parents; she was the oldest of eight children. Although she had a turbulent young life, my mother was remarkable in her dedication to my brother and me. She graduated from high school, which was not easy, because she rarely spent an entire year in one school. At a very young age she was expected to take responsibility for her brothers and sister. Her family moved often, and she lived in all but one of Hartford's housing projects. The projects in Connecticut are two-story duplex buildings with black shutters and bars on the first-floor windows.

Her brothers were infamous in the projects for causing trouble, and they were kicked out of several apartment buildings. Several of my family members still lived in the projects or other run-down apartments while I was growing up, and they seemed to always be in trouble, especially my uncles. My mother always made sure there was distance between us because they were sometimes violent and jealous because of her ambitions. At about the time my mother and father decided to move away from my grandmother's house, others in my family turned to drugs and violence.

My uncle Juan's death was the event that most changed the family; it even affected my parents' marriage. On a sunny Easter Sunday when I was six years old I woke up and asked my father, "Dad, where are we going today?" He answered briefly, "Probably to your grandmother's house." Just then the phone rang. My mother picked up, listened for a short time, and hung up as quickly as she had answered. "We have to go to Abuela Maria's house, something happened to Juan," she said.

It was a long ride to my grandmother's house. My father turned up the radio and was silent the entire way. As we pulled up to her house, nothing looked unusual, except that no people were hanging out on the front porch and the dog was in the house instead of the yard. I can still remember seeing the flies on the huge puddle of blood rippling in the wind, like an ocean on the concrete driveway. Gauze bandages and medical tape were scattered around the lawn. In the backyard, the clothesline was dangling from its post. I thought to myself, "What happened to my uncle Juan?" I could hear people crying in the house, but nobody appeared in the windows.

Juan was special to me because he had shown me a kind of attention that usually only my mother displayed. He was a special uncle, not blood, but married to my mother's sister. Everybody looked up to him as the "man of the family" because he was smart, strong-willed, good-looking, always the person to settle an argument or cheer everybody up.

Daydreaming while staring at his blood, I woke up when my father called me, "Bobby, let's go! I have to drop you off at the house because we have to go the hospital." Wanting to know more, I asked, "What happened to Juan?" A few silent moments passed when my mother softly said, "Juan tried to kill himself this morning. He was sad and did not want to live anymore. He might not live."

Juan died soon afterward. At first I had no reaction. It was the first time that anybody so important in the family had died, so I did not know how to react. I can't remember any feeling but just a curiosity about why it had all happened. What would happen to his kids, my cousins Juan and Melissa? What would happen to the family? How did he do it? Why was he sad? What did it all mean?

In the end, it meant that my mother's family would never be the same. My aunt Angela, his wife, was pregnant when he died, and that baby, Angela, died two weeks after birth because of a brain abnormality. Overhearing a conversation, I learned that Juan had been using drugs heavily, mostly crack cocaine. Aunt Angela and Juan were having conflicts that destroyed their marriage even before he died. Years later my mother told me, "Bobby, he killed himself using drugs because he was sad that Angela did not want to be married to him anymore."

That one event haunts me because its secondhand effects altered my life. Everybody in the family was devastated. It happened on Easter Sunday, and every family event after that was just a sad reminder of how happy we used to be. Aunt Angela found solace in drug use, then evangelical Christianity, and was finally institutionalized for several months for severe depression. Even my uncles, who put on a face of toughness, were shaken and saddened by Juan's death. My uncle Anthony, the most gifted man in the family and the most troubled, was incarcerated for burglary months later. Almost every time Uncle Anthony drinks, he mentions how great Juan was. My cousin Juan Jr. did not have a father anymore, and he was a timid kid who desperately needed a father. Nearly everybody drank more heavily after Juan's death. What was once a happy, working-class Puerto Rican–Peruvian family turned into a sad group of people searching for a way out of their sadness.

Other problems made the situation worse. In our suburban home, my parents looked like an interracial couple. In Puerto Rico there are skin color categories, but they are not as rigid as the American system of black and white. Puerto Ricans have brown to green eyes, red to black hair, and pale to chocolate brown skin. If you saw my mother on the street, you would think she was white. If you saw my father you would think he was black. The product of my parents' physical differences is my light brown face, with pronounced cheekbones, full lips, and dark almond-shaped eyes. I could be taken for Latin American, South Asian, North African, or Middle Eastern. In some places, the way you look means more than a culture or nationality; it can be a call to misunderstanding and hate.

My father left us soon after Juan's death. Almost a year and a half after Juan's death, my parents began to fight. In retrospect, I think the stresses of work, the self-destructing family, and the neighborhood hatred were too much for my parents to handle and remain together. All of a sudden, I would hear screaming coming from the bedroom. I cannot remember what they were saying, but I hid under my blankets, scared, every night. At one point my father stormed out of the house in a rage. The entire house was awake, my two-year-old brother screaming in his room. I peeked into the kitchen and saw my father in such a state of anger he looked like he would hit my mother—something I knew he would never do. Instead he just turned and left.

I can still hear myself crying my heart out those nights alone, hiding underneath some blue blankets. I shed a lifetime of tears when I was seven. The arguments between my mother and father were not the worst part of it all; it was being alone and worrying that the most important people in my life were in danger. I had nobody to talk to then, not even an imaginary friend; my cousins to whom I felt the closest lived too far for me to reach them. Uncle Anthony, my cousin Jessica's father, was in jail, and Juan was dead, so they were alone too, and going through similar things. By the time my mother told me, "Bobby, me and your father are getting a divorce. But you will be OK," I had cried all that I could and emotion had left me. I answered calmly, "I know, Mom, but where are we going to live?" She replied, "Until we find a place we are going to live with Tia Angela." I think she was shocked at how calm I was, but since then I have taken bad news in the same way.

Aunt Angela was just getting back on her feet; now my mother, my brother, and I had to get back on ours. We lived in the city for a few months, and then my mother found an apartment inside the town line of a good school district. In this new place I found a new way of dealing with emotions: crying so much during that year drained me, and I chose not to let things bother me anymore.

Entering a new school in sixth grade after a tumultuous two years, I began to experience new challenges. I began to learn something in school that has little to do with math, reading, or writing. I realized that I was in a white school and that I was different. I recall a classmate asking me, "Are you Portuguese?" I said, "No." I thought that the kids might laugh or say something mean if I said where my family was from, so after a few seconds' hesitation, I said, "I am Puerto Rican." "Really?" he asked. "You don't act like a Puerto Rican: you're different. Right, Mike?" Mike responded, "Yeah, you're not like the rest of them. That is why we like you." How was I different? I looked around and saw that my face was different from the kids in line. Until then, I had never really noticed that I looked different from the white kids and two Chinese kids. I thought to myself, "What are Puerto Ricans supposed to act like?" Because I did not fit the stereotypes, I could not possibly be Puerto Rican to them. So for a long time, my philosophy in school was to prove to other people that Puerto Ricans can do well and that we are smart. In short, I had to do better than the white kids.

In the midst of adolescence, I had to reconcile two worlds. In middle school I was nerdy, awkward, and in the minority as a Puerto Rican kid in an all-white school. Coming home from school in seventh grade, I turned on the TV and saw a white, three-family house that resembled my abuela Maria's house, where my uncle was living. The reporter noted, "Drug dealer arrested after FBI seizes drugs and weapons." I yelled, "Mom, Tio Miguel is on the news!" Looking back at the television, I saw my uncle, handcuffed, being escorted by law enforcement people—the Hartford Police Department, the DEA, the FBI, the ATF, and the bomb squad. I thought to myself, "I hope nobody sees this at my school. It must be a secret." A few minutes later, the phone rang and my mother was speaking with my aunt Angela. At my grandmother's house, papers were scattered across the floor, boxes were emptied, all the furniture was moved, and the doors had boot marks on them from being kicked in. My grandmother kept repeating, "Ay, Dios mío, se lo tomaron" (Dear lord, they took him). The police had left the house a disaster area, without any explanation. According to the news report, drugs and weapons were found in the house.

Overhearing a conversation between my mother and Aunt Angela, I learned that 160 bags of heroin, some marijuana, several shotguns, a pistol, and a grenade were found in Miguel's closet. The police were tipped, but the circumstances were shady because Tio Miguel insisted that he was just holding the drugs and weapons for somebody else. He was involved in the Los Solidos gang, the rival of the Latin Kings, in Hartford, at the height of gang membership in the early 1990s. Everybody in the family knew about his gang membership and worried that he would be killed. My uncle's involvement in a gang never bothered me, but it was always something that made me feel out of place at school. Friends would come to school and say, "Did you hear about that Latin Kings murder of a Solido last night in Hartford?" Another would respond, "Yeah, all those Puerto Ricans are in gangs. Some of them are even coming to this town. I hope they keep them out."

At that time I did not know how to confront such racism. I could have said something, but what? Puerto Ricans were in fact in the gangs, and they were killing one another. All I could think to say was, "There are white gangs, too, like the Nomads." After that the topic would change. I had to find a way out of those awkward situations. I did not want to challenge anybody; I wanted out of that kind of interaction. The weirdest thing about having an uncle who sold drugs and was in a gang was not the criminal part of his life, but that he was normal and good to me in our everyday life. Miguel always talked to me about the latest video games and what I learned in school. He was a second-generation Puerto Rican who sold drugs, but he was a good uncle too.

Back in school, I did not have anybody I could tell these secrets to. I had several girlfriends, but none serious enough to share my secrets with. My male friends were all people I knew from sports teams, and they were hardly confidants. For schoolwork or getting in trouble, I had plenty of friends, but I had no one to talk to about problems a Puerto Rican family might face, such as drugs or gangs, because my white friends discussed them as if they were far-away fantasies. I felt isolated because I could not imagine that anybody else had such outrageous family issues like my uncle Miguel's incarceration. In high school, my other uncles were all incarcerated for some period of time, mostly on drug charges. I was embarrassed, but I also felt that nobody wanted to hear about my family and certainly could not understand. The last time I saw Miguel, I was on the other side of a corrections facility visitation booth. Looking at him through a plastic window, I spoke to him through a phone and said, "Come home soon. Don't forget to write me."

Besides the "What are you?" question, I had to answer ignorant wealthy white kids' questions such as, "What do your parents do? Where are they from?" I would answer, "My father works for the bus company and my mother for the insurance company." Most people did not ask more. My greatest fear was that somebody would say to me, "Tell me about your family." Luckily, I managed to get out of that question most of the time. I could talk to others about math problems, novels, and what was on TV the night before, but when it came to having fun with them, I couldn't do it. I was afraid of saying something they might think was strange, and of letting my secrets out. I didn't feel like anybody in my classes knew where I was coming from or who I really was. They mispronounced my last name and butchered it. I don't know who they thought I was, but whatever they thought could not have been right. My best option was to have just a few friends within the limited interaction of sports or schoolwork. In some ways, the window I saw my uncle through is what I put up around myself. People could look at and speak to me but never really get inside to touch me.

At times during middle school I was a class clown, cracking jokes and rebelling against teachers and administrators to distract myself from the real things bothering me. I got away with it because I was in the higher-track classes. I was a nerdy runt at school, an awkward, brown anomaly. People never guessed and were even shocked when they found out that I was Puerto Rican—although I didn't look anywhere near white. I heard often that I wasn't like "those other Puerto Ricans" and I "didn't get into trouble." My academic success kept me outside of the lower-track classes filled with other Puerto Rican and black students. Middle school was lonely, in that I had people all around me, but my depth of friendships was shallow. I wrote lots of poetry, and had three girlfriends, two black and one Chinese, to ease my loneliness. But for the most part, while my academic life flourished, my social life suffered because of my own insecurities.

After a socially difficult freshmen year of high school, feeling more and more isolated in school, I returned for summer football practice in August. Despite my starkly different home life, which placed a premium on family togetherness, I was geographically separated from the majority of my family on an everyday basis. My mother urged us to do well in school, but I was losing interest in school because I rarely connected with anything being taught or any of the people in my classes. If I was on a racial island early in high school, then I needed to find a way off, or at least to learn how to survive. Being a short guy playing football and the only Puerto Rican quietly succeeding in advanced placement and honors classes proved to others that I was capable of any school activity. Socially, however, I was in

Puerto Rico and all of my peers were on the mainland; I had few friends, but many acquaintances. Being so emotionally detached from people took its toll on making new friends and becoming comfortable with white and other brown students. I rarely trusted people with my thoughts, feelings, and especially family secrets. I think I may have been a typically socially uncomfortable and awkward adolescent trying to answer the identity question, "Who am I?" What made being a teenager more difficult was also having to answer others' question, "What are you?" when I was in the process of trying to figure that out too. I felt like an exotic creature in the midst of my classmates, and my family culture and humbler means exacerbated that feeling.

Playing football saved me from getting in trouble and becoming absolutely withdrawn from school. I did not have to try to hide emotions or information about my family from my teammates. It was pretty easy to hide myself behind my helmet and pads. Although I would not say that I was a friend of my teammates during my time on the squad, I trusted them to protect me on and off the field, and I would do the same. It was an important group that helped me survive high school.

Dirty and tired after one long, cold November afternoon of football practice, I immediately showered and started my homework alone in my bedroom. My mother came in and asked, "How was school?" I answered, "Boring as usual." In the background, my mother had Spanish music playing. I was very cranky after school and football, as usual, and the music was bothering me. I snapped at my mother and yelled, "Can you turn the music down, I'm trying to read!" Shocked, my mother said, "That is the music of your people, you are Puerto Rican." I answered just as quickly, "Well, what if I don't want to be Puerto Rican? What have Puerto Ricans ever done that was good?"

Besides my father's family, who I saw less and less of as I grew older, the only Puerto Ricans I knew were my uncles in jail, my alcoholic father, and the other brown kids in school who wanted to fight me for being nerdy. In my ten years of school, I had never read about one Puerto Rican in any history, literature, or science textbooks. The closest thing to seeing Puerto Ricans being validated was watching *West Side Story*, but those characters were nothing like my family. So I told my mother, "I will just tell people that I am Peruvian; the Inca empire was in Peru." It was sad, but I became convinced early on that I was on a social island because my skin color, facial features, and family life seemed to leave me out of the social loop of my classmates. I was confident in my abilities to do well in school and to play football, but I did not fit in well otherwise and I had no Puerto Rican role models. My mother had always been my best role model, but I was too deep in adolescence and conflict with her to see her as a person to emulate. That evening my mother simply answered by saying, "You are Puerto Rican, and nothing can change that no matter what you say."

Later that year my mother asked, "What would you like for Christmas?" I said, "I don't want anything." She insisted, "You must want something?" I said, "Well, a CD player would be nice." She looked at me and nodded. By that point it seemed the entire world had a CD player except for me, and I was getting into hip-hop and Latin music more. To my surprise, my uncle on my father's side bought me several Spanish music CDs in conjunction with my new radio. Mother told me, "Put them in and see how they sound!" From that first merengue CD, I was hooked on Latin American music. Although I had heard all kinds of Puerto Rican music as a kid, after my parents divorced we spent less time with my father's side of the family and I was less exposed to that part of our culture. That Christmas morning I was excited to have something new in my hands that I could say was Puerto Rican culture. I loved the music for the wonderful percussion sounds and fun Spanish lyrics.

What I did not realize at that moment was that Latin American music was something tangibly, indelibly, and remarkably positive about Puerto Rican culture and that I needed it to find value in being Puerto Rican at a crucial time in my life. The music was fast, recognizable, happy, fun, complex, and artful; salsa, merengue, and *bomba* became a symbol for me of Puerto Rican achievement. It meant more than just music to me. I collected as much Latin music as I could, searching for more information on what great Puerto Ricans had made and left for me to find. In order to figure out who I was and what I was racially at the same time, I found solace in Latin music that even my family members knew little about. Understanding my Puerto Ricanness was not just listening to a particular type of music, it was accepting the differences that I knew existed between me and my classmates, and feeling that achieving academically could be possible at the same time.

Perhaps my mother's most important advice came during my junior year when my outlook was becoming more positive, thanks to my success in academics and sports. In my senior year I was selected cocaptain of the football team, which I had lettered in for two years, and I was chosen for the National Honor Society.

A turning point came when my mother saw me throwing an application to a summer college program in the trash and yelled at me, asking why I was doing so. I began to rethink my decision to ignore the program—perhaps this was an opportunity I should not pass up. More than anybody else in my life, my mother has shown me not to let opportunities slip through my hands; she has always pushed me to seize chances, no matter how unreachable the goal may seem. Taking that application out of the garbage and sending it in was perhaps one of the most important decisions I made as a result of my mother's influence. That influence has shaped my trajectory into college and beyond.

I was a bit scared of what to expect at a minority business program at a graduate school of business. Would the kids be from the suburbs like myself, or would they be from big cities? I imagined that the kids in the program would be child prodigies who started their own Internet businesses and were definitely on their way to Ivy League schools. Just thinking about college, not to mention Ivy League schools, was an exciting prospect. At that time I was starting to realize that, as a Puerto Rican kid with great grades, above average test scores, and some ambition, I was a commodity. The packet I received said that I would be going to Dartmouth College for the month of July, all expenses paid.

The other twenty-nine participants in the program were from everywhere in the United States. They were all black, Latino, and Native American, and many of them had gone to mostly white schools. Most of my friends in the program had gone to white schools and done very well. For the first time I felt that there were other people similar to me in the world, which changed the way I looked at things. Instead of a world of solitude, I began to feel I was part of a network of brown people in a white academic world. I am grateful for having had the chance to participate in the program and wonder how things might be different today if my mother had not persuaded me to apply. Again, I look back and realize how lucky I am to have my mother. Even if I was the luckiest, smartest person in the world, I would not be where I am today without her.

On the first day of classes in my freshman year of college, I walked into my sociology class on the issues that Latinos face and saw a rainbow of faces. I had not been in a classroom with so many brown people since my summer program. After giving an outline of the course, the Hispanic professor went around the room and asked our names and where we were from. There were names like García, Velasquez, and Ramírez from places such as Chicago, L.A., Boston, and New York. Although the class was racially mixed, I was amazed there were so many other brown people. What struck me most was the professor and the course content. She was commanding, intelligent, and sharp. She got to the heart of what I think many of us were trying to find out—how we all got to such a good college and what it meant to be Latino. In that first class the professor said, "We will be studying the experiences of Dominicans, Mexicans, Puerto Ricans, and Cubans in the United States." I remember being absolutely impressed that this woman who reminded me of my mother was in charge in a class-room because of her intelligence and ability.

However, early on I knew something was wrong. I didn't feel like I was a part of anything at college. I was doing well in school, but something was missing. With all of my baggage from home and the past, I thought I could never be a part of my college. I didn't have the desire to do the things most people seemed to be doing. During the day, groups of four to six people would go to the dining halls together, while I liked to eat alone, or with one good friend. To me, college seemed like high school all over again. The athletes all sat together, fraternity brothers sat together, and all the brown kids sat together, with a few exceptions.

I quickly saw that at my college there were two schools of thought on Latino identity. There were people who embraced the political label Latino and believed in the goal of a united community, much like the black or Asian communities. And there was the camp that thought they didn't want to "segregate" themselves on the basis of having Latino ancestry. I was stuck somewhere in the middle. The social spectrum was either hav-ing all brown friends or being a random brown kid mixed with a group of white kids. That was how I saw it, so I chose not to do either. I had a lot of Latino friends and acquaintances, but I never had a group of friends, and I didn't feel comfortable alone with only white kids. To this day, most of my friends are people of color, but I have branched out. Ironically, many of the Latino students who avoided me the first two years of college are my friends today. As time went on, they found me open to their insecuri-ties and we became friends. I know my mother prepared me to face the white world by teaching me what it means to be Puerto Rican and how to have pride in that. Many of the people around me did not have those cul-tural foundations; how might things have been different if I had had an-other family?

That year school became less important and my own insecurities needed to be addressed, especially I needed to open up and show my emotions. For most of my life I had chosen not to become emotionally involved in family mishaps. My uncles' incarceration, my mother's hysterectomy, my grandmother's cancer, and my two cousins who were young and pregnant were things that bothered me, but I tried to forget them. During college, these issues began to eat away at me and I did not know how to deal with them.

I met a girl during freshman year who helped heal my emotional insecurities. Nandini, an Indian girl, listened to my family stories without criticizing them, which was therapeutic for my emotional well-being. I appreciated her love for two years, but our relationship exposed other problems that we would each face. At a dinner with her family, Nandini's mother asked what my ethnicity was. She guessed Mexican, but I said, "I am Puerto Rican." From another room I heard Nandini's grandmother ask, "Don't all you people eat rice and beans?"

Who were "all you people"? Equating Mexicans with Puerto Ricans is like equating Pakistanis and Indians. There are some similarities, but also significant differences, which I explained to Nandini's family. After that conversation, I felt kind of sick because I didn't feel wanted there. Nandini felt it and apologized for her family, and she gave me a wonderful hug and kiss when nobody was looking. I appreciated the comfort she gave me, but there was a lump in my throat.

Before I went to sleep, Nandini told me that she told her parents that I was dating a friend of hers because they were very curious about me. I was hurt when she told me that. I am a man who made it to an Ivy League school from a very modest family. Although I did not make it completely on my own, I did a lot to make it here. In my eyes I am similar to her parents, who worked to become doctors and to come the United States from modest families in India. To Nandini's parents I was good enough to be her friend's boyfriend, but not their own daughter's. I know culture and tradition were important to her family, but her parents had married because of love, not arrangement. It seemed that Puerto Ricans were good enough to be her mother's patients in her medical practice, but not her daughter's admirer. I had to love her daughter in secret because of culture. I had never felt so undervalued in my life. Nandini asked me if I was OK before we went to sleep, and I said I was fine. I slept on the bed in the basement guestroom. Our relationship eventually ended because of differences in the way we saw the world, particularly about race, but the contrast provided me with a mirror to see my family background and life history as distinct.

Nandini was an important person in my life because she listened to the stories about my uncles Juan, Anthony, and Miguel with compassion. More than anything, I was attracted to her for being so understanding of my family problems. But that understanding was also entwined with a physical relationship that was not meant to last. I have dated other women since then and have had a few fulfilling relationships, especially with Latina women whose cultural and class experiences are more compatible with my own. My most important friends in college have been other students of Latin American descent.

My most important friend until this day has been Joey, another Latino student, because he can also understand the necessity of having to emotionally detach himself. After three years of friendship, he finally opened up to me, though it took a catastrophe. On the day I was scheduled to fly to Madrid for foreign study, the September 11th terrorist attack took place. I called to let Joey know I never got on a plane that day because the flight was cancelled. He was silent for a moment, then said, "I was worried, man, that you might be in trouble. Thanks for calling." And he cried for a few minutes on the phone. He followed up by saying, "I'm sorry for crying, it's just been a crazy day. I was worried about you." Since then we have never talked about it, but I know that we are very alike in how we deal with our emotions.

Around that time my family life was again deteriorating. My brother had to have heart surgery, and my father was drinking more heavily. After a night of drinking with my brother in the car, my father got arrested for fighting with a policeman. The police officers were unnecessarily rough with him and even sprayed Mace at him. My brother was left without a ride home, and the police only noticed him after my father was arrested. After bailing my father out, I confronted him about his drinking.

As we stood on our porch, I searched for the words to talk to my father. "Dad, do you want to end up like Abuela? I asked. My father's mother suffered from alcoholism before she was diagnosed with cancer. Ever since my grandmother died he had been drinking more heavily than ever, and I was worried, but I did not know how to approach him about the problem. My father began to sob, then I burst out in rage, "You're going to be sick just like Abuela by drinking so much! Don't you get it? Matt and I do not want to have to take care of you like you had to take care of your mom. You need to stop drinking so much!" Maybe I should not have attacked my father so soon after his mother's death, but his drinking began to remind me of my grandmother's. The worst part of that night was when my father began to cry. On top of feeling bad for confronting him about his drinking, I had to comfort him. It was a humbling moment for both of us—we had never been so emotional together since my parents divorced. That night I became my father's equal. I think I became a man in his eyes because he treated me as an individual capable of taking responsibility for myself and for him. In many ways, I began to feel like the father in our relationship. I had to confront him about his actions, especially with my brother. Up to then, my father had been passively supportive of my brother and me, but that night he had begun to disrupt our lives.

At the same time, my brother was scheduled to have major surgery. My brother and I have had a distant relationship, even though we have shared a bedroom our entire lives. He told me, "I want you to be with me when I have my operation." As he was mentally preparing for his surgery, he decided I was the person he wanted to stay in his hospital room the night of his operation. I was surprised because I did not think he really liked me at all, but I learned then that he looked up to me more than I could have ever imagined. More importantly, I began to appreciate my brother as somebody who has experienced challenges at almost every stage of his life. As a child in grammar school, he had chronic ear infections and a learning disability that affected him profoundly. Matt's tenuous relationship with my father complicates his life in numerous ways. When my father is in trouble, Matt is beset with worry, whereas I have learned to detach myself emotionally from negative situations, which has created its own problems. My way of accepting or ignoring emotional issues has often been problematic in my relationships. The summer after my freshmen year in college I began to realize more about myself by paying more attention to the people in my family. Rather than ignoring family problems to save myself and succeed in school, I was beginning to learn that caring about other people was important and could be more fulfilling than apathy was.

Learning to care more about my brother and father gave me some direction in college during my sophomore year. I caught my academic stride and I began to think about my professional future. Several classes in education and two important teachers helped me find my way toward my own definition of success. My academic work improved that year despite having had a tough first year, during which I struggled to find something meaningful to pursue. What was I here at college for? How would that goal honor all the people that helped me get here? I needed to find a justification for my expensive education.

In the winter of my sophomore year I met with my sociology professor about a final paper for her class on the educational issues of immigrant children. I told her I was interested in learning about schools specifically for immigrant children. "Why would you want to just learn about schools like this? Think about creating one yourself!" I was a bit taken aback, but I was also immediately excited. Educational issues and theory were becoming a large academic interest of mine, so creating a proposal for a newcomer/immigrant charter school would be a challenge to apply what I learned in class and add some imagination too. Professor Ramírez continued to talk to me about going to graduate school and starting my own school someday. She reminded me of my mother because she would not let me settle for half of a dream. I left her office excited and optimistic about my future. I finished my proposal for a Spanish/English bilingual school in New England at the end of the term.

During an off term after a long sophomore year that included a trip to Spain, I chose to do practice teaching at a school in Spanish Harlem in New York City. Working at the small private middle school for Puerto Rican and black youth was very fulfilling. I began to learn the skills necessary to be a great educator. Most important, I found teaching youth of color to be extremely rewarding emotionally and professionally because I filled an important role in many of the children's lives. The children looked up to me because I was a man of color, in college, passionate about learning, and attentive to their needs. In other words, in a school I am the Latino man that I never had to look up to as a kid. One particular night solidified my commitment to working as an educator.

That night put me in the middle of a situation that could have been part of my own childhood. Standing between a yelling student and three armed drug dealers, all I could do was scream, "He's only a kid, what the hell are you doing?" As we stood near school, the student said, "I'm running away from home because I can't live with my mother anymore." What if the principal and I had not been there to protect Michael? The uncles I love could have been those drug dealers, Michael could have been my brother, his mother could have been mine. What if I had lead poisoning like my cousin, or was an alcoholic like my depressed and incarcerated uncle? I took the train back to my apartment and broke down sobbing. I had been scared out of my mind during this incident, but I had put on my mask to stand up to the drug dealers. I thought about the effort it had taken over the years not to cry or show my worry about my cousins, uncle, father, or brother being hurt. It felt like the nights I cried when my parents fought after Juan's death. For the second time I was broken emotionally. However, this time, instead of hiding, my outlook changed about my future goals. I began to wonder what I could do to help the other people in my life who are emotionally broken.

My path in life and education often seemed a result of chance, like that night with Michael. When I see my family work hard every day and still struggle to pay for groceries, I have to stop and think how privileged I am to be at college, and ask, "Why me?" Sometimes I feel guilty for being here, and other times I feel proud and accomplished. However, I am undeniably lucky to be the only person in my family to complete a college degree. I have found peace, not in a resolution to these questions, but in my decision to work so that young people succeed because they are educated, thoughtful, and skilled.

Despite my love for teaching and what it meant for me, the decision to pursue it as a profession has been challenged even by the people who have inspired me. I can still hear my uncle Anthony two years ago yelling at me, "You think you're better than us, Mr. Ivy League?" He screamed and waved the Budweiser in his hand as the salsa CD switched to a hip-hop song. Even though I tried to ignore his taunting, I was bothered by the idea that my family thought I might be trying to escape. If being successful meant leaving my family behind, then what would I really be left with as a "success"? On that same night my uncle George asked me, "Are you going to be a lawyer or politician when you're done with school?" I turned toward him, looked him in the eye, and said, "No, I'm going to be a teacher." George stared at me, uncomprehending. I didn't feel the need to defend myself, but now I was in the spotlight of the entire family. They sat in their seats awaiting my reply. I said in a low but confident voice, "What if you had the opportunity to have a different life? I want to be a person who helps other people fulfill their potential and stay out of jail. You know, have choices in their life." He laughed and said, "I *want* to be a thug. I hustle on the streets, and that's all I know!" Before he left the room, laughing in his own intoxication, I said, "What if you knew something else?" A few months later he was in prison again.

On the other hand, my uncle Ricardo has been very supportive of my choices in life. Before my senior year of college, I decided to take a trip to Puerto Rico on my own. Arriving in San Juan, I was apprehensive about what to expect because I had not been to Puerto Rico in nearly twenty years. Ricardo and my other uncles showed me around the island. We went from one end to the other every weekend. My brother and I spent time together that we rarely get because I have been away at school all the time. Ricardo asked me about my plans for the future. I learned that he had attended college in Chicago, then had finished his BA in Puerto Rico.

Although I look up to my father, Ricardo serves a different role. Ricardo is an ambitious Puerto Rican man with whom I have much more in common. My brother loves him even more because he is a strong male figure, which my father often is not. In Puerto Rico that month, I learned about what it means to be Puerto Rican on the island. It was not a culmination of understanding my identity but an addition to my rich experience of figuring out what it means to be a college-educated Puerto Rican and American man, and the responsibility that comes with it. I still have unresolved issues with my father and brother that I must work through. Because I will soon graduate from college and plan on attending graduate school in education, I worry that I will not have time enough to spend with my family. In addition to wanting to help other kids of color become successful, my other challenge in life is to remain involved with my family because without them I am incomplete. I am a Puerto Rican from New England who attended an Ivy League school. Because my family has kept me down to earth, I know how lucky my life has been. I never had to find myself culturally; my main challenge has been trying to understand that I can be Puerto Rican and ambitious without fulfilling negative stereotypes—despite having family members that often exemplified those very stereotypes.

My mother and the inconsistent men in my life have made me a Puerto Rican man in search of helping other people of color. I wish to empower them to answer the question "What are you?" with confidence. At the same time I seek to acknowledge my emotions and integrate them fully into my being and into my relations with my family.

After my long first day in Puerto Rico, I heard a constant sweet chirping sound outside the bedroom window. I asked my brother Matt, who was back in Puerto Rico for the third summer in a row, "Matt, is that some kind of bird?" He answered quickly, "No, stupid, it's the *coquí*!" I thought to myself, "How could I not recognize the sound of the *coquí*?" The *coquí* is a small tropical toad that is named after the sound it makes every night. I felt embarrassed not to recognize the *coquí*'s sound, but I was proud that night because that part of Puerto Rico is the only thing I could not have known about firsthand in the States. The *coquí* can only survive on the island of Puerto Rico, but because of my family, our culture has survived under difficult circumstances in the United States.

After graduating with an undergraduate degree in sociology, Robert Cotto earned a master's degree in education. He is now a public school teacher at an interdistrict magnet school in his home state. In addition to spending time with his family, Robert enjoys traveling and participating in local politics. In the future, it is his hope to earn a second graduate degree and establish a school that addresses the needs of the growing Latino population.

Viana Turcios   A Latinidad I Cannot, Will Not Hide

"Yeah, the thing that I like about SEEDS [Scholars Educators Excellence Dedication Success] is that it's based on economic status instead of on racial status," I say as Lisa and I walk to lunch. "They have cut-off points. Your family has to make no more than a set amount according to the number of people in your family. So we have white kids in the program too. I think colleges should do something more like that rather than just look at race."

"See, I still have problems with that," she replies. "If I were to have applied to SEEDS, I wouldn't have been accepted. See, my thing is—what about those like me who are in the middle class and can't get help because we make too much money, but aren't rich enough to go to boarding schools and stuff? . . . It's not fair that we don't get any help just because we have more money than you."

Frustrated, I say good-bye and walk away, pretending I am in a rush to get somewhere. I cannot help but feel that Lisa was upset that I was able to get into a program like SEEDS, and somewhat envious that I went to Phillips Exeter Academy. She thought it was unfair for people like me who "don't make as much money" to get help. Sometimes I feel like yelling, "*I'm poor*! It's not that we make slightly less money than your family, who owns a house in the suburbs and can afford to take family vacations and buy all brand-name clothing and go tanning and get their hair done all the time. *I am poor*!"

Too often, I hear the white middle and upper classes argue against affirmative action. I, too, disagree with the proposed admissions decisions that are based on race; but I support programs that base aid on economic status. Many white people are poor and could use the kind of help I have received. I believe Lisa thinks that only a few people of color deserve to attend selective schools and the rest who go are granted free rides. Does she think I deserve to be there?

"You went to Exeter?" That is the shocked response of almost everyone, no matter whether white, black, or brown, once I reveal that I attended Phillips Exeter Academy. Yes, it is a prestigious, elite, majority white school, but it, too, had to join the trend of diversifying its student population. Therefore, a little poor brown girl from a little poor city was the perfect answer for Exeter. I was the exact opposite of the stereotyped rich white male Exonian. However, I was not accepted into that school or into my Ivy League college just because I am "brown" or Latina, and this is something I have had to prove to myself and to many around me over the past seven years.

Growing up in poverty, survival was a challenge. The oldest daughter of a single mother, I helped her raise the three younger children since the two fathers did not. I worked hard in school because I knew that was what was expected of me. I was the typical overachiever who worries and stresses, which I do to this day. Somehow I have succeeded academically, but no matter where I am in the world, I am always reminded of the money troubles that my family faces.

What has gotten me here? Why have I made it all the way to college when so many others from similar backgrounds have not? Maybe it is my mother's strength or high expectations. Perhaps it is because I am the stereotypical overachieving oldest child. Could it be because of my teachers and their support? Could it be my determination and resilience? Maybe it is the poverty that I am fighting to get away from. Perhaps it is because I can project myself into the future and plan accordingly. Could it just be fate or luck? This is what I am trying to understand.

My first memory takes me back to when I was almost four years old. By that time my mother and father had split up. My mom, my first younger sister, Isis, and I relocated from New York City to Paterson, New Jersey. My father had court-ordered visits and was allowed to take Isis and me to his apartment on weekends. One weekend, instead of returning us to my mother, my father abducted us to Honduras, my parents' native country. He moved us from concrete hut to concrete hut in the countryside of Honduras every two weeks. I am told we were in constant motion for six months during which two-year-old Isis and I ate white rice every day with Honduran black beans in a bowl full of black bean water. While Isis always remained at home with our father, I was allowed to walk down to the *pulpería*, or market, across the street by myself, but Isis and I were never together without our father around.

My memory of my rescue is that I am four years old when a woman with sunglasses and two men in suits walk into our dark, concrete hut. Running through the darkness with me in his arms, my father and I reach the backyard and he propels me over the concrete wall, in an attempt to hide me in another yard. The woman shrieks, "Danilo, what are you doing? Don't let her go!" My shirt lifts up and my belly and chest rub against the rough concrete wall. My toes desperately search for a solid surface to rest on, but all I feel is cold water in the deep laundry sink full of water beneath me. A man runs to me, wraps his big hands around my tiny waist, and thrusts me back over the wall into my father's hands. "What the hell are you doing? Are you crazy? She would've drowned! Take her back!" he remonstrates. I am now back in my father's arms and we are in the living room. Isis is hiding, crouched behind the sofa chair my father and I are sitting in. I am perched on his lap, head buried in his chest and arms wrapped tightly around his waist. "Danilo, let her come to me! Let her go!" the woman demands. "I'm not holding her back!" My father lifts his arms to demonstrate my freedom.

The strange woman with sunglasses speaks directly to me, "Mamita [Sweetie], don't you see who it is? Don't you recognize me?" She pulls her sunglasses off. "Mami? Mami!" I scream. "Isis, it's Mami! It's OK!" Jumping off my father's lap, I dive into my mother's arms. A huge smile stretches across my face as I squeeze my mom with my skinny arms. Isis deserts her hiding spot and dashes to my mother to join the reunion. We go to a hotel room where we shower and put pretty dresses on. My mother has told me that Isis and I ate with such hunger it seemed we had not eaten in months. The next time I saw my father was through court-ordered, supervised visits in the United States when I was eight years old.

My father has been a big part of my life, although he has not been around for most of it. He never held a steady job because he would hardly ever go to work; when he did, he was usually late. Because of him, the man I marry will need to be ambitious and motivated, not just *seem* educated like my charming father. He must be a man who seems likely to be with me forever. I will not be rushing into any weddings! And I know that I, too, will be ambitious, motivated, and making my own living in case things do not work out as planned. I cannot be dependent on him because I will not allow myself to need welfare like my mother did when she left my father.

I have spent much time wondering why I am so resentful and unforgiving toward "that guy," as Isis and I have termed him. Is it because I blame him for our poverty? Is it because I feel I grew up fatherless? I think it is because he had nothing to complain about and yet he could not handle being a father. I am mad because of all the lies he told us. He had three beautiful, smart, good, loving daughters; spent four years gaining Isis's and my trust and love back; had a second chance when Jasmine, his third daughter, was born; and yet he chose to throw it away, chose not to fight for it, to give it all up. When I was twelve, he took another trip to Honduras and never returned, losing his U.S. residency. Luckily for him, this means he does not have to worry about the fifty-thousand-plus dollars in child support that he owes my mother.

I just thank God for giving my mother the strength to leave my father when she did, because I cannot even imagine what my life would have been like if we had stayed with him any longer. Although my mother has been human and thus not perfect, she has been my fuel, my inspiration to accomplish all my goals. I have never met a woman with my mother's relentlessness and strength, and I hope to emulate even half of it. At age seventeen, my mother left Honduras for Paterson where she had family. She and an aunt, Concha, hired a *coyote*, a man who helps people get across the border for a living. They trekked through northern Mexico and swam across the Rio Grande at the U.S. border. When I was seventeen, my challenge was to finish my fourth year at one of the world's wealthiest schools. Deportation and death were not real concerns.

My mother has four children and has raised all four alone. Although she is still with the father of the two youngest children, we do not all live together, not because we do not want to, but because of circumstances. Mario has his own business, a Laundromat, in Brooklyn. He has provided financially for all of us, especially his own children, but my mother has raised all four without him living with us. "Mario, you need to sell the laundry and just move in with us," my mother asserts. "The day you want your children's love and affection they're going to give you a kick in the ass and they're not going to want to deal with you. They haven't had their father around like they should have." His living arrangement has been one of the few sources of arguments between my mother and stepfather.

Maybe if Mario had lived with us, I would not still be resentful toward my father because I would have had a replacement father. Mario has been involved with my mother since she left my father, but I did not truly feel that I loved him until the end of high school. In order to survive, my mother went on welfare and was able to go to school to learn English while welfare paid for Isis's and my private preschool and day care. My mother never had a steady job but always had odd jobs that ended quickly. For a while she cleaned apartments and worked in a department store. She then sewed in a clothing factory with her sister Lydia and many other immigrants, most of whom were illegal.

My mother continued to apply her knowledge of sewing by making dresses for her girls and sewing beautiful stuffed bunnies, which she sold for sixty dollars each. Sewing is my mother's education. She became a seamstress at the age of fifteen because her parents could only afford to send one child to school. My mother dropped out so that her older brother could graduate from the military academy, Escuela de las Americas (the School of the Americas), an academy based in Central America but headquartered in Georgia. He was supposed to become a great general and be successful. Fortunately, he dropped out of the school, which produced heartless killing machines for Latin America. Although he did live as a wealthy businessman in Honduras, he is now an illegal immigrant in the United States, earning less than my mother. Unfortunately, my mother was never fully educated. She took adult classes to learn English, but she cannot write grammatically correctly in either Spanish, her native language, or English, and she cannot get her General Educational Development test (GED) because she does not remember algebra or geometry.

However, sewing and all her odd jobs were not enough for her to support the family. Mario did give my mother money, but he also did not make enough to support himself and all five of us. The real problem was that there was a six-year difference between the youngest of the first pair of children, Isis and me, and the second pair of children, Laura and Anthony (Tony). Isis was finally going to school when Tony, the youngest child, was born. That meant my mother had to stay at home until Laura and Tony could attend school because she could not afford a babysitter or day care. Therefore, my mother stayed on welfare, a system with security that also assured her three hundred dollars a month in food stamps; WIC (Women, Infants, and Children) vouchers, which gave us free food such as dairy products and baby formula; Medicaid, which covered medical expenses; and Section 8, which subsidized our housing.

Many people believe that those on such public assistance wish to live that way and enjoy the free money. I hated it. It still brings such pain and tears to think about being on this assistance for ten years. My mother did not find a job and get off assistance until I was fourteen and on my way to

Exeter. Welfare had a program that sent people to a vocational program for a few hours during the day and then into a part-time job in the afternoon. The proudest I had ever been of my mother was when she was placed in "Food and Nutrition" at a nearby hospital and was no longer in the welfare system. While preparing trays of food, taking them to patients, and then picking them up, she plodded throughout the hospital for hours each day. My mother's joy and relief at getting off welfare compensated for her tired feet and achy back. Tears filled my eyes at the thought of my mother having a job and us getting off welfare. I did not have to go to Exeter as a child on welfare. When people asked me, "What does your mom do?" I could proudly reply, "She works in a hospital." I did not care what she did; I told them honestly that she brought people food and worked in the cafeteria. What I cared about was that my mother had a job, finally.

In order for my mom to work, and since I was leaving for boarding school, Isis had to help around the house. Isis and I—well, mostly I—had been babysitting the younger kids for seven years. I was definitely nervous about my daydreamer sister watching over them, but it all worked out. My mom regularly worked twelve-hour shifts. A few times she did not get home until two in the morning, but it all paid off because she was given a full-time position with benefits. After five years of working at the hospital, my mom and a manager got into an argument, which resulted in her simultaneous quitting and firing. While she got her license for commercial driving, my mother collected unemployment checks. For a few months she drove a school bus, but was then hired by New Jersey Transit, the state's public transportation company. She is once again starting at the bottom, working part time and fighting her way to a full-time position with benefits. This job seems to be the one she is going to keep because the hourly wage is in the teens, and once benefits kick in, everyone in the family, including Isis and me, will be covered.

Honestly, what keeps me going is knowing how much my mother was able to handle. With all the pressure she had to support us and keep us fed, clothed, and healthy, my mother never turned to inappropriate behaviors such as prostitution or drugs. She taught by example and she taught me to work hard and keep a positive attitude.

As much as I love my mother and as much as I consider us to be friends, there is one thing that we will never see eye to eye on: her racism. Although she says she is not racist, my mother holds racist views. Ironically, her family is dark-skinned. I am one of the lighter members of the family because of my father's fair complexion. I am the color of creamy peanut butter, and my mother, like many of her siblings, is the color of cinnamon. My aunt Lydia has pleaded with my mother to understand and accept that we do have black ancestry, but it is always to no avail. "No, Lydia, our grandmother was not black. She was a bit dark but we aren't black. That's it!" responds my mother firmly.

Two of the biggest arguments I have ever had with my mother centered on our views on race. The first happened the summer before my first year of high school. Isis and I had been contemplating how to raise the topic for weeks. That weekend we were in Brooklyn visiting Mario at his apartment. Knowing what I was about to say, I took a deep breath and we walked into the small, dimly lit kitchen. Mario, with his back resting against the wall, sat on one of the little chairs around the square table. My mother sat next to him at the round corner of the table. "Mario, we wanted to talk to you and Mami about something. Now, I know that sometimes you guys might just be joking and stuff, but Isis and I . . . well, we were just feeling that sometimes you guys sound racist. I just don't like how you guys say some stuff sometimes." I stood in front of my mother darting my eyes between their faces and the floor as I passed this judgment on them. "What?!? No, we're not racist! I mean, I understand what you're thinking, but we don't hate black people or anyone. Whatever, if you don't bother me I'm fine, ya know," Mario defended himself. My mother's response, which was in itself racist, was: "I tell you all the time how I played with the black kids in Honduras. We would jump rope and go to school together. We don't have anything against black people."

My mother and Mario sent us away, as we held our tongues and remained unconvinced by their replies. On the way back home to New Jersey at the end of the weekend, my mom secretly admitted, "You know, Mario might be a little racist because his uncle had a restaurant in Honduras and his uncle hated the blacks that went to the restaurant. So I think that attitude rubbed off on him a bit. But I did play with the black kids."

Three years later, after finishing my junior year of high school, I am watching some talk show like Ricki Lake, when my mom comes in and sees a black woman and a white man kissing and says, "Ugh, what a sight." My mother looks down at my brother, who is about eight years old at the time, and says, "Papito [Sweetie], you know you can't marry a black girl, right? It wouldn't be good." She continues speaking, laughing deeply from her belly as she makes an inappropriate joke I cannot remember now. She added, "People should just stick to their own races." My brother looks up at me from his spot on the carpet. With furrowed brows he asks me, "That's not right, right Viana? What Mami said isn't right, right?" I looked at Tony as I shook my head and rolled my eyes in disapproval of my mother. "No, Tony, Mami isn't right. You can marry a black girl if you want to. As long as you love a person it doesn't matter what color they are."

Hearing my comment to Anthony, my mother yells from the kitchen, "And don't think I don't know about the boy you went out with. I know that black friend of yours was your boyfriend, don't deny it!" "Yeah and . . . so?" I defiantly reply. I knew what her issue was, but I had had enough. "So? So!" my mother echoes in astonishment as she returns to the bedroom and begins screaming angrily at me. "Everyone should be with their own race; blacks with blacks and whites with whites!" I get off the bed and scream back: "Yeah, except that you'd prefer I be with a homeless, dirty white guy! Just as long as he's not black, right Ma? Whatever, I'm never gonna think like you. Just accept that! We should all stick to our races except that all of us should be with white people."

As I beat the mattress with a plastic soda bottle, Isis runs into the room and pushes me away from me mother. Having been screaming so close to each other, we had one another's spit on our faces. Anthony crouched on the floor in a corner, wide-eyed, not believing what he was seeing. "But being with a white guy is different!" my mother asserts. Isis, tired of being caught in the middle, yells, "Yah! That's enough! Stop it, both of you! Look, poor Tony. You OK, Tony?"

If we were cartoons, my mother and I probably would have been bright red with steam coming out of our heads. She left the room and I wiped my face of the tears that had spilled out with my anger. I still had one last thought, and I was not going to hold my tongue because she was already mad and I wanted to piss her off even more: "And what you don't know is that I have had white boyfriends, and Hispanic boyfriends, and mixed boyfriends! I don't care whether they're brown, black, white, green, yellow, red, purple! As long as he treats me good and we like each other, I'm happy!" I proclaim myself the winner of this argument since I had the last word. Later, when she heard about the ordeal, my aunt Lydia confessed that the thought of me being with a black guy kept my mother from eating for two days. Since that day, my mom and I have not spoken about race and race relations.

In Paterson I went to elementary school with other Latino children, but also with blacks, East Indians, whites, and a few Asians. Paterson is a racially mixed city with a mixed public school system. In high school I was surrounded by people from places like Saudi Arabia, Japan, China, France, Mexico, Colombia, as well as most of the United States. I was also exposed to students in homosexual and bisexual relationships. This diversity has continued in college and has shaped my open-mindedness.

In the seventh grade I and eight other Paterson students were accepted into the program that led to my argument with Lisa—New Jersey SEEDS, which was for disadvantaged children with academic talent. It involved intensive summer sessions and Saturday classes during my eighth-grade year. I recall my excitement in telling the news to my seventh-grade homeroom teacher one Monday morning. "Mrs. Mitchell, I got in!" We were in the hallway, getting ready to go into class and start the day. When she heard my news, her eyebrows, cheeks, and lips all moved upward, as she let out an excited squeal. Mrs. Mitchell was a strong-looking woman with broad shoulders and must have been almost six feet tall. She grabbed me by the wrists and began flinging me up into the air while she jumped around in circles, forcing me to jump with her. She laughed, and all the students looked confused about all the excitement. At the time, Mrs. Mitchell was the only one who really understood the implications of my acceptance into the SEEDS program.

That summer the nine of us, along with another fifty or so students from West New York, Jersey City, Passaic, and a few other cities in New Jersey, were bused to a private day school in Englewood, New Jersey. After a tough but fun summer, the group was reduced in size by half based on the quality of our work, each student's effort, and how well each student got along with others. Phase 2, the worst of the three phases of SEEDS, was dark, cold, and way too early. Every Saturday morning I caught the bus at 6:30 for classes that began at eight and ended at three. I had my SEEDS homework, which I did every Friday night, along with my daily eighth-grade work. During this phase we learned algebra and prepared for high school English and the Secondary School Achievement Test (SSAT). We also applied to and interviewed with private secondary schools.

When I asked two classmates who had been in phase 2 why they stopped coming to the program, the male said he had to get a part-time job and help around the house and the female said her parents did not want her to go away to school. They were both Latinos. Of the nine Paterson students that had started out, six were Latinos. I was the only Paterson Latino to make it through the whole program. Two boys did not accept the offers they were given by private schools because not enough financial aid was awarded and because of long bus trips. That means that out of nine students, only two of us attended a private high school. I was honestly just lucky with Exeter.

I showed up to my Phillips Exeter interview in blue jeans and a T-shirt because I was so unexcited about interviewing that I did not bother to change my clothes after school. Worried that her broken English would not be good enough for the interview, my mom seemed more nervous than I did. I went into the interview and honestly do not remember doing anything other than just relaxing and talking to the woman as if we were hanging out eating ice cream. I have no recollection because I truly did not care, and for once I was not worried. After the admissions officer spoke with my mother privately, both women reappeared, laughing so hard and being so moved by their talk that my mom was wiping tears off her cheeks. "What the heck just happened?" I thought. We said our farewells and went home.

After a few months, the admissions officer who had interviewed us called our house. She left me in shock when she told me I had been accepted to Exeter, and she left my mother crying tears of joy. She also informed us that we were getting a free train trip to visit the school. My mother called Mario and all my family members to tell them that I was going away to New Hampshire to attend private school. As soon as I arrived on campus I fell in love with the school. I was lucky: I later learned that my grades and SSAT scores were not necessarily Exeter level, but they were great for a student from Paterson. I also learned that the SEEDS staff had only asked me to interview to fill empty time slots because the Exeter admissions officer had been nice enough to make the long trip to New Jersey.

My acceptance into SEEDS was very different from my acceptance into Exeter, but both had similar goals. Each wanted to help out underprivileged, bright, hard-working students. However, SEEDS accepts students based on economic status. Basically, if you are a promising student and your family is near or below the poverty line, you are accepted into SEEDS. At Exeter, grades were definitely a factor; my SEEDS advisors had to vouch for me because of my C in algebra. But instead of taking only economic status into account, Exeter considers race.

Every April, when college acceptance letters were coming in, affirmative action became the most controversial topic on campus. "You don't have to worry, you're Latina. Everyone's looking for Latinos. It's easier for you to get into college. But I'm Asian so it's gonna be really hard for me because I have to be so much better than all the other Asians," commented a friend nonchalantly. During high school I heard this regularly. The problem with affirmative action is that, too often, those who do need that extra help do not get it. Instead of accepting poor blacks and Latinos into these elite schools, those who get in are usually well off.

People who claim a Latino background often come from wealthy families that do not even acknowledge this heritage until it is time to "check the box" on an application. This fuels the idea that "you are only here because you're Latina." I have been very involved with clubs and extracurricular activities at school since my elementary years. However, in high school I did it in part because I enjoyed them but also because I thought they were my main ticket to a good college. I also thought they would give me some value, importance, credibility at such a fancy school that I "wasn't supposed to be at."

I was accepted at an Ivy League college, but during my freshman fall trimester I thought that I was not capable of surviving and would have been better off at a non–Ivy League school. That term I earned a high C average. I did not believe in myself and started believing what people had said: that I was only accepted because I added color to my class, not because I am capable and smart. That winter I worked hard to see what some effort would get me. My average that term was 1.22 points higher than my fall average. I started believing.

My involvement with nonacademic activities is how I demonstrate my value to myself and others. I have not only mentored and done research but also volunteered at the local public schools and been a teacher's assistant for a college course. By the end of junior year in college, I won a national scholarship, was granted a prestigious summer internship, and was tapped into a senior society. This is how I show others and remind myself that I am capable of being at such a great institution. It is not just because I am Latina but because I can bring a different experience, intelligence, and drive to the table. I *am* worthy. I must never forget that.

At college, I am very aware that I am Latina. Although I am light skinned, I am still darker than most of the students all year-round, despite their artificial tanning. My hair is long, wavy, dark, and very thick: I "look Latina." My *Latinidad* is so apparent that I cannot hide it, nor do I wish to. When I walk down the paths here, I hold my head high and look straight ahead. I have to show that I am proud to be who I am, even though I am different from most.

During my first year I was more involved with the Latino community than I am today, in my junior year. I attended meetings of the student Latino organization and enjoyed going to the dinners and dances put on by the Latino fraternity and other groups. Although I am still friends with a few who are involved and am still friendly with most in the Latino community, I have drifted away from it. Nevertheless, I am still known by most of the community members and as a Latina on campus. A few weekends ago, when newly accepted high school seniors visited the campus, I stopped by the reception at the Latin American, Latino, and Caribbean Studies house. I did not recognize the female giving advice to the visiting Latino high school seniors in the living room, but I thought it was my own fault because I never hang out with the community.

I whispered into a male Dartmouth student's ear, "Yo, Mark, do you know who she is?"

"Not a clue!" he immediately whispered back. Then he added, "I've seen her around, but all of a sudden she wants to show up at something and hang out with the Latinos. You know after this weekend she'll disappear and we won't see her ever again."

The Latino community at my college is somewhat unforgiving if you do not make your Latinidad always known. What is funniest about Mark's comment is that he never hung out with the Latinos his freshman year. The statement he made about the female in question is how I felt about him when he all of a sudden decided to join the Latino fraternity, even though he had never made himself a part of the community. Knowing how hard it could sometimes be to accept the group and have the group accept you in return, Mark was still as unforgiving of the woman as I, who had accepted the group and was accepted from day one. Logically, ethically, I know it is not good to reject people like this woman, because it can be a hard community to break into. People have their personal reasons for not being involved, and sometimes it is just because they do not like the others or because they are afraid of being rejected. Instead of helping these people make a smooth transition into the community to make it stronger, we talk about them behind their backs and fulfill their suspicions. We might act like this because we are bitter toward those who "checked the box" just for admissions purposes. Claiming Latinoness to better their chances of admission, they deny it once they are on campus. It is frustrating because my college boasts that 7 percent of its student body is Latino, when in reality only about a third to half of that percentage self-identify as Latino. The college believes we have made great strides and that diversity is at its peak, but in fact it is not.

My strong Latina identity is interesting to me because I have not always felt I embodied the culture. At home I have always been the skinny one in the family. My aunts and uncles called me *flacucha* or *flaca*, skinny girl, while growing up. They called Isis *gordita*, little fat girl. After years of this, we accepted our roles—Isis has accepted that she is the chunky one and I have always tried to be the skinny one. Thinness is the thing that all admire and try to achieve in my family. Therefore, Isis has been harassed by family members like our aunt Lydia, who would tell her to stop eating because she was too fat and would warn me whenever I looked like I was gaining weight.

Isis's chunkiness, though, provides a body that many Latinos admire, with curves that our culture has accepted and that are typically beautiful features. Many give Jennifer Lopez credit for showing off her body and making a curvy body acceptable, but they fail to realize that her shape is newly acceptable only in the white community. A voluptuous, curvaceous body is what Latinas have always desired and what Latinos have always been attracted to. On Spanish-language television, thin women show off their hips, round bottoms, and breasts that add to the curves.

Perhaps more significant to my family than Isis's body type is the challenge confronting Tony. My brother has been diagnosed with a learning disability in reading and as having both attention-deficit/hyperactivity disorder (ADHD) and oppositional defiant disorder (ODD). Having been told that he learned differently, he felt that it meant he had a "mental problem," as he puts it. He believed that he was innately dumber and less capable of succeeding in school. Therefore, he struggled to learn how to read, and when it was too hard he became frustrated, yelled at whoever was helping him, and walked away from the reading session. He eventually stopped trying because he was afraid of failing.

Having read Tony's individualized education plan (IEP), which informed teachers and parents of what the school was doing to attend to Tony's learning difficulties, I noticed that a few things stated in the doctor's report were not addressed in the IEP. Fortunately, I had taken a great course on special education in my freshman year of college. Taking the course to better understand my brother, I learned the laws and practices and the steps a parent could take if their child was not being adequately served. Sophomore year, in early September, I was at home when Tony's fifth-grade teacher called on three of the five days of his first week of school. I talked to the guidance counselor, school psychologist, and Tony's teacher on my mother's behalf. They were convinced that the school was not enough for him and that he needed to attend a special education school with kids at his intelligence level. Although Tony has many difficulties, he is a very bright boy, but because he has very little self-control, he is unable to put his intelligence to good use.

After hating his new school at first, he has just finished his second year there, completing sixth grade. Now he is only a few months behind his reading level rather than two years behind, and he has become more confident that he is smart and capable of succeeding. Striving to do well, he has started stepping in the right direction to overcome some of his insecurities. Anthony has been my inspiration for my career choices.

Seeing the struggles that both my mom and brother have gone through with school makes me really angry and passionate about helping those who may be in similar situations. Although my first language, Spanish, is not as good as I would like it to be, I can still communicate effectively with Spanish-speaking parents. I hope to advocate for people who struggle with the laws or with the language and who are impeded from understanding their situation because of them. In my teacher certification courses, I am learning techniques that would include all children and even make a child who believed he was dumb feel adequate and capable. Much of my brother's low self-esteem comes from school, and I hope to boost children's self-perceptions while they are my students.

Although education is a great passion of mine, becoming a child psychologist is my goal. I believe that education and psychology are intermingled and that my passion for both is due to that belief. Speaking about his thoughts and feelings, Tony and I do not come to definite decisions and conclusions that "fix" the problem, but he always seems to feel better and at least listened to at the end of our conversations. I understand that it is easier for him to talk to me because I am his sister and he knows and trusts me, but I hope I can bring such comfort and relief to other children who just want someone to listen to them.

When I started my teacher education courses, I wondered how my mom felt about my becoming a teacher. People of color often choose professions such as business and engineering, fields other than education, that will bring them more money. I fully understand their choices and that sometimes they are influenced by parents, and although I do sometimes think I should just study business, it is not where my heart is. I decided to talk to my mother about my decision, in part to seek her approval but also just to inform her.

"Ma, now I don't know if I've talked to you about this but . . . how would you feel about me becoming a teacher? I mean, I still want to become a child psychologist, but before that I'd like to teach. What do you think?"

I asked apprehensively. "You know that I have always told you that I don't care what you become as long as you're somebody in life," she replied. "Graduate and be somebody; that's all I ask! You don't want to continue living this life. When you're a professional, you're not gonna have to worry about money anymore. That's what I want for all my children."

The most I can do to repay my mother for her sacrifices and all she has provided for us is to work hard to achieve my goal of becoming a professional. It will not only be a gift to her but to me as well, for all of my hard work and strife. I understand more than most how important an education is to make your life happy and successful. Although I'm a rising senior at Dartmouth College, my family is still in Section 8 housing. No matter how much money we receive through assistance and from Mario, we are still just as broke and penniless as ever. My forty-year-old uneducated mother is currently earning close to fifteen dollars an hour. My twenty-three-year-old boyfriend who has a master's degree is earning about thirty-three dollars an hour. Mami has a job; he has a career.

I am also proof of how important a supportive network is. I have had family and friends encouraging me and believing that I will succeed. In my senior year of high school, I met a freshman girl who is half black, half Dominican. She was a foster child with many blood and foster siblings. At the age of twelve she was raped, and at the trial her biological mother went against her, stating her daughter was never raped. The girl's boyfriend was in jail for selling drugs. This life is unimaginable to me, with hardships I wish on no one. Yet, she was accepted at a great boarding school. I promised her that I would return for her graduation. A few weeks ago, I kept my promise and returned to Exeter's 2004 graduation. My boyfriend thought I was crazy to return because of some silly promise I made. When I found Maria in line for the procession, she screamed out, "You came!" The people there to see her graduate consisted of three black female graduates, three teachers from her junior high school, her principal from junior high, and myself. We were her family, her friends, her support. She is off to Spelman College, a historically black female college, in the fall. She has thus far succeeded, and I know she will continue to do so.

I appreciate my life with all the ups, downs, and obstacles handed to me. I love all the people who are a part of it and am actually grateful for having had a humble upbringing. It has given me drive and has made me truly appreciate the little things. Many say this, but I get excited when a friend brings me a chocolate bar or when my mother makes my favorite meal, or when I see a chipmunk while I am walking around campus. However, I am exhausted. I am tired of struggling to survive at the elite schools I have been fortunate to attend. Seeing so many people in Gucci, Ralph Lauren, and Prada apparel does bother me and make me jealous. Yes, I wish I had Prada bags and Gucci shoes. But it also bothers me because it reminds me, makes me aware that even though my family is no longer on welfare, we are still at the poverty line. We still have to struggle every day and do not even come close to having the kind of wealth many of the people who surround me daily enjoy.

Because of my ethnicity, I have had to prove myself. On campuses where my Latino features have made me very visible, I felt that I had to step up and do as well or better than those around me. Luckily, I had many experiences in my younger years that made me strong enough for this challenge. I have family support and a reputation to uphold. I also have self-motivation and self-pressure that come from striving to be an exemplary oldest child. I know who I am and where I want to go. I will continue fighting to get there.

While at Dartmouth College, Viana Turcios majored in psychological and brain sciences and became a certified elementary school teacher through the Teacher Education Program. She was awarded the Rockefeller Brothers Fund Fellowship for Aspiring Teachers of Color. Subsequently, she earned a master's degree from the Harvard Graduate School of Education in human development and psychology. She is currently teaching in Manchester, Connecticut.

LATINO IDENTITIES

BECOMING AND UNBECOMING LATINO

Alejo Alvarez   The Strange Comfort of an Unknown Future

The tube of sun block had been sitting in the sun far too long. As I drip the lotion onto my body, it scalds the thin line of skin it covers until I rub it into my arms and shoulders with my hand. I drop a puddle of the white ooze onto my hand, smearing it onto my face and ears. The mixture of hot lotion and warm sweat instantly begins to drip down my forehead in narrow streamlets, inevitably bound for my eyes.

I wipe my forehead with the back of my arm before replacing the sun block in my backpack and looking up at my fellow lifeguard standing on the wooden chair eight feet above me. His sunglasses obscure his eyes, but they are clearly directed in an unyielding gaze at the stretch of brownish-green ocean in front of him. He raises his whistle to his lips and blows out two short, sharp blasts. His hand points toward two young boys wading in the water, throwing handfuls of sand at each other.

"No tire la arena!" he yells.

The boys, their attention caught, quickly stop their activity and run to another section of the beach. I smile and turn to walk down the sand. I've mastered that command, "Don't throw sand!" I repeat the phrase slowly to myself, "No tire la arena," the words rolling off my lips with ease, yet at once sounding somehow alien. I squint under my sunglasses as the sun assaults my eyes. I look down the line of beach, brown sand meeting darker brown water, the air above the sand rippling as the midday sun makes the day's intense heat ever more oppressive.

As I walk, micro-dunes of sand flatten and crunch under my steps. My gaze drifts from person to person in the water of Long Island Sound, searching for anything out of the ordinary—flapping arms, bobbing heads, violent splashing. The music from a radio a quarter mile down the beach pounds a *merengue* rhythm, the volume so obscenely loud that the words are almost unrecognizable: "Algo en tu cara me fascina . . . me da vida . . ." I silently mouth the lyrics to myself. After spending hours on a lifeguard chair with radios tuned to New York's Spanish music station, I have become well-versed in the latest salsa and merengue hits. Any meaning that the words to these songs have for me only came after a lot of thought— and some time at home with a Spanish-English dictionary. But I enjoy the music. It sounds familiar. It is all I hear, working at Orchard Beach in the Bronx, a summer haven for New York's Puerto Rican and Dominican working class.

I stare across the water, eyes moving from person to person, couple to couple, one person swimming a sloppy back stroke, two others in the throes of a passionate aquatic embrace, two children wrestling. A drop of sun-block-tainted sweat rolls into my eye. The salt and chemicals begin to burn. As I struggle to rub vigorously enough so the burning will stop, another song begins on the radio: "Dime porque lloras . . . de felicidad . . ."

I also know this one. A little on the cheesy side, but I mouth these words too, looking at the water again, my eyes still burning, two men talking, a woman treading water, two children wrestling.

"No me ames porque estoy perdido . . ."

Two children wrestling.

I have never watched anyone drowning before. For a moment of realization and disbelief, it is actually quite interesting to note how much the actual event resembles what I have been shown in videos during training. And then a loud, thoroughly intrusive voice reminds me that during training we were taught to do something when encountering such a situation.

I blow my whistle, two short, piercing blasts. I sprint, water splashing as my feet leave dry sand and invade the ocean, sinking deeper into the surf with each step. I swim. I grab the forms enveloped in the hail of splashing that I had seen as wrestling children, first a girl, then a boy, and then another boy I had not seen. Their small bodies feel impossibly light.

I kick my way toward the sand, my movements feeling sluggish. The music is gone, replaced by hysterical crying. Land comes quickly and I find myself standing, ankle deep, in water, three small children crying and stammering on the sand in front of me. The girl, apparently the oldest, speaks in Spanish, trying to tell me something, "Salvevida . . . gracias . . . mi hermano tiene miedo . . . papi . . ."

I cannot understand a word of what she is saying. I hear just that, words, but no meanings, no clarity . . . just words. I try to answer in my broken Spanish, "¿Dónde están tus padres, mija?"

She responds clearly. I can hear the words she is saying, recognizing them from years of high school Spanish. I simply cannot make sense of them. I can decipher meaningless pop songs, memorize short phrases, but I cannot communicate with the frightened young girl standing in front of me.

"She's looking for her parents. Her brother is scared and she wants her father, but she can't find either of her parents." My friend, another guard, appears beside me and begins speaking to the girl. She understands him. He understands her. She meets his eyes and he meets hers. They are communicating. My friend says he will walk the kids to the lost and found. The three children toddle next to him down the beach. I stand in one place for a long time, water dripping from my body, salt water in my eyes, burning them again. I feel accomplished and proud, and incompetent and lost, all at the same time.

I am Puerto Rican. Yet, standing on the beach that summer day, as much as right now, I felt in many ways like an invisible presence within my cultural community, as if that culture were not entirely mine. Until recently, I never thought of myself as having "grown up Latino." Growing up in a predominantly white, upper-middle-class world, I always considered myself, perhaps unconsciously, part of that world. For me, Latinos, Hispanics, and minorities were groups labeled *them*. I knew on some level that I was one of *them*, but for all my daily purposes, I lived in a world where my Latinoness was simply unnecessary. I had no need for a culture other than the one in which I was living. Yes, some people could not come to terms with my name. They mispronounced it, shortened it, Americanized it, and otherwise bastardized it.

Some assumed that I spoke Spanish as my first language. They were surprised to discover that until I was twelve, I could not communicate in Spanish, and even now my knowledge of what is supposed to be my language remains at an elementary level. "Latino" and "Puerto Rican" for me were concepts on a distant horizon rather than a culture close to my heart. Hence, for me, being Latino has been a recent process of creating a cultural definition that comes to terms with who I was, who I am, and who I hope to be. It is a journey both of *being* and *becoming* that allows for a cultural placement from which I can look toward everything that is Puerto Rican, while shedding my cloak of cultural invisibility so everything Puerto Rican can also see me.

Exploring the different directions in which my journey has taken me is a process that must begin by looking at the places and experiences from which I have come. It is difficult for me to define myself solely in terms of "me." Self-definition, for me, is only possible by incorporating others into my perception of self. Perhaps this stems from growing up close to many members of a tightly knit family. Or it may be a result of my tendency toward solitude when not in the company of those close friends with whom I feel deeply connected.

If defining my life begins with others therein, exploring me, my life, my culture, my identity must begin with my parents. "Remembering" my parents is a concept alien to me. "Memory" seems to imply a past, a moment gone by, whereas my mother and father are anything but moments in my past. They are my best friends, my confidants, my heroes, teachers, guardians, and guides. My parents are present not only in all that I do, but in all that I am.

This is not to say that I am particularly like my parents. Often, at the most unexpected times, in a restaurant, in the car, on the beach, my mother has given me a quizzical look and asked, "Where did you come from? Two such nutty, fiery parents, and then you, subdued, level-headed, and low-key." I have not the vaguest answer to her question because in so many ways her words ring true. It is at such times that I look at each of my parents and wonder how much of them I want, what of them I want to be? Not an easy question to answer, but strangely enough, one made easier to explore by my parents' separation when I was ten.

My parents raised me together, though for much of my life they have been apart. They began to divorce when I was ten years old. The process finished when I was thirteen and remains one of the most powerful, deeply influential events in my life. It was a heated, spiteful, vindictive, searingly painful process that brought out the worst in the two humans I admire most in my world. For a long time they were able to live in the same house, my father on the third floor, my mother and I on the second, in a state of constant tension. Outbursts of loud fighting were frequent and unpredictable. During those times, which always seemed to last for an eternity, I would try to find a place where the voices were muffled, where I would not be able to hear the venom being hurled through the air. The worst battles were the ones at night, after I was in bed. I felt trapped, in a hole, absolutely alone. They yelled. I cried. All I could do was cover my head with my pillow and huddle deep under my blanket. Eventually their voices would become more fluid, words melting together into mere sounds, the vulgar symphony of their angry passion becoming my profane lullaby as I slowly drifted into sleep.

I have never questioned the depth of my parents' love or investment in me. They have always offered me unconditional love, putting me even before themselves. Perhaps out of guilt, or maybe respect, I have never spoken with either of my parents about my single worst memory. Sometimes I think they still feel guilty for granting me such a recollection. One or the other may occasionally bring it up:

"What do you remember about that night in the house?"

I push the night away. It is never a good time to talk about it. Sometimes I think they look disappointed at my calm rejection of the topic. However, they never push. They simply move away from a door that is very clearly locked to them. The conversation simply moves on.

It was Sunday night. I do not know why the fighting began. I think that I should have clear memories of every moment, but I do not. I know I was scared, sitting in my room, trying so hard to block out the verbal violence with music. I played song after song on my stereo, hoping that by the end of the next one, the fighting would stop. The voice of a Disney character vied with the sounds of war in the hallway: "Well, master you're in luck 'cause up your sleeve, you've got a brand of magic that never *fails* . . ."

I wanted magic. I wanted reality. I wanted silence. But the battle raged on. My music continued to fight the good fight. "Have a wish or two or three . . ." I only needed one. And then my mother's voice. She was yelling, but I could tell she was crying too. She said something incomprehensible but for one word: my name. Immediately there was a sound like a person running down a flight of wooden stairs, but somehow different, higher and sharper. Hearing my name made me open the door to my room. I saw my father fifteen feet above me, at the top of the stairs leading to the third floor, an expression of stunned disbelief on his face. My eyes followed his. His gaze fell on my mother, sliding toward me down the stairway, the deep, dull, cracking sound of her skull hitting each stair echoing through the hallway. She slid to a stop at my feet on the second-floor landing, crying, reaching out to me.

The flow of tears from my eyes ceased. I looked from my mother, in a crying heap at the bottom of the stairs, to my father, frozen at the top. The moment's silence was met only by the obnoxious glee of the music, still pulsing forth from my room: "You ain't never had a friend like me!"

I stepped toward my mother, overly calm. Helping her to her feet, holding her hand as we walked **toward** her bedroom, I felt very detached from myself, thoroughly unlike **an eleven-year-old** boy. My father rushed down the stairs and touched my arm, trying to explain the inexplicable.

"It's OK, Dad. Just stay," I said to him. My own calm was asphyxiating me. I wanted to scream.

Emerging from my mother's room minutes later, I found my father sitting on the steps, his head in his hands, staring at the floor. I put my hand on his shoulder, and he looked at me with tears in his eyes.

I saw the faces of my parents in the backseat of the police car in front of our house, not understanding the sight. I have no measure of how much time went by as I was standing on the sidewalk, looking at my parents' faces through the window, close enough to the glass so the reflection of my own tear-streaked face superimposed itself on my father's eyes.

A family friend arrived to collect me. The police drove into the night with my parents. I cried myself to exhaustion, standing on the sidewalk, lost in the arms of a mother not my own.

"What do you remember about that night in the house?"

I push that night away as my parents offer it up to me. The guilt in my parents' eyes is clear. They are aware of the impact that night had on me, and they feel responsible. Their eyes apologize each time they want to talk about it. Perhaps the most selfish side of me does a dance in the shadow of their guilt. The part of me that wants to blame them revels in their sorrow for the past. Those moments at the door of my room, at the foot of the stairs, on the sidewalk under a dark night sky deconstructed my life as no other event had before. I returned to school four days later feeling different, perhaps somehow darker if not deeper in the ensuing feelings of emptiness. For the first time in my life, if only for a split second in the night, I felt abandoned, alone, and irrevocably lost.

There are times when I want so much to pass judgment, to make a decision about what happened as I sat in my room. I do not speak of that night with my parents for many reasons. I would not know where to start, whom to believe, or why. I respect them too much to lay honest blame. I love them too much to forego understanding, even if I know it will never really come. For all that, I am torn, forever wondering. I do not want to know the truth. Moments come and go when a chain of events seems so very clear. But these moments pass quickly. As they come, visions of a single truth, I hear the voice of my mother or my father dispelling the ideas, speaking to me in a voice that I am compelled to believe. In many ways, it is in such confusion that I find a certain peace, peace in the unknown. Whereas I used to take refuge from my parents' conflicts under my pillow, wrapped in my blankets, I now find asylum from the answers of which I want no part in the warmth of self-imposed ignorance.

A witness can only know so little, though. I can only deny so much. I try to hold that night at a distance. I intellectualize it and objectify it in order to reconcile it with what I wanted my life to be. I sugarcoat my putrid pile of rotting memory so that I will not smell the essence that lingers in my soul.

There are moments, though, when I hold that night close. I relive those minutes. They flood through my mind and wash out my eyes with quiet tears, long overdue. I feel the hurt, the anger, the loneliness, the love, and the confusion of a frightened young boy talking to me. For though that night does not define me, so much of who I am with myself and others has been shaped by those moments in my past.

I stood on the second floor in my house six days after my parents had been taken away. It was the same house, but so much had changed. I smelled the soft, sweet wood of the floor. I could hear cars slowly passing by on the street outside, the familiar sound of engines purring, sputtering, or roaring down the hill into the distance, telling my ears to believe that all was the same. The night-light in my room was still burning from nights before. On the floor lay a doorknob of heavy glass, rolling ever so slightly as I stepped toward it, sounding a deep, hollow rumble of glass against wood. I could not remember how it got there. I did remember the sound though, a soft, hollow drumroll as I walked down the stairs, hand in hand with a police officer.

My father stood behind me as I stared at the doorknob rolling at my feet, hearing in its deep rolling sound the voices, the screaming, the crying of the night's bitter symphony. My father leaned down and kissed the back of my head. I did not move, but simply stared, listening to the rumbling, looking for what was lost.

I never wanted to allow myself to be angry at my parents. I was though. So angry. I felt betrayed, hurt, and damaged. And I hated feeling this way. I hated the fact that I was so angry at my parents, the ones who had always taken care of and loved me. They were supposed to be my safety, not my threat, the healers of my hurt and not the source. Whatever I told myself, the anger was still there and would be for months, perhaps even years, just under the surface, along with something else that had changed. My parents suddenly became flawed, fallible, and strangely human.

My parents' divorce and all that went with it no doubt affected my relationship with them and with others. My anger caused me to distrust my parents for a time, to hold myself at a distance. I took pride in being quiet, in distancing myself from others. I did not want to have to trust anybody. Even now I grant my trust to very few; perhaps some part of me expects them to fail me. Although some wounds never completely heal, my pain slowly subsided. With more maturity I gained some understanding of my parents, and over time we were able to restore trust and develop the strong relationships we have now. Despite periods of detachment, I have always been very close to my parents. In the long run, this did not change.

Even when I most wanted to distance myself, I could only do so to a certain extent. In many ways, I remained anything but detached from my mother. Our relationship has always been wide open. I tell her everything. Sometimes I wonder if I tell my mother so much because I actually want her to know, or because I am constantly looking for her approval. In her role as my close friend, I want her to know what is happening in my life. As my mother, I respect her so much that I do, in fact, seek her approval. My mother knows most of what there is to know about me, at least what goes on in my day-to-day life.

In our relationship, honesty is not a one-way street. As far as I know, my mother hides very little from me. I am one of the few people with whom she shares many parts of her life. I am the first person she tells about exciting events, the person to whom she vents her anger when something frustrates her. Occasionally, she even tells me about what saddens her. But I never feel that my mother tells me too much, more than a son should hear. It is important to her not to overstep the boundaries of our primary relationship of mother and son. Hence, even in talking to my friend, my advisor, I am first and foremost talking to my mother.

Sharing truth, especially truth that is difficult to accept, can require a certain amount of strength and integrity. However, accepting truth about one's self often requires even more strength, and a good deal of courage. This is what I admire most about Mom: her acceptance of all that she is and her courage to advocate, sometimes to fight, for what she believes to be a worthy truth. For Mom, honesty and truth are not abstract concepts one can learn from a book but a source of strength and power.

I remember a cool summer evening when I was twenty-one, standing in the emergency room of a hospital as my mother's father lay dying. My mother was livid because one of her siblings had, out of fear and confusion, delayed allowing a doctor to explain to my grandfather his terminal condition. The family had agreed that a doctor should be the one to tell him because none of us, his loved ones, could bear to tell him his own sad secret. I could not see him that day, nor could my mother. How can you talk to someone you love when the simple act of looking them in the eye becomes an unconscionable lie?

Later that night, I stared at a shadow on the ceiling of a room in my cousin's house. My mother was looking at the same shadow, of a tree waving in the wind. From the bed she said it looked like snakes on the ceiling. From my spot on the floor, I agreed. That night we spoke as freely as two children at a slumber party, yet of matters no child could understand. We spoke about family. We talked of fathers. We spoke about men and women. She talked about small people. I told her about very big people. Most of all we talked about truth, about power, about being human, being flawed. I learned nothing new about Mommy as we talked into the early hours of an uncertain morning. However, I did see her struggle. I saw *her* truth. I saw so many of the roots of what she had taught me over the years. In her sadness, her vulnerability, my mother appeared with a human clarity as she never had before in my life. The moment was one of absolute sincerity, in which I saw my teacher living her teachings. Truth was real. Honesty had weight. I saw my mother humbled, and for a moment in the night, under a tree's serpentine shadow, she made perfect sense.

Sense, on the other hand, is something that has eluded me when it comes to my father. In many ways, my father makes very little sense. However, sense has never been a prerequisite for my understanding of Dad and our relationship. My father is my own personal tragic hero. His flaw, though, is not hubris, it is just that he thinks, perhaps cares, about others more than he does of himself. While he loves to do for others, he often feels the emptiness of self-neglect. At times this makes him intensely sad, even depressed. At others it feeds the anger inside him, bringing it to the surface of his personality's ocean. He is a comic, even a jester of sorts, making fun out of almost anything that will make people smile, often at his own expense. He is also a man with demons deeply entrenched in the heart of his being. His darkest days are pitch black nights. Many of his brighter days are lit merely by a faded moon's glow.

I sometimes think that I idealize my father, harboring a hopelessly romantic notion of what he is that defies reality. But I do not fool myself—

there are many parts of my father of which I want no part. However, there are more parts I reach out to. Perhaps my father has taken on this larger-than-life persona in my eyes because he has set such a high standard as a father. "Father" has come to have such a rich meaning for me because of the way he has defined it. Father has meant caretaker, the man who gives me what I need to live. Dad protects me and makes sure that I protect myself, not only from people who would physically harm me but also from those who might take advantage of me in other ways. My father has been my mentor, emotionally and intellectually. He may not always have answers, but he always finds a way. Dad is the man who offers me a most rare commodity, unconditional understanding. My conception of "man" is tied inextricably to the nature of my dad's existence. He does not judge. He is a listener, a friend, a teacher, a counselor, yet he never expects humans to be free of fault. He accepts people as they are—flawed, bruised, and battered. Nor does my father hide his own flaws.

My father also has a side that few people see, an inner rage. Ironically, only those closest to him have ever experienced this part of him. Some of my most vivid childhood memories are of my father yelling in my ear, his words uncontrollably vicious. Sometimes there was a reason for his anger —at least I could tell myself that I had done something to spark his fire. A word, a look, a childish lie, something that brought on the terrible squall of anger and rage. Other times, though, I did nothing wrong. I was simply there.

I am in the passenger seat of my father's car, parked in the lot of my elementary school. I stare at the teardrop on my shirt, my head hung, eyes fixated on the liquid clinging to the fabric on my abdomen. I do not remember what I did to unleash my father's beast that morning. It did not matter then and it does not matter now. If it was not one thing, it would surely have been another. I could feel my father staring at me, his breathing accelerated, his voice momentarily absent, but his rage so very present.

"Get the hell out of the car and go to school before you piss me off any more!"

I could not say a word. "Daddy, I don't . . ."

"Fuck you kid! Go to class and maybe I'll see you at the end of the day."

My father knew that one of my eleven-year-old irrational fears was of not being picked up from school at the end of the day. Even in his rage, he played his cards like a pro: not only to win but to demolish. I tried to push out a word before escaping, tears flowing, scared and embarrassed, into my school. "Bye Daddy. . . ."

"Get out of the car."

At such times my father hurt me like no other man could. He had the ability to make me feel as small as I ever have, precisely because he is the same man who could make me feel larger than the world.

When I was young, I felt bad after experiencing my father's anger. I was hurting inside and didn't understand why Dad would treat me that way. As I grew older I felt more angry than hurt after these episodes. I do not know when my anger began to die. Perhaps it was when I began to mature enough to see that my father's rage was something much deeper than a reaction to anything I could do. Maybe it was when I started to understand that my father was sick, not physically, but psychologically. Maybe it was when I began to see that there were parts of my father that I could not understand, parts of him in pieces, in pain.

As I grew up, slowly, year by year, it became clear to me that, as had always been the case, my father did not hide his flaws from me. Looking at my father the idealized protector, the mentor, the friend, my hero, went hand in hand with looking at my father the flawed, tragic, hurting man. I think my father knows himself. Perhaps by teaching me to take people as they are, he was also asking me to take him as he was, is, and will be.

My parents are both highly educated and successful. However, having come from poor, uneducated backgrounds and having experienced the benefits of education firsthand, my education was always of the utmost importance to them. Having two parents who are in the business of education does not allow a lot of room for their child to neglect school. I realize, though, that perhaps the most important learning I did in elementary and high school was not in math or writing, but in building, through my relationships with others, a concept of me. My school years laid the foundation for my journeys of today, toward being Latino, and toward being me.

I was one of a handful of minority students at my school from pre-K through eighth grade, one of an even smaller Latino subgroup. All of my friends, save one whose family was from the Philippines, were white. On those rare occasions when the question of cultural background arose I became confused as to how to answer. Was I white? Was I American? Or should I answer Puerto Rican? My parents told me I was Puerto Rican, but I was never quite sure what that meant when I was young.

My school tried hard to inculcate all of its students with a sense of a larger world. It attempted to erase considerations of color, nationality, and origin from our mind, teaching us to see only the *human* in front of us. It was a curriculum for an ideal world, though in retrospect I have to ask, whose ideal? For me, someone not in the white majority, the message was essentially that who I was, what I was, didn't matter and was not to be examined. My school did not suppress who I was, but it did, however subtly, teach me to neglect a part of myself.

My parents would talk to me about small aspects of being Puerto Rican or about some cultural tidbit, and I would think to myself, "What does it matter? We're all the same so why should where I come from make a difference to me or anyone else?" The entire cultural construct was foreign to me, the importance of identity entirely unclear. I had lots of friends, I enjoyed school, I did well in school, I played the violin. None of this caused me to think about what it meant to be Puerto Rican or what that meant to me. Trying to remember my days in elementary and middle school in light of issues of cultural identity is intensely difficult because such considerations were not even in the back of my mind at the time. In my world, being Puerto Rican was unnecessary. I was getting by without it. In fact, it was not until I left private school for a New York City public school that I began to wonder about being Latino. Private school education became too expensive for my parents, and the public school option, despite the mediocrity of most city schools, became appealing when I was accepted into one of the city's selective, specialized high schools.

I walked into the cafeteria of my new school on my first day as a freshman and stood at the door for longer than I would have liked. The noise was overwhelming, the voices of seven hundred restless fourteen year olds echoing off the dull, yellow-tiled walls and checkered floors of what seemed to me a cavern of a room. Every few minutes, names would be called over the crackling speaker system and directed to collect their schedules. The names were barely audible over the din of the students. I felt utterly detached and yearned for the quiet of the brick-and-glass halls of my former school, the familiarity of the campus, of faces in the crowd. However, despite my reluctance, I remember what seemed a small detail at the time, though it now strikes me as a most momentous observation: I noticed the people. Lots of them. Lots of *different* people. Black. White. Latino. Asian. Indian. I had never seen so many different people, some of them who clearly looked like me, at school. Only in the subway or on a street corner. I suppose at the time this was a passing observation, but as time went on, I came to learn that, unlike my private school, the students, my peers, at this new school recognized difference.

This recognition was not a form of racial or cultural discrimination. On the contrary, I always experienced Science High as a very open, accepting community. The recognition was more a kind of social placement, an ID card for a particular in-group. Often, the answer to such questions as, "With whom am I an insider?" or "Where is my inner circle?" related to what part of the city one came from or what elementary school one attended, and therefore who one's friends were outside of school. Nevertheless, these same questions were often answered, if more subtly yet not insidiously, in terms of one's culture, one's ethnicity.

Walking into the cafeteria every day, I became keenly aware of these distinctions. There was a black table, a Japanese table, a Chinese table, a Puerto Rican table, a Dominican table, an Indian table, and two Greek tables (I later discovered that one table was predominantly Greeks from Queens, while the other was almost exclusively Greek kids from Brooklyn). I had entered a world in which people were different. This was a curiosity to me at first, but after meeting people, sitting at different tables, talking to friends who sat at other tables, I slowly realized that "difference" was not an issue of bad or good, but of familiarity. People sought others with similar upbringings, similar values, sometimes similar parents, and often similar language. In trying to figure out this new system, the questions became, "Who am I?" and "Where do I sit?"

I did not feel I fit in anywhere. I thought about sitting with the Puerto Ricans, but that seemed odd. They all looked Puerto Rican, came from Puerto Rican communities, and, most intimidating of all, most of them spoke Spanish. I felt like an outsider before even setting foot inside, but I was only vaguely aware of these feelings on a conscious level. However, others saw it even if I did not. I was a bit of a curiosity to the Puerto Rican and Dominican crowd in school. I was clearly "meant" to be one of them, but I suppose I acted more like *los blancos* (white people) than like any "typical" Latino. The guys tried to talk to me in Spanish, testing me, I suppose, to see just how much I fit in to their world. The girls seemed more aware that I was a bit lost as a Latino man, so they took on a distinctly maternal role, doting on me in class and trying to teach me Spanish any way they could.

I spent my years in high school with my foot in many doors, but feeling truly at home with very few people—there were only two or three with whom I became close. I never really connected to a group, through my ethnicity or otherwise; my status as a Puerto Rican remained an enigma in my mind. Three years of questions—of wondering, of a long process of coming to terms with the differences I was experiencing and the familiarity I desired—brought me to another place where I also felt like an outsider, the beach. This time, however, the impact of the experience came not because I was unlike everyone else nor from any intense diversity of people. On the beach, the power of the experience emanated from the very homogeneity of the population and the fact that I was expected to fit in. I was Latino. Everyone was Latino. I was one among many.

Walking along the beach that hot summer day after pulling the three children from the water, I mulled over how ridiculous I felt. I worked at a beach in the Bronx with a Latino population, with co-workers who were for the most part all Latino. I am Latino, yet it was apparent that I could not handle some of the basics of being Puerto Rican. I could not even communicate with another person of my culture when it really counted. Until that summer, I rarely gave significant thought to who I was, who I *am*, within my culture.

That summer, being Latino became real to me. My culture took on meaning beyond just a casual expression of heritage. Being Puerto Rican, *truly* Puerto Rican, meant being part of the crowd, an insider. Anything else kept me on the periphery.

I often wonder how I became so far removed from a part of me that seems to be inextricably linked to who I am. I feel as if I have lost something, though it is something that perhaps I never really owned. Both of my parents grew up Latino. They grew up with other Puerto Ricans. They grew up with Spanish in their ears. They grew up where being Puerto Rican was the inner circle. At times I ask myself why I do not feel that I "grew up Puerto Rican." I always knew *what* I was, but never knew what it was supposed to mean, to me or to others. Worse than being rejected, my cultural identity had been neglected. I simply never allowed it to speak to me because its voice was one that, in many ways, I was never taught to hear.

This was not for any lack of effort on the part of my parents. For them, my own recognition that I was Puerto Rican and that this had a meaning always seemed important. However, I think because of the environment in which I was growing up, learning, and socializing, I failed to understand why it would ever be important to me. Somehow the culture, the language, never quite settled into me. I knew the food, the dance, some of the customs, but I never meaningfully internalized any of it. However, that summer on the beach in the Bronx thrust me out of my soul's half-hearted classroom and into a world in which being Latino, meaning Latino, and living Latino *was* reality. Anything else was simply not enough.

I was not, however, lost all summer. Perhaps I never became an "insider," but I did become real to others. I became not only visible as a Latino but identifiable. Sometimes it is difficult to pinpoint exactly what I learned that made me feel more at ease, made others feel more at ease with me. I learned words. I learned attitudes. I learned what to say and how to say it. I found myself engaging people in English and in Spanish. I became able to communicate. I adapted. I learned.

I make no claims that I found my ethnic identity, my Puerto Ricanness, my Latinoness, in the course of a single summer. I would say, however, that over that summer I gained awareness. I found, or perhaps was shown, another part of myself, an alternate voice whose language I had never learned to speak or hear.

Returning to school in September, I felt subtly transformed. I knew just a bit more about myself, a little bit more of who I was. I felt more confident, somehow bigger. In having seen another side of myself, I felt more ready for others. I spent much of my senior year in high school wondering who I wanted to be in college. I felt ready for a new me, though in fact, I think that the *me* I was planning for college was nothing truly new. It was simply what had always been silent.

Dartmouth College is four and half hours north of Orchard Beach and five and a half worlds away, in every way. Orchard Beach is a mecca of working-class, inner-city culture. Dartmouth stands hidden in the woods of New Hampshire, a bastion of academia and intellectual curiosity far removed from day-to-day life at a beach in the Bronx. Somehow, my name at Dartmouth has been transformed into a nickname with little relation to my real one. On the beach, my name flowed off people's lips as rain drips off a leaf, smoothly, without effort, naturally.

I think I arrived at Dartmouth blind. People asked me why I was going to Dartmouth. People ask me today why I chose Dartmouth. As much in the twilight of my college career as at the end of high school, I have no real answer to this question. I say it felt good when I visited, on a whim, with my mother one summer day after work at the beach. I say I fell in love. And as much as this is all true, in retrospect I wonder if the love of place is what has made my experience at Dartmouth, this leg of my life journey, truly extraordinary. Perhaps while the place has been a prime setting for my own growth and search for self, it is in fact the people I have met, those with whom I have spent the better part of four years, who have had the most impact on my identity formation.

I have few close friends. I have a core group of people with whom I spend time, yet there is only a handful of people with whom I am truly close, with whom I feel I share myself. Among those at Dartmouth who are dearest to me, the one who most shaped me and my college experience is, without question, a single girl.

I met Emily during my freshman year and we remained close friends until a year later, when we began dating. Our relationship is difficult to define because it includes many different roles for each of us. She is my best friend. She is my girlfriend, whom I love. She is my adviser and confidant, and in many ways a favorite teacher. We learn from each other and learn together. Essential for me in our relationship is the invitation I have felt to invest myself. It has always been difficult for me to trust, to commit, to give of myself. However, with Emily, I think there was never an expectation, never a demand. Emily is one of the few people I have encountered, save for my family, who has made an investment in me with no strings attached. Any questions of who I wanted to be or should be were suddenly dwarfed by considerations of who I was at that moment. While I wondered who I was, Emily always seemed simply to accept the essential, present "me." She allows me to enjoy "me" as I am in the presence of another, and forces "me" to take on a greater meaning in the context of an "us." In this way, self-definition takes on an entirely new dimension, whether in defining me as a Latino man or just a man, as looking for myself becomes a journey on which I have intimate company.

Becoming Latino for me has turned away from assimilating and instead is about realizing, internalizing the fact that I *am* Puerto Rican, despite the relative lack of meaning this has had to me until the past eight years. There is no way for me to escape that. I carry it everywhere I go, into every new day. Defining that identity, then, becomes a four-step process: accept what is, define myself, allow the two to exist at once, repeat indefinitely. In many ways, the process of becoming Latino has slowed as I struggle to define other aspects of myself. What am I doing after college? What do I want from my life? What kind of career might work for me? Who am I as a son? A friend? A boyfriend? Who is the man that I want to become?

In many ways, that summer on the beach epitomizes my experience as a Puerto Rican. My experience is often empty and detached, complemented by moments of fulfillment. The beach was a moment of encounter, a turning point, although my Latino experience has been defined as much by discovery as it has been by desire and neglect. That neglect has been driven by ignorance, and as I learn more about myself, the more I desire to learn, the more I yearn for meaning.

I am looking for a way, a way to define and redefine myself, a way to walk with myself and others. And while many things in my life neither begin nor end with being Latino, I still look for a way to integrate being Latino into being me. Yet, I am lost. So many years of thinking and searching has left me with less of an idea of what to do with myself than is comfortable at times. Somehow though, in being so lost, I think I find more of myself, my identity, my *me*, my *I*, every single day, as I move forward into the strange comfort of an unknown future.

Alejo Alvarez grew up in New York City. He graduated from Dartmouth College and hopes to pursue a career in law.

Antonio Rodríguez   Me against the Wall

As a first-generation Latino male, I have been forced to be the miracle child of the family. Being the son of two educated parents who emigrated in the hopes of obtaining success and prestige, my parents have fought hard in the hopes that I would someday fulfill their dreams. In aiming for success, I have had to confront, like my parents, the stereotypes of *Latinidad* and my place within the broad pan-ethnic label of Latino. Growing up, I often felt like my ethnicity and identity were predefined. Although I am a pale-skinned upper-middle-class white Latino, I have experienced the struggles that many Latinos face in trying to get ahead in a society that deems Latino people underqualified.

Being Latino and coming from a Cuban-Colombian heritage is unusual within the constructed definition of Latino. Having roots in Spain, my Latino identity has been strongly tied to Spanish cultural ideals. Unlike Latinos, who come from a blend of Spanish, Native American, and African blood, my cultural roots are more closely associated with being European than the stereotypical Latino. So when I find myself being grouped with blacks or dark brown Dominicans, for example, on the basis of my ethnicity as Latino, I often feel uncomfortable and alienated because the assumptions made in these narrow classifications are often incorrect. Although we may have certain similarities such as language and some religious beliefs, we are two separate entities that are identified as one in the eyes of the ethnically ignorant white population. As a white Latino who has grown up in a different class than many first-generation Latinos in the United States, I have lived among Latinos who share a different set of cultural values, tastes, and beliefs. However, regardless of my personal struggles to identify within the broad spectrum of *Latinidad*, the common link that binds us all ethnically has been the struggle to be accepted and to incorporate ourselves into American society.

In writing this story about my life and reflecting back on what has given me the will to fight hard to get ahead, I recognize foremost the battles my parents fought to give me a better life, especially the sacrifices my father has made. My father was born in Cienfuegos, Cuba, and came from a hardworking merchant-class family. From an early age, my father worked in the bustling city of Cienfuegos during the day, selling groceries—fresh cut meats and fish, as well as fruits and vegetables. At night he went to school to learn to read, write, and do math. For my father, that was the extent of his daily life. In the late 1950s, when Castro came to power, my father's life changed dramatically. He no longer had the privilege of being schooled and was forced to work more jobs—assisting mechanics, helping construction workers build homes, and driving a taxi on weekend nights—in order to put food on the table for a household of eight. As the last young man still living in his parents' house, my father was expected to lead the family and support the household. Although my father had older brothers, they were already supporting their own families and pursuing their own careers.

Although it was becoming tougher to maintain the family, Castro continued to take away our family possessions and bank accounts in order to create "an economically stable Cuba." My father, in the hope of pursuing a career and helping his family flee, petitioned the United States for permission to emigrate. Because he had been watched by members of Castro's regime outside of the American embassy when he went inside with his petition, my father lost his freedom for the next three years. He was arrested and sent out to the sugarcane fields in the center of Cuba to work like a slave, day and night, with only bread and water to eat, until he either died or was rescued by the arrival of his departure papers. Because of his light skin, my father was treated worse than other prisoners; he was seen as part of a working-class elite that stomped on lowly underpaid workers. Cutting strands of sugarcane, reading by the fire, writing poems, and singing alongside the other workers, my father struggled to survive, buoyed by the hope of one day reaching the United States.

Five months into the third year of his enslavement, my father obtained his freedom. There is a small black-and-white photo that sits in the middle of my father's Bible inside his bottom dresser drawer—a photo taken prior to his departure from the camp. The day the papers came, a camp official handcuffed him and shipped him off to another consulate where they disrobed him, probed him, and humiliated him. Wearing a pair of worker's shorts made from potato sacks and a white guayabera shirt, my father was left in the middle of a road ten miles from the Havana airport. He found his way and boarded the plane assigned to those leaving Cuba, swearing never to return again.

It often baffles me how my father was able to endure so much, and I marvel at how lucky we are to be living in this country. As a child I did not have to worry about getting a job or fearing for my life. I never had to be concerned about anything; my parents gave it all to me. Sometimes, thinking about my early childhood, I feel guilty that I never realized at the time what I had, but instead often wondered why I did not have more. Hearing my father's stories as a child, I took them with a grain of salt. Because I had never seen or had to live through what he described, his stories seemed more like haunting legends than truthful accounts. It was not until I grew older that I started to appreciate his grit and wanted to learn more about his life and struggles. Realizing how my father's battles influenced my life and my sense of wanting to fight harder, I vowed to never let anyone undermine my personal pursuits.

Growing up, I would often sit on my father's lap and ask him to tell me stories of my early childhood. My mother and father often told me I was the special blessing that God had given them. After many failed attempts and a painful late miscarriage, my parents prayed for a child who would fulfill their unfinished dreams.

As a young child, the first obstacle that I encountered in my education was learning how to speak English. I remember not being able to speak or communicate with anyone outside of my house in New Jersey, since no one around me understood Spanish. As time went on, through the help of teaching assistants at the day care center my parents took me to, I began to pick up English and soon enough became fluent. Although I spoke English by the time I entered kindergarten, it took me years for my speech to lose the Spanish accent that distinguished mine from the flawless English spoken by the other kids in my class.

After we moved to a new town in New Jersey, known for being the city of *los blanquitos* (white folks), I got ready to begin my schooling. It was my first day of kindergarten and I was six years old. My mother had just dropped me off in the courtyard of the old red brick building that created the divide between our town and the neighboring town, where the blacks and Puerto Ricans lived. There were policeman everywhere, holding back a large group of women holding signs reading "Integration Now!" I followed the other children into the large auditorium where I looked for my assigned teacher; my mother had told me she would be wearing a red sign. I found my teacher and joined her group of children in a single-file line. As I looked at the children and the teacher, I began to feel uncomfortable. As I gazed around, I realized no one looked like me, that I was like a marshmallow in a glass of hot chocolate. I thought, "I don't belong here."

Why was I the only white face in this sea of brown children? Why wasn't I allowed to be with the other white kids who lived near me? Why was I put here? Reflecting back on this event, I can still feel how out of place I was in that auditorium; yet in America's eyes, it was where I belonged. As a young Latino being forced into this alienating classification, I realized how different I was from the norm.

Incidents like these during my early years at school made me question where I belonged. I often saw myself as different from other black and Latino students in terms of cultural tastes; I grew up listening to boleros, tango, opera, and learning how to appreciate art, acts that were pretty atypical of American-born Latinos. Throughout my early childhood, my mom played a big role in teaching me about the world. She frequently took me to cultural fairs, Broadway shows, and museums, opening my eyes to the richness and beauty of the arts. My mom had a huge wooden trunk that was always filled with colorful books, beautiful fabrics, and her most treasured belongings from Colombia. My fondest memories of my mother are those days when we went to the living room and opened her beautiful carved trunk and began to explore a world I didn't know existed. While the other kids at my public school enjoyed spending their lunchtime breaks braiding hair, playing double Dutch, rapping, and bebopping to songs, I confined myself to my own world and focused on my academics.

When I reached fourth grade, I was moved by my parents into a school system that was made up of students like me: white, Latino, and middle class. My middle school years were about learning as much as possible, improving my English, and just trying to be the best. I was a pretty smart boy, always bringing home straight As and having teachers acknowledge me for my hard work. My parents always said I had the gift of "ability" and that I should use it to the greatest extent. I knew I had to push myself extra hard because, unlike my parents, I had the weight of two people's dreams on my shoulders and felt I could not let them down.

When I was not in school worrying about my grades or trying to be the model son, I dreamed about escaping into the world of music. The lights, the cameras, the dream of being up on a stage belting away musical standards was a constant daydream I would often fall into while watching my favorite singers perform on television. I still slip away every now and then into these grandiose visions in the midst of my daily routine. I began singing when I was about six years old, joining the church choir where I sang the lead to Spanish hymns. Unlike most of the kids around me, who hated to get attention or were scared to perform their songs, I never found it difficult to sing. After Mass, people would come up and touch my throat, blessing and giving thanks to God for giving me the gift of song. I hoped that one day I would have the chance to climb up on a stage and receive the love of an adoring crowd.

I took every opportunity to sing and practice, but the more I sang the farther I drifted from my studies. I would eat, sleep, and dream about becoming a professional singer. My dream was not of fame but of being able to sing on a stage. The more I focused on my voice, the harsher the arguments became between my parents and me. My parents did not value singing as a career. In their eyes, a singer was nothing more than a clown with a talent who would always live at the mercy of some unknown audience. Being a Broadway star was not a career. Being a first-generation Latino male, I did not have the privilege of choosing my career. The arts were not for Latinos; we had not gained enough respect as a group in the United States to have that luxury. We needed to strive to become lawyers, doctors, engineers, careers that would distinguish us and gain us respect in the eyes of American society. In my last year of high school my parents began to tighten their grip, making sure acceptance into an Ivy League institution was my only priority, and singing a mere pastime.

However, in the midst of my newfound worries about getting into an Ivy League institution and finding a lucrative career, I was given the opportunity of a lifetime. The singing coaches at my high school were invited to fill a spot in the Christmas Classic at a prestigious concert hall in New York City. I was asked to sing the opening song, "Ave Maria," but my heart sank when I realized that it would probably be my first and last experience on the New York stage that I always dreamed of owning. As excited as I was on the outside, inside I knew that this would be one of those situations that I would have to go alone, without the support of my parents.

The long-awaited day was finally here: the conductor took his spot in the center of the pit, looked up, gave me the sign, and there I confronted my worst fear: myself. The orchestra began; I closed my eyes, hoping that my voice would come out. I began to sing in my tenor voice. As I reached the final chorus I opened my eyes, inspired by the power of the violins and the harp, and I felt myself lost in this wave of song. Almost out of breath, I took one last deep gasp and gave it all in this last lap. In what the local papers called "a climactic rendition," I hit the notes and finished strong. As I stood there feeling my heart pounding and my legs shaking, I looked up hoping to see the face of my nervous mother and the stern look of my father. But there was nothing, I saw two empty seats. The two people I had hoped would share my biggest dream had not come to support the very thing that had driven me away from theirs. That night, I chose to give up singing and make my parents proud. I was going to graduate with honors and get into an Ivy League school if it was the last thing I did. I would finish up their lost dream of integrating into the upper class of American society, and then one day I would find a way to finish up my own dream.

The next fall I left for college. We arrived at my dorm and I unpacked. About an hour later, I heard the sound of a key and saw the handle of my door begin to turn. The door opened and in walked a tall boy who was somewhat thin with a protruding belly. His father, who resembled Charlton Heston, stood behind him in the doorway. They walked in, looked around at my side of the room, and then began placing small grocery bags on his bed. The boy said, "Hi, my name is Barry. I guess we're roommates, huh?" His father brought in three bags and then they shut the door. I wondered, did he have anything else? He had a duffle bag with the name "Exeter" on it, a rack of freshly dry-cleaned button-down shirts, and another rack of freshly cleaned khakis. His father looked over at me, realizing I had been staring at him, and then walked over and introduced himself to me in an extremely formal manner. I extended my hand to introduce myself. He looked at my hand, and then at me, but he did not shake it. He told me his name and where he lived in South Carolina, and concluded with, "I hope that you find your experience at Dartmouth a fulfilling one." I wondered why he did not shake my hand, but didn't think much of it at first. So I smiled and continued fixing up my side of the room as Barry and his father hung up a little banner of Exeter and set up his computer. I took out my Colombian flag and began to hang it at the foot of my bed. As I was trying to pin it to the wall, I overheard the father whisper to his son, "I can't believe you are living with a spic! Be careful, don't you leave your wallet lying around and make sure you keep that laptop with you at all times. I paid too much money for you to get that thing stolen." My mouth dropped. The tack in the wall holding my flag fell off and down came my beautiful flag.

My stomach turned and I could not believe what I had just heard. I kept thinking, "Did I misunderstand him or was I going crazy?" But as I tried to turn my head, I froze. It was like I was shot in the brain; the words stopped flowing to my mouth. My body pumped with adrenaline yet my speech was impaired. My eyes began to water, yet my tears did not fall. I picked up my tack and got back to putting up my flag. How dare he imply to his son that I would steal his money? Did he not look around the room? My closet was filled with the latest trendy clothing from New York in the colors black, red, and dark gray; his was filled with button-down shirts in light pastels and khakis. His bookshelf was barren, his dresser was empty while mine was overflowing with things: an altar, pictures, trinkets, and things that gave my side of the room a sense of homely clutter. Did he not think that maybe I should have been afraid of him stealing my stuff? The more I tried to make sense of what had happened, the angrier I got. Everything was slowly starting to make sense as I realized that they were not looking at me but at my ethnicity. Not shaking my hand should have made me realize that this man thought me inferior. It should have immediately made me retaliate, but I would not have known what to say. I felt like a mosquito in a glass of milk.

As a student, I concentrated on empowering and developing the school's Latino community. I began making my first moves to change the perceptions of what being Latino was all about. Taking from European ideals of glamour, style, and beauty, I became motivated to try to transform the Latinos around me from being plain to looking attractive, respectable, and professional. I tried to get them to do away with the baggy jeans and T-shirts, and I encouraged people to wear more fashionable, well-kept clothing. Coming from a world that valued people based on the way one looked, I knew that if one looked good, one would feel good, and ultimately would gain the strength to command the respect of any community. It was during that effort to change the perceptions of being Latino that I came to find the woman who would ultimately be my college sweetheart and future wife.

Tall and radiant, like an ancient carved Maya figurine with almond-shaped eyes, a soft and pudgy nose, and wide cheekbones that marked her face like that of a Mexican princess, Marissa astonished me. With her long curly hair that hung on her head like a helmet covering her innocent face, I saw a striking woman who was hidden underneath a baggy T-shirt and tight blue jeans. Her demeanor was tomboyish. She hung around two boys who were also clearly Mexican and who looked similar to her. I would often see them from the window of my dorm, wrestling in the grass, or messing around with each other much like a group of boys. In their company, she was full of energy and always wore a big smile, yet outside of that clique, she was quiet and not very amiable.

Marissa and I first met during an Alianza meeting in the early fall. After the meeting we broke up into little groups and began introducing ourselves. I went with a group of other Latinos to meet the Mexican clique. I remember introducing myself in Spanish along with the rest of the people around me and that Marissa looked at us funnily. She introduced herself and said she was from L.A. and then jokingly remarked, "I don't speak Spanish!" We all looked at each other in confusion, and then I asked, "Are you Latina?" She responded, "No, I'm Chicana." I looked at her, and all I could think was how she could look so indigenous and yet not speak a word of Spanish. In my mind she was one of those paper Latinas who look and act the part but have none of the stuffing; a half package, if you will.

My parents had taught me that the day one loses the ability to speak Spanish, one loses the ability to be a real Latino. Without having the essence of our language, how could a person be able to call themselves a proud Latino? The culture, so richly connected to the language, would lose its meaning to a person who could no longer carry with them the *orgullo* (pride) of our heritage. As I remembered my parents' words, I began to dislike Marissa, thinking she was nothing more than an assimilated sellout. How could she claim a Mexican heritage when she was nothing like the Latinas on the telenovelas? I was confident that on Saturday nights she sat at home renting movies and eating potato salad, rather than congregating with her family to watch *Sabado Gigante* while eating *carne con papas y arroz blanco*. After this meeting I did not see her; she rarely attended any of the Latino events, choosing instead to hang out with the other indigenous-looking Mexicans who worked hard at being Latino, the "brown" way. It did not bother me to not see her at events or at our meetings, as to me she was clearly not Latina.

In the winter of our sophomore year, Marissa became a resident of the Latino house and thereby my neighbor. She was still lost in the baggy disarray of her clothing and hidden behind her curly hair, and I could not help but want to teach this girl about being Latina. As we became more comfortable as friends, I slowly began to implement a process of change. We were going to go get lunch one morning before our classes, and as I was telling her how hungry I was, she replied, "Oh, don't worry, I just have to put on my sneakers and I'm ready to go." I gasped and made the blunt statement that started it all: "You aren't going to go out like that, are you?" She looked at me as if I had slapped her across the face. "What do you mean?!" she responded. I looked at her and smiled, saying, "Aren't you going to fix your hair and put some makeup on?" Marissa was extremely pretty with unmistakable natural beauty, yet underneath the curly locks no one would ever see it. I told her, "If you don't mind, could you let me fix you up sometime and make you look a little more fashionable?" She surprisingly took it well and said, "Sure." That was all it took. I told her, "Grab your wallet and let's go and make you fabulous."

After purchasing a lot of makeup and a few outfits, we rushed back to the house. Drawing on my theater experience, I sat her down and began to apply makeup to her face. After giving her a thick, creamy foundation, black eyeliner, a rich purple shadow, and glossy pink lips, Marissa's face was ready to grace the cover of a magazine. I put her hair in a high ponytail, which stretched her newly painted eyebrows to give her a sense of majesty and elegance. Dressed in a black top and boot-cut-leg jeans, a pair of heels, and two large silver hoop earrings, the new and exotic transformation was complete. As Marissa stepped out of her room that day, the old Marissa who hid underneath the baggy clothing and helmet hairdo died, and the new Marissa was born. And just like that, our relationship began, first as friends and then into something more. I knew that deep down inside this clam existed the perfect pearl, waiting to be discovered. As we allowed each other into our hearts, we learned how to love and be each other's new family.

The closer Marissa and I got to graduation, the more we started to think about what direction we would be taking in our personal lives. We began to discuss marrying after graduation but nothing was definite. The more we spoke about becoming a family, the more this very concept would be tested on our journey to graduate college. As we planned our lives, we began thinking about taking that next big step and having a child. Although the idea was not something we had set in stone, we had mentally prepared ourselves that if God gave us the gift of a child, we would know that it was time.

In November of our senior year, Marissa told me that her menstrual period was late. We went to the local pharmacy and bought a home pregnancy test. As if time had slowed down and everything began to move in slow motion, the e.p.t stick began to reveal a small light pink line that ran across from one edge of the window to the next. As I picked up the thermometer to look at it closer, something inside me finally reacted. With an uncontrollable smile, a desire to cry for happiness, and a feeling of something miraculous happening, I grabbed Marissa, and there before our eyes, we found out we were no longer a pair of young students but rather soon-to-be parents.

As Marissa's eyes bulged and her mouth kind of dropped, she grabbed the e.p.t and quickly began walking to her room crying and shaking as she acknowledged the results of the exam. She sat at her desk and out came the tears. I picked up the phone and called my mother, knowing she would be the best person to talk to about this. As the phone rang and rang, I started to cry. My mom picked up and I told her the great news, and soon both of us were a mess of tears.

Looking back now, I recall these memories and contemplate the hurdles, and wonder about what is going to be next. Having had to play the dual role of being a Latino and, more important, being an upper-middle-class white Latino, I have broken the stereotypes. I have shown that I too can succeed in a world that deems me less intelligent and worthy of success. And I will graduate with my head held high, the product of my family's American dream. I have shown that as a Latino I do not need to embody the cultural stereotypes to be real, and that the color of my skin is only an extension of my ethnicity and the history it carries. I will not be told how to "act Latino," nor do I need to conform to society's stereotypes. Instead, I will create my own interpretations.

But then again, as I think about my anger, my pride, and my happiness at finally having finished this grand hurdle, I cannot help but feel the pain and anxiety in my heart begin to boil up. I count the days until I receive my diploma and thereby break the awful spell that prevented my parents from realizing their dreams. I am now capable of fully integrating into American society, which, though it completes my parents' dream, makes me wonder when I will be able to fulfill my own artistic dreams. Will I pursue my dream of the stage, or will I have to endure the loss of my dream to support and push forward the dreams of my family?

I have accepted a job after graduation that will require a great deal of international travel. It makes my stomach turn to know that I may not be able to know my daughter more than in passing. My dream of being her friend, her confidant, her father, and giving her the power to do whatever her heart desires, may not come true. Will she be burdened with the curse of feeling obligated to live the last generation's dreams, or will she have the opportunity to be the woman she wants to be? I fear I won't know the answers to these questions anytime soon.

After graduating from Dartmouth College as an art history major, Antonio Rodríguez went on to become a consultant at a large professional services firm in New York City. This summer he and his family will be moving into their first home.

Norma Andrade   On Being Canela

I remember very clearly the day my brother went off to college, simply because that was the last day I ever saw him as Michael—the next time I saw him he would be Miguel. He was the first person in *mi familia*, immediate or extended, to attend college, and no one could imagine what kind of journey he was embarking on.

When my brother walked into our apartment six months into his freshman year, the first words he uttered were, "¿Dónde están mis papitos? ¿Dónde está mi hermana, la fea?" (Where are my parents? Where is my ugly sister?) My parents and I were both excited and confused: We were so happy that he was home, but we hadn't expected him to speak to us in Spanish, or to hug us like he had never hugged us before. He didn't speak much about his college experience; all I could tell was that he was going through drastic changes. This was clear in his face and his new behavior and in our verbal exchanges, which were both weird and refreshing. I observed an air about him that had never been there before—a kind of uncertainty that I couldn't quite place. These changes bothered me tremendously because I couldn't comprehend where he was coming from.

Ever since we were little, my brother and I had spoken to each other only in English, not in Spanish. We grew up speaking to our parents in Spanish, but my brother, Michael, eventually felt more comfortable speaking with them in English. After he went to college, however, he started to speak to us only in Spanish. Even more interesting was that he reverted to using words in Quechua, the Incan language that my parents grew up hearing from their parents. For example, for "parents," instead of using the Spanish *papás*, he used the Quecha *taitas*. It was as if his college experience allowed the cultural and ethnic traits that had been absent during his early life to be born. He embraced the indigenous richness of our family heritage, which we had never really celebrated. Something apparently led him to look inside himself and dig out his *raices*—his roots. When I look in my brother's eyes today, I see weariness and pain. It seems to me that his quest for his past, for his identity, should not have been that hard. However, I also see a beautiful peace reflected in his eyes, and it is clear that the person he is today embraces all aspects of himself and tries to give them life.

After going to college myself, I was able to understand where my brother's weariness came from. In college, I had no choice but to place myself within the context of American history and identify myself as Latina. I never felt I had to prove anything to anyone. Maybe my appearance (dark skin, wavy black hair, and indigenous features) protected me from intra-ethnic pressures—though not, of course, from white pressures. Nevertheless, I was never scared to show who I really was. My brother, and my own college experience, taught me to take pride in and honor the changes my family went through when they made the leap to *los* Estados Unidos. I link everything that I have experienced back to *mi familia*.

La historia de mi familia—my family's history—is in many ways a classic immigrant experience, characterized by a patchwork quilt of custom and assimilation, of resistance and complicity, and of understanding and confusion. I saw much more clearly how I fit in to American society after reading a book on immigrant European women at college. I wouldn't have guessed that the experiences of Jewish and Italian immigrant women a century ago would be so closely related to my family's and my own experience, but in an American society where I am supposed to identify first and foremost with *mi gente*—Latinos—I found myself readily relating to these poor white women from 1890. I knew then that I would forever consciously identify myself as a child of immigrant parents, and my life began to change in promising, yet sad, ways. I embarked on a quest to hold on firmly to memories of the past in order to reconcile my past with my present.

My first recollections of *mi familia*, and of myself, were *las fiestas*, big family parties. When I was a *mocosa*—a term of endearment in my family that literally means "snot-nosed kid"—*mi familia* encompassed everybody who was in any way related to us, including long-lost aunts, close family friends, *tios*—our many uncles, sixth cousins, and whoever else shared our family history in some way. Numbering around two hundred—or so it seemed—we would gather for family birthdays, weddings, showers, and on any other occasion that gave us reason to celebrate *familia* style. These events, which occurred nearly every other week, brought us laughter, tears, sweat, criticism, and happiness all under one roof and sky.

I especially remember the parties to celebrate *cumpleaños* (birthdays). *Hay, pero* those were something to see. It was like being in a child's fantasy world: colorful *piñatas* hung from trees and *cumbia* music with a splash of salsa pumped in the background. Our birthday parties took place in Flushing Meadow Park, a beautiful spot for us *ecuatorianos* (Ecuadorians) to spend time with *la familia*. We all brought food—pots of rice, big bowls of potato salad, lots of fresh corn to be roasted, containers filled with chopped tomatoes and onions, pounds of *sazón* (seasoned) chicken and beef to barbecue—even roasted pig, enough to feed an entire village.

We children had the time of our lives just chasing each other around. The spacious park gave us a sense of liberation, and the birthday parties allowed us to release the tension from our little lives. Although I wasn't aware of it then, most of us lived in tiny apartments, and only the park could provide enough room for our whole family. Dancing gave the grown-ups a chance to escape the monotony of their jobs, and the parties enabled them to meet up with others of their own kind who also felt the burden of the working life. Meanwhile, we children got dirty and smelly while playing on the ground, or dancing with the grown-ups, or moving our hips, arms, and legs to Lisandro Mesa's "El Siete."

At these family *fiestas* I was able to express who I was. As a young child I was the family *atrevida* (daredevil). I would play with the boys, hang out with the grown-ups, make jokes with everyone, and dance like a crazy little child. My mother would yell at me, saying I should stop running around so much or else I'd become a boy. But the more she yelled at me, the more I ran, and the more I ran, the more freely I entered into the world of child's play, where the sky is your only limit.

I also remember parties held at relatives' homes. I loved them just as much because of their opposite nature. While the park provided open space for all of us, a small hole of an apartment provided comfort and intimacy. The minute you stepped into the apartment you smelled the aroma of the food. The little kids would drool with hunger, expecting to be fed like queens and kings. We first went through the formalities, saying hello to everyone in the room. First we had to kiss the cheeks of first cousins, aunts, uncles, great-aunts, close cousins, distant cousins, and even cousins who weren't really cousins but were called cousins; then my brother and I would run to the table and dig into the bags of *papas fritas* (potato chips).

We would then splurge on the main course, finding a nest on the couch where we would be stuck like sardines between some smiling great-aunt and favorite cousin.

The room was filled with the chatter of *chisme*—the gossip that was spread from one person to another. *Las mujeres* would talk about what someone had the nerve to wear to the party or share the latest news of family back in Ecuador. They would entertain themselves by commenting on how others' daughters were developing nicely or not, or even by complimenting one another: "Estás linda hoy. No estás tan gorda." (You look pretty today. You're not so fat). *Los hombres*, on the other hand, would talk about politics in Ecuador or current conditions in the workforce, whether work was picking up or not. Even if it was a child's birthday party, it always ended up being a party for the adults. Still, the smaller kids also had fun. The older women would arrange a game of Pin the Tail on the Donkey or play Spanish children's music so we could bop around. I would take part in these festivities at first, but when I got bored playing with *los niños*, I sought the company of the older kids.

When I was ten, my older cousins Catalina, Denise, and Isabella were my idols. They didn't really mind my being around, although I knew I bothered them at times. They would talk about boys or the latest fashions in music and clothing. They set themselves apart from the rest of the family by chatting in English while the rest carried on in Spanish. We had the idea that speaking in English would separate us from the older generation, and we children took much pride in speaking English: We all had Spanish accents, but we took no notice of that.

The older cousins would let me in on their secrets once in a while, which I loved because it made me feel I "fit in" with the cool crowd. I was fortunate that *mi familia* provided me with female role models. I knew that some day I wanted to be like my cousins. However, I knew that somehow I couldn't fit in completely because of my skin color. My older cousins were all pretty. Denise and Isabella, who were sisters, had long black hair, fair skin, and small facial features; some people would mistake them for Spaniards, Italians, or Argentineans. Catalina was the prettiest. She had green eyes, pale skin, freckles, light brown hair, and a long face with small features. I thought she was beautiful, mainly because I loved her as a person, but family members also often told me she was. I would hear Catalina this, Catalina that from old *soltera* aunts (spinsters). Although I love my aunts dearly, I never felt pretty enough for them, which I blamed on my color: *canela*—cinnamon—as my family would call me. Although I loved to eat cinnamon sugar, as a child to *be* cinnamon seemed silly. My family believed in the notion of *adelantar la raza* (improving the race) simply by looking white. I was always referred to as *la morenita* (brown-skinned girl) or *la prieta* (the blackish one) in a family where most are light skinned. As a kid I took little notice of these things—at least consciously.

Once we were older, we would make trips to the sea at Orchard Beach, Far Rockaway, or Sunken Meadow to get some sun. My cousins would apply baby oil and bake their skin like *cuchifritos* (fried pork skin) under the sun for hours. I, on the other hand, turned to roasted *canela* within minutes. Although my cousins wanted to get darker, I know that they didn't want to be as dark as I was. In winter, their complexions returned to normal, while my skin darkened all the more as the years passed. Nevertheless, those girls were my *primas* (cousins), and I loved them.

At our indoor family gatherings, after chillin' for a while, the atmosphere would be lively and hot, from both human heat and the kitchen oven. After hours of chatter, the food was ready—always at odd times of night, perhaps around ten o'clock. Everyone filled their paper plates with *arroz con frijoles, mote con tostado* (hominy with fried kernels of corn)—an Andean dish that *serranos*, or Ecuadorians from the mountains, love to feast on, roast *puerco*, and beans of all sorts. Our staple foods were rice and beans, along with some type of meat. I joke about this now because among my friends such food is known as poor people's food. After the food was tucked inside everyone's *barrigas*, our stomachs bulging out of our dresses, skirts, and pants, we sat in silence for a while.

Then, suddenly, some crazy vivacious relative, like my *tia* Rosario or my *prima* Amparo, would wake the crowd by grabbing some man to dance. The music would fill the room and spill into the hallways, the entire building booming with its sound. When one couple got up, the entire herd rose to dance, joking that they had to lose a few *calorias* after eating so much. Everyone danced: the kids who were falling asleep, *los viejitos*, the old folks, and the rest who came together to dance and celebrate our rich lives and culture. No space, however small, could confine the life and energy of *mi familia*. I became energetic myself. Seeing all the life that surged forth from my relatives' bodies and minds fostered an ambience of joy and love that allowed me as a small girl to be a small girl. *Mi familia* provided comfort and familiarity.

More than anyone else, *mi mamita* has been the backbone of my life. In my mother's childhood, my *abuelita* (grandmother) geared her toward cooking and cleaning houses. In fact, she was forced to drop out of school because her family was too poor to afford books and clothing, and so she could attend to the duties of the home. My mother would tell me stories about walking to a stream a mile away to wash her family's clothing on the rocks. She could not protest, because at that time women simply did not leave home. The woman's place *was* the home, and that was what they were brought up to believe, with village life reinforcing such ideas. Of course my mother dreamed and felt and yearned, but, as she told me, "when there are no possibilities for a woman to leave unless you marry, then you just have to endure life." Over time, she mastered all the techniques of keeping a house immaculate—scrubbing floors, windows, and ceilings. She also cooked meals for her family morning, noon, and night. It's interesting that my *abuelita* denied my mother freedom but allowed her to attain the powerful family position of bread maker and bread giver, if not of breadwinner. When my parents married and emigrated to the United States, they brought these traditions and beliefs with them and tried to instill them in us.

Ever since my mother arrived in the United States she has had to work. Because of her upbringing, she excelled exclusively in domestic skills. Since she neither spoke English well nor was accustomed to the traditions and mentality of U.S. society, she sought help from family members who were already living in this country. There were about thirty of them, through whom my mother found jobs cleaning "gringos'" apartments in New York City. My mother worked Monday through Friday, cleaning a different apartment every day. I came to know her employers, some of whom she worked for almost fifteen years, either by their last names or by some fact associated with them. There were the Greenbergs, *la rubia* (the blonde), *los de* Roosevelt Island, and *los de la cuarenta y nueve* (those from 49th Street), among others.

My mother would often take me to work with her, but never my brother. I was very young, and I really only recall when I was older and helped her at work, but my mother and her employers later told me about my first visits. My mother would wake up every morning to feed us, and then she would sleep for an hour or so. She set out around eleven o'clock, saying that she needed to attend to her own apartment in the morning. When I went to work with her, I never left her sight. I was shy—very different from how I was with *mi familia*—and intimidated by the people she worked for and often hid from them under her skirt. When she vacuumed, I would sit on top of the vacuum in order to be close to her.

Back home, my father would arrive around six o'clock after a long day in the picture frame factory, covered in white dust from the machinery. In the summers he arrived home dehydrated, since there was no air-conditioning in the factory. My mother wouldn't come home until seven o'clock, which was one reason why I spent so much time at *los* Benavides—a family with eight children. Mrs. Benavides was a skinny little woman who already had wrinkles from all the hardships she had endured. Behind every wrinkle on my mother's face there is a story waiting to reveal the joys and the hardships of my own family's story. My mother's wrinkles are mostly around her eyes, like two windows into our world.

My mother would come home, hang her clothing in the closet, change her clothes, and then walk around to make sure everyone was home: Papito (Daddy), Miguel, and me. Then she would begin her amazing cooking. Even after long days of hard work, she cooked for her family every single night. She still tells me that her heart does not feel right unless she knows that her children have been fed. She raised my brother and me to eat everything offered us; doing otherwise is an insult, especially among poor families. My mother knows that while she cannot offer material goods or gifts to her children or guests, she can always offer pieces of her love through her cooking. After dinner, she would tidy up around our own house, doing the laundry, washing the dishes whenever we had homework, or preparing desserts like *arroz* con leche y canela (rice pudding with cinnamon). As a little *mocosa*, I took my mother's expressions of love for granted. Perhaps most important, I also took for granted what she did at work, partly because I had yet to internalize what she did.

I must have been around twelve when I started to work with my mother during the summer, while other kids were traveling or just running around. Initially, my mother asked me if I could help out. I was reluctant because I was a kid and didn't want to work, and also because around that time I was rebelling against anything and everything, especially my parents. But somehow, even then, I knew that helping out was something that I had to do for my mother.

The first apartment I remember cleaning was on Monday at the Greenbergs. The Greenbergs lived in Riverdale, in the northwest Bronx, which by car was only five minutes away from where we lived, though on the other side of the subway tracks. Tree-lined streets meandered through their neighborhood. Entering the Greenbergs' building, I would see a doorman, a highly secured entrance area, and flowers and plants everywhere. At that age, a peak time for my mind to question everything in sight, I couldn't believe the prettiness of these people's lives. I always knew that other people lived nicer than we did—I did watch TV quite a bit—but I never thought much of it. I lived in a happy little world of family and friends where concerns revolved around trying to fit in to a lively environment. That summer, when my mother first asked me to help at work, I saw our lives—my family's and mine—as poor, and I tried to understand why we were poor. I don't remember the first time I began to judge my mother's job, but at some point I did, and in retrospect I hate myself for having done so. I looked down on my mother's job for many years and was ashamed to tell people what my parents did for work.

My mother trained me to clean someone else's house. She had her own "plan of attack" for each apartment. She would first change out of her regular clothing and put on raggedy garments. She began with the bedrooms, vacuuming the floors. She didn't miss a spot. Next, she dusted everything that could possibly be dusted, including picture frames and strange objects like exotic wooden birds that looked very ugly to me. She always used really strong chemicals that forced her to wear gloves to protect her hands. She made the beds and put everything up into a pristine state.

She then moved into the "book room," as I referred to it, which seemed endless, as we attended to almost every single book and the shelves as well. In the bathroom, we both got down on our knees and scrubbed. I did not want to help with this but in the end I suffered through it with her. My mother had such a delicate manner that I could never picture her performing such grueling tasks. She eventually scrubbed the kitchen, including the oven and stove, and sometimes even the walls. She ended her day by doing laundry and ironing all the shirts. It took about nine hours to finish everything, and by the end of the day my mother was famished. I realized that she stayed so thin because she was constantly moving, with little rest.

My mother was paid in cash, "off the books." Although this is illegal and could entail dire consequences, no one who mattered ever knew. Anyway, I considered it more illegal that my mother was paid such miserly amounts of money. It was unjust for her to have to go down on her hands and knees to clean someone else's toilet and then get paid close to nothing—not enough to get by on her own. It made me angry and resentful at society. But I channeled that anger toward helping my mother with her job. After spending the entire summer cleaning houses, some two stories, others three, I began to understand what it meant for my mother to have to do this every day of her life. She worked so hard both at home and at work, but she was never commended for what she did. I had taken what she was doing for granted, and I began to see how others did as well.

Still, I would never tell anyone what she did. When someone asked, I would say that my mother was a housewife, denying that she worked at all. My mother would even deny it herself to teachers from my high school. She knew that I was ashamed of it when we were both in public. I would ask her to get dressed up a little to go to work, so people wouldn't think that she cleaned houses, and so we could hang out in the city after a long day of cleaning. Society taught me to respect the jobs of lawyer, doctor, and professor and to look down on the kind of work my mother does. I came to ignore those jobs that were never seen or commended as respectable.

In the end, through my mother I gained an enormous amount of respect for all of the women in my family. The pride they have in their jobs inspires me to become a better person and understand our position in this society. I remember reading a book on El Salvadoran women who came to the United States and filled a specific labor sector in Washington, D.C.: that of domestic work. It fascinated me because it was the first time I had seen a documented account of the house cleaners and maids who have been stereotypically portrayed on TV for so many years. Most of the women immigrants in my family have formed a similar sacred kin network of labor, looking out for, encouraging, and supporting one another. They all clean and have even made an art out of it, and it's amazing how they have used their jobs to make themselves partly American. Today I look at these women and see strength, perseverance, and love.

Juanita, my godmother and also my third cousin on my mother's side, was the first woman in my family to gain a foothold in domestic labor. She is now about sixty years old and in my opinion is one of the strongest women ever to have existed on this planet, in addition to my mother. She is married and has one daughter, Catalina. She worked two jobs every day, just like Christina, Patricia, Elisa, Sandra, Carmensita—who passed away two years ago due to breast cancer—Marinita, Rosita, Soraya, and many others. Juanita is a *mujer* with a lot of life, energy, and creativity. She suffered badly in her low-paid work so that she could pay the bills and give her daughter opportunities. She additionally used her work as a means of acquiring the American traditions and customs found in the households she cleaned. She first learned English at work and has since mastered it, enough to practice her rights in court, such as when serving in jury duty.

When Esthercita, a close family friend, first arrived in the United States, having been pretty well off in Ecuador, she landed a job in a travel agency for the airline Ecuatoriana. As the years progressed she ascended the ranks. She eventually decided to return to school to attain more managerial skills; after successfully completing certain courses, she got a job as director and manager of a travel agency in Queens, tripling her salary. At this job, however, she experienced extreme discrimination and disrespect from her employees—all were Italian. It made her life unbearable, leading her to quit, as she could not believe that she could be treated as so low. After twenty years of studying and trying to succeed, she ended up cleaning houses. When she recounted her story to me, she was very disappointed and upset, but she did say that she was happier cleaning houses, where she received respect, than she had been working with the employees who drove her away from her aspirations.

Juanita, meanwhile, has formed bonds with her employers that have helped her in many ways. One employer, who had retained her services for fifteen years, helped her make a down payment on her new house. Another, a very wealthy woman who owned thirty acres of land in the Berkshires, allowed Juanita to vacation there whenever she needed to. This provided her whole family with the opportunity to escape the noisy life of the city and enter a peaceful place; it was a safe haven for many of the members of *mi* familia who have longed to return to Ecuador to experience the liberty of roaming around in a natural habitat untouched by machines. The women could relax and do nothing but tend to the plants, go cherry or apple picking, or buy corn for roasting. No one would have experienced this place if not for the intimate connection formed between Juanita and her employer.

My mother adopted many customs learned from cleaning for other people. She would see the kinds of things they bought, especially food; she wouldn't snoop around the fridge, but when her employers offered her things to eat she took particular notice of a newly discovered dish that would wind up in our refrigerators some weeks later. She trusted these people, since they supposedly knew a lot of things—since they were *americanos* and had money. She trusted their judgment on furniture and at times even bought things that she first saw at work. Once she persuaded my father to buy chairs that she knew to be very reliable and of very good quality. Today, we still sit on these chairs, which are now raggedy from years of family gatherings. Sometimes she would go to poetry readings and art performances because she had been invited by her employers. In general, I saw my mother becoming American in small ways through her work. As I think about it now, my mother is just as much a hybrid as I am. She has devoted, unwillingly at times because of her longing to return to Ecuador, more than thirty years of her life to this land. The difference between us is that she formed *raices* a long time ago. It came with her territory unquestioned. I, on the other hand, am learning what it means to have *raices*. My mother will always be Ecuadorian, but living here for many years and having close relationships with her employers has acculturated her to American traditions. She learned English very quickly and eventually excelled in it. It became her passageway onto the U.S. landscape, a place where she has learned to believe in herself as more than a housewife and domestic worker.

More than anything else, the discrepancies between my mother's Americanization and empowerment and my own have led me to feel like a marginalized person within my own family. With my parent's decision to enter the United States and raise both my brother and me here, it became inevitable that we would be very different from them. I was destined to live in two worlds—the world my parents were brought up in and which they brought to the United States with them, and the rest of society, where I gained a sense of "Americanness." At college, I do not readily claim to be American, but when I juxtapose myself with my family, I *do* see myself as American. I am still undergoing a process of assimilation. For me, it has been selective assimilation, because I choose what I want to embrace from American culture as well as that which I completely reject.

The factor that has contributed most to my marginalization has been the English language. When I was an infant, my *cuidadora* (babysitter) was an old Colombian woman who only spoke Spanish, so prior to entering kindergarten I only spoke Spanish. Nevertheless, as children my brother and I were able to pick up English very quickly, without which we would have been isolated from the culture that existed outside of our home. We began living double lives, speaking Spanish in the home and English in school. This duality created a gap between the two cultures; Spanish is very personal to me, while English is public and open. Even as I write this account, I wish it were in Spanish so my parents could understand it fully. . . . so we can share our memories over dinner and take pride in them, laugh at the joyful memories and ponder over our distance as children of immigrant parents.

Another part of the immigrant experience contributing to the marginalization of children from their parents is the reversal of leadership roles. We children became teachers to our parents. We would read and translate their English mail, write letters for them on the typewriter, and teach them about American culture. My brother and I taught my parents about the procedures involved in applying to schools, and I guided them through the process of school selection as well as my school experiences, as opposed to them giving me advice.

I further see myself living in two worlds when I identify myself as Latina. This identification alone shows how different the world I live in is from *mi familia*'s, as well as how close I can come to being American in *mi familia*'s eyes. It is only in the United States where being "Latina" is necessary, because of the way the United States has presented its history through a "white" lens. In fact, I have come to reinterpret all of U.S. history integrally, without indiscriminately employing cultural or racial indicators. My own identification with being Latina is a form of resistance. I had been trained to look at people's color my entire life. I would go to school and hear people say, "Look at the black girl," or, "Check that white girl out." I would turn on the TV and hear black people this, white people that. On the streets, my friends would utter, "Don't go talking to that *blanquita*— she's too *white* for us." I heard these statements—and eventually uttered them myself—day in and day out.

Of course, although identifying myself as Latina could only have been necessary after my family came to the United States, the issue of race is not present in this country alone. The "colorism" that exists and is discussed in the United States is present but just never spoken about in Latin America. In *mi familia*, certain relatives with racist mentalities would perform cruel deeds in order to make me look "white," since I was *prieta*. I remember being bathed in milk so that my skin would lighten up. One aunt disowned her only son for marrying a black woman. I heard comments that were so derogatory toward indigenous and black people that I did not know what to do; I just let them slide. The feelings of guilt and hatred that I developed toward myself for being too dark for my family should never have been present, but they were. While my family has big problems when it comes to skin color, luckily I was able to learn from their mistakes.

Another experience that led me to pay particular attention to skin color and inequalities took place in my junior year of high school. For three months, as we watched on our classroom news channel from what seemed the longest distance, Rwanda experienced a genocide. Few elaborate discussions took place and no specific details were reported. But each day, after seeing a clip or just imagining one, I cried. I cried for our complacency as human beings and for my own inability to do anything. The world I was living in was not one I wanted to be a part of. Once the TV was shut off, girls continued gossiping about other girls and their sexual escapades with boys, and teachers followed the agenda of the day. I knew then that schools were machines and that we were both its components and its products. When I tried to bring up the topics of war and injustice—the ones that exist thousands of miles away as well as the ones that exist outside our front doors—it was futile. I needed to find explanations for what was occurring in the world. I needed to know why close to a million people had been slaughtered in such a short period of time. I needed to know why the United States and the rest of the world did nothing. I would never accept the African syndrome response: "It's the way Africans are." I knew my family couldn't help answer the questions, nor could my schools, so I sought refuge in my own learning, in gaining awareness—in the kind of education *not* found in schools.

Later, identifying myself as Latina gave me the ability to take pride in who I am as a woman of color. I no longer feel ugly or destroyed every time my aunts call me "india fea" (ugly Indian) or saying "Even though you are black, you are still beautiful." With respect to the need for and development of "Latinoness," white American society first collectivized itself as being apart from others. Therefore, those "others" had to make sense of their place in society as groups of people. Although this country is very individualistic, the group is much more powerful than the individual, and when people act collectively it makes an impact—such as with the civil rights movement. In the conventional telling of U.S. history, many of these "others" are excluded and ignored; even worse, many are given histories based on lies. Buffalo Bill's telling the story of the Wild West and "them Injuns" is atrocious, but sadly enough many people have believed such misrepresentations. American history had been manipulated to hide the rich legacies of brown-, yellow-, red-, and black-skinned people. Even the histories of those white-skinned people who had to lose parts of their culture and identity in order to "become American" are rarely recounted in the classroom. Therefore, efforts by immigrant Filipinos, African Americans, Japanese, Koreans, Mexicans, Puerto Ricans, Chicanos, Chinese, and many others to affirm their status in the United States became necessary. People of diverse backgrounds now write stories incorporating themselves into U.S. history, unraveling the oppression that has long remained hidden. Uniting as group—such as with *mi familia*, in the greatest sense—allows people to appear as a strong force against the white American society that always tried to oppress them. Of course, this, too, is problematic, because these groups also become monolithic. Being "Latina/o" dilutes the inherent differences among all of those who claim to be part of this group.

My own identification as Latina is more of a social and political statement. This, in essence, I associate with power. I have never heard people from my old neighborhood talk about themselves as Latinos. On the other hand, in college, a place of elitism, I feel I had no choice but to place myself and my family's experience within the context of U.S. history and identify as Latina. Since being Latina only exists within the greater context of American society, my identifying as such makes me more "American." In fact, when I call myself Latina, I am reminded of the status that I am entering into—that of privilege. There is no kind of look or trait or anything that can depict what being Latino or Latina is, but I do believe that there is a "certain something" that makes me Latina. I make up the essence of and believe in that state. It is a personal reflection and reaction to the circumstances surrounding me.

After twenty-one years of living, I have learned a lot about myself and continue to do so every day. Becoming Latina is one facet of myself that I am still learning about, because I know that it has built barriers between me and the world that I grew up in. Unintentionally, identifying as Latina disconnects me from most of my family, as they can never experience such a revolutionary identification. It is the process through which I was able to finally understand why Michael became Miguel. My large *familia* provided the foundation of my livelihood and existence, and I cry knowing there is some distance between us. It has been difficult for my parents to try to understand who I am today and why it is that I have chosen to resist the status quo found in heterosexual relationships, linear career paths, and religious devotion.

My mother especially has had the biggest problems with me, as she judges me according to her paradigm of what women should be and ought to do. Catholicism has pervaded *mi mamita*'s life since her birth. Her church was like school: an indoctrinating system. She cleaned the floors, polished the pews, and joined the rosary meetings, all under *abuelita*'s stern and watchful eyes. She learned the Catholic codes: to be obedient and have blind faith—to never question or doubt, just be. She learned that good is whatever is not bad, and bad is whatever is not good. In such a polarized perspective, fulfilling female obligations had to be good, no matter how confined she felt, because it surely was not bad per se. Thus, her Catholic fervor runs deep in her bones, and she judges me for not believing. She feverishly asks God to guide me in life, protect me, and forgive me for my nonbelief. She blames my nonbelief partly on my education, partly on my free will as an American-raised woman, and partly simply on me. Regardless, I don't judge her, because I know that the years she has spent believing can never be erased.

Although I have come to know her well, my mother still often cries and cries for reasons that I have yet to fully understand. Her tears especially pain me because I have made efforts to help other women who have been oppressed by society's imposed beliefs, but I cannot help the person whom I love most dearly. Many people are able to share everything with their parents and savor crucial developmental moments, but many cannot do that. I know that my mother is very proud of me, but she does not understand the true importance of my college experience learning about *mis raices.* Still, when she tells others where her children are, she sees their facial expressions and is satisfied. Being marginalized in society is a beneficial experience, but being marginalized within my family has made me lose a part of who I am. My identification as Latina has been a part of my assimilation process, just as language and school have.

The immigrant experience involves not only resistance and assimilation but also complicity as a way of survival. My family was forced to accommodate to the work that was presented to them. Although they picked up menial and manual work—"bottom of the scale" jobs—they have taken great pride in their work. My mother is no longer ashamed of cleaning homes because it is an honest living. I, on the other hand, was embarrassed by my parents' work; as such, I gave in to society's views of which jobs are and are not respectable. Being embarrassed for so many years about what my mother did only impeded my growth. Now, I see the beauty in her work. This is a living that the women in *mi familia* have shared and will continue to share. They made the best out of their experiences, and I admire them for it.

The extent to which my mother has taken advantage of her own situation was evident when she went through menopause, which terrified her; she had no idea what she was going through and suffered from many symptoms. Thankfully, her employers helped her out. Through them, she obtained and read books on menopause, in English. They advised her to be a lot more demanding when going to the doctor. And this empowerment is evident elsewhere in her life as well. She readily expresses her discomfort in discussion with my father and goes to the theater on her own to watch films. Overall, while my mother may just clean and scrub their floors, her employers have utter respect for her and love her. I do not know if that kind of bond can be fostered in the corporate world or in other professional settings. My mother's experience has been symbiotic; she has learned from her employers, and they have learned from her. During my last visit home, I found out that she is applying for U.S. citizenship. She was encouraged by her employers to demand rights for herself and begin focusing on the future.

My mother and her stories of survival guide me throughout life. I see her as a superwoman who went to work all day long, then came home and attended to her family. The life that she has led for her children and the experiences that she has gone through as an immigrant to the United States for the benefit of her children are a constant reminder of why I *need* to wake up every morning. I would be throwing my mother's life away, disappointing and belittling her, if I did not. When I find myself at home caressing her work-worn hands, we grow closer as *madre e hija* (mother and daughter). It is imperative as women to find camaraderie among those who nourish us with love. Although my mother and I are linguistically distant and educational strangers, I need to be connected to my *raices*—my roots.

I choose to get up and face the day so my family can live through me and I through my family. My family has not been endowed with monetary wealth, but they have been endowed with pride in their existence and love for others. I see their lives in me, and I will share their lives with others so that their experiences live on. Further, I am driven to find the voices of the many women who continue bending their backs, of neighbors who have died as a result of drug selling, of people who were denied an education, and of all women and children who have died in war. I have chosen to fight for and preserve their memories and dignities.

I remember something very hopeful my father told me. He said, "I plan to be a citizen to vote for a president, to put in the good and take out the bad." I immediately thought to myself, only if life were that simple and that sincere could that really happen. But my father believes in the good in life, as he should—as we all should. Like myself, *mi familia* is forever changing and assimilating, but like me, they selectively assimilate in order to retain a rich culture.

After graduation, Norma Andrade spent four years working in the field of adult literacy in Zambia, in Canada, and in her hometown of New York City. In 2003, she worked and acted in a theater company, Teesri Dunyi, creating and producing migrant and refugee stories from community members living in Montreal. Since then she has earned a master's of arts degree with a cross-disciplinary study of language, literacy, migration, and education at Columbia University. She is presently living in Seattle with her husband.

Alessandro Meléndez　Living between the Lines

My pleasant experiences of a happy childhood in Puerto Rico were interrupted when my father lost his job and moved to the United States. At the age of eighteen, my oldest brother, Ricardo, left to go away to school. Finally, my mom, my sister Juanita, my brother José, and I emigrated from Puerto Rico to New Haven, Connecticut, in order to keep the family together. At age eleven, I was excited to see a brand-new place and couldn't imagine ever being able to return to my homeland.

As the oldest child, Ricardo had the responsibility of opening up the road of opportunity for his three siblings, especially for my sister. Ricardo was only a year older than Juanita; he was five years older than José, and seven years older than me. He began his studies in the state university without even knowing how to communicate in English. Living in New Haven was a tough transition for all of us. Although we had a few family members in New Haven, we were largely on our own trying to settle in the unknown, unfriendly environment of a small city in a foreign culture.

Ricardo enrolled in the U.S. Army Reserve and worked at a fast food restaurant to pay for his college tuition. At nineteen, he tackled the English language, his first year of college, a job, and the army. After five years, he was the first in our family to graduate from college, and he graduated with honors. From Ricardo, I learned I had a long and arduous road ahead in school, but I knew I would make it as long as I put all my efforts into what I wanted to accomplish.

Essay previously published © 1999, *Souls Looking Back: Life Stories of Growing Up Black*, edited by Andrew Garrod et al. Reproduced by permission of Routledge/Taylor & Francis Group, LLC.

Juanita graduated from her high school at the top of the class, as everyone in my family must do, and entered college. When Juanita began to attend college, my mom placed her in Ricardo's hands, expecting him to protect and take care of her. I still remember attending their college graduations, where my mom's tears showed how proud she was of her children. In school, her children were expected to be the best in their class; no report card could be brought home unless straight As appeared on all subjects. We knew that receiving anything less than an A meant a whipping with the thick leather belt. When my mom punished me, the red imprints of the belt flared on my legs for hours. In my entire elementary school career, I received only one B on a math test in second grade and one C on a science test in fifth grade. I knew what I had coming to me if I came home with a C on my test, but I never received a whipping for being lazy and not doing my work in school. I graduated at the top of my class every year.

Disobeying our parents was the one rule we simply could not break. The only reasons my brothers and I could leave the house were to attend Catholic school, go to church, play baseball, or deliver newspapers. My mother's strict rules extended to our social lives, or what little social activity we were allowed to have. My brothers and I had friends in school and on the baseball teams, but interactions with the opposite sex were essentially forbidden. My brothers delivered newspapers around town and they were able to talk to girls then. As for me, I didn't have a relationship with a woman until my sophomore year in college. Although my mom's guidelines for our social development were rather strict, I believe she gave us a strong basis for our own personal moral standards. Therefore, the only relationships we have with members of the opposite sex tend to be extremely personal and serious.

As for my dad, he always provided for our well-being and established a secure place for us to accomplish what we could accomplish, both in Puerto Rico and in the United States. Although he never received his high school diploma, my dad has put four children through college. I truly admire him, and although we have never discussed our problems with each other, he has always been a pillar of strength I could hold on to. When I have needed courage and confidence, he has stood by me and helped me in every way he could, especially when the opportunity to attend prep school came along.

As my father and I drove into the town of Lewisburg, New Hampshire, I stared at the picture-perfect snow sparkling in the bright winter sun. The application I received a month before showed a great lawn on which a group of students from different ethnic and racial backgrounds sat in a circle, books open, and a teacher sitting in the middle of the circle read to them. This was the picture I had in my mind the day I visited Lewisburg Academy for my final interview. (Lewisburg is not the school's real name; suffice it to say that the school is among the top five prep schools in the nation.) In the brochure, the students were dressed in casual clothes to attend classes, so I thought that I should try to fit in to this image.

As my father parked our red '77 Pontiac in the visitors' parking spot, I did not even feel a nervous twitch as I slammed the rust-ridden car door. I felt confident in the brand-new high-tops, blue jeans, and gray sweatshirt I had worn that day to public school. My father wore something similar, except that his jeans were quite faded and worn in places where patches were needed. The receptionist showed us to the waiting room, which looked like the living room of a rather expensive house. Gazing around the room, I marveled at the antique sofas and chairs, the fragile coffee tables, and the gray stone fireplace. I carefully sat down on one of the sofas, afraid that it might break under my weight. As my father and I read the brochures about the prep school, another prospective student walked into the waiting room wearing a blue coat and tie, khaki pants, and brown leather shoes. I first thought, "Hmm, he's overdressed!" but I remembered the receptionist's comment—"Hey, your sneakers match my dress. I should be wearing those"—as I looked down at my discount sneakers and realized that I was the one wearing the inappropriate clothes.

The interview itself seemed short and pointless, as I answered with the same responses I had written on my application. As we drove away from the campus, my father told me that he had answered the questions he understood with the little English he could fragment together. I knew he had tried his best. He cared so much about my opportunity to get admitted that he would have done everything he could do to present me in the best light. After describing his interview, he asked me, "Do you think they will accept you?" Looking at my father's concerned expression, I knew he wanted me to reassure him that he had done his best. I responded solemnly, "I don't know, Dad. I don't think I did very well in the interview. But we'll see what kind of letter they send with their decision." I didn't want to disappoint my dad, but I also didn't want to raise his hopes without knowing for certain that I had a chance to attend prep school.

When I received the letter of acceptance from Lewisburg, my excitement was overwhelming. Since my parents were not fluent in English, I knew I would be the one handling all the financial, academic, and commuting arrangements. It would be my responsibility to read and translate all the application forms my parents had to sign. I realized that if I had decided to go to public school, my parents and I would have had an easier time. Not only was the high school within walking distance from home but the community and the school were both tightly intertwined with Latino culture and the Spanish language. I knew that I would definitely have an easier transition going to the public high school. However, I couldn't turn down this opportunity, offered to only one member of my junior high school graduating class. I knew the decision had been made even before I made up my own mind. Such an opportunity for a prep school education was hard to turn down.

Although the prep school owned acres of green land on which stood buildings for every academic subject imaginable, I never felt as safe and as wanted there as I had in the long, three-story public school building that held classes for inner-city students. As soon as I was accepted to prep school, my junior high teachers and guidance counselor warned me that it would be a tough and challenging environment for me. However, they also encouraged me, saying, "Don't worry! If anyone deserves to go to Lewisburg Academy, it's definitely you. Good luck next year!" I arrived on campus as the smartest student from my junior high school, which really didn't amount to much in a class full of intelligent students from all over the country and the world.

The only person who introduced himself to me at the day-student orientation seemed like a good-natured guy. I had no idea then that he would turn out to be my best friend and crucial to my personal growth and success. Looking at the tall, blond, blue-eyed boy who stood before me, I remembered meeting him the day we took the national test required to apply to prep schools. With a warm, welcoming smile, he said, "Hey, how are you? Remember me? I'm Ben, and this is my grandmother." I smiled back and introduced my parents, quickly explaining that my mom couldn't understand English very well. My dad ventured into a small conversation with Ben's grandmother, who seemed rather patient trying to understand him. After saying good-bye we got into our cars, and I felt relieved; I had survived the first experience with my parents at prep school without any major embarrassments. I promised myself, however, that I would keep social engagements involving the presence of my parents to a minimum.

As I think back, I realize that my family and I lived in two distinctly separate worlds. My city flourished with the Latino culture, Spanish language, and the bonds of community. Over the hill, the town of Lewisburg operated under the guidelines of the American culture, the English language, and a sense of individual success. Remembering my mom's fearful eyes masked under her smiling face, I now understand her feeling helpless in a world she could not comprehend. She did not possess enough English to express her feelings or concerns. As for my father, he always made a brave attempt at making people understand him. Although he has a thick Spanish accent, I have always been proud of how my dad has been able to take care of his own affairs with little or no help from me or my brothers.

My parents always taught me the importance of speaking in my native tongue. My mom made it clear that she expected us to speak only Spanish at home. She thought that the only reason we kids spoke English at home would be to discuss things we didn't want her to understand. I must admit that my brother and I usually did talk explicitly about girls in English, which always kept my mom in the dark. However, she encouraged us to speak Spanish in order to help us retain our culture and heritage. She reminded us every day, "I know you have to learn how to speak English, but don't forget your own language. Remember that you're my sons and that you are Latino. You will be able to get more in your life if you are bilingual." Speaking Spanish at home reinforced my Latino identity. Although I spent most of my day in the English-speaking world, when I came home from school at the end of my day to tell my mom about what I had done, I felt reassured to know that I would always be able to return to my community, no matter what happened in the English-speaking world.

The town of Lewisburg was very different from the city I lived in. In Lewisburg, the streets gleamed with the beauty of spring. The sun barely shone through the trees whose branches spread over the streets, providing a cool shade to those walking on the sidewalk. Green grass covered the front and backyards of the single-family homes. The houses were painted in bright, vivid colors that contrasted with the dull red bricks of the chimneys. The prep school proudly boasted about its great lawn and its beautiful fall and spring seasons, which could only be fully appreciated in the New England setting. On the other hand, in the city where I lived, the streets were too dangerous to walk at night. Covered with trash, they wore the nocturnal skid marks from the tires of yet another stolen car. Trees were only seen in the common park across the street from the junior high school. Only narrow driveways divided the houses that were still standing; most of the houses on the block had either been boarded up or demolished.

The three-family homes that were in good condition were painted dark, dead colors. But no matter how awful the city was, it was the place I called home, where I yearned to return every night after the school day.

From the first day I arrived at Lewisburg, I felt intimidated by the enormous campus, the classes, and even the students. Like every freshman, I was lost in an unknown place in which we were told we either had to swim with the rest of the fish or drown. Prep school was a whole new world for me. The system I had learned in junior high school was simple. In order to get good grades, you behaved in class by not talking to other students and turned in your homework. Everything you needed to know to get a good grade would be on the board, and our chairs were all set in rows with the teacher's desk placed at the front so that we could only make eye contact with her. The public school assumption evident in the seating arrangement was that all we needed to learn would come from the teacher, so that was the only person we needed to see and the only person we should speak to. In the prep school system, the chairs were set in a semicircle around the room, with the teacher's desk placed at the opening of the semicircle so that everyone could see one another equally. The school assumed that we would learn from one another's ideas, so we needed to be able to see and speak to one another.

Waiting for the teacher to come in that first day of prep school, I sat silently, not saying a word to any of my classmates. I had no idea what to say and could only repeat to myself over and over, "I don't belong in this place. Everyone here is smarter than I am. They'll just laugh at me if I speak in my Spanish accent." I was completely intimidated and petrified, wondering whether my fears would all come true in front of me that morning. As the bell rang, the teacher walked in to the room with nothing in her hands but her purse and house keys, which she dropped on the desk. I must admit that I was not expecting an African American teacher for English class. She introduced herself as Mrs. Brown and gave us the list of books that we would be reading for the term. Then she laughed and said, "Now that I've covered the course, do you think it would be all right if I spent the rest of the period getting to know you?" No one objected, and I felt some of the tension diminish. Mrs. Brown was the first teacher I had met who wanted to get to know her class. After writing journal entries for her for a year, I knew that she knew me better than any other teacher on campus. After four years, Mrs. Brown knew me well enough to recognize that Lewisburg had been a different experience for me as a Latino day student in a predominantly white prep school than it had been for most students. It was Mrs. Brown who asked me to write about my experience at Lewisburg, which I was happy to do. During my first year at Lewisburg, I didn't risk taking any high-level classes. Every course on my schedule was carefully picked as the lowest-level course I could possibly take. My first term at Lewisburg was the toughest academic transition I had ever experienced. Even when I arrived in the United States and entered the sixth grade, I at least had the confidence that I could do well if I applied myself. At Lewisburg, I saw that hard work did not always pay off. I convinced myself that I obviously had not worked hard enough. In order to do well, I promised myself that academics would be my only priority and everything else, including sports and social life, would have to be accommodated to fit my academic work schedule. Although my mom didn't approve of me getting up at dawn and returning home well after dusk, she eventually understood I was trying to work hard and stopped nagging me about not spending enough time at home. I eventually compromised with my mom and decided to stay at home on the weekends when I didn't have any athletic events.

As a sophomore, I thought I finally had a handle on what I needed to do in order to earn good grades. I never thought I would stay up all night writing for my English class, but regardless of the length of the paper I would be up all night trying to figure out how to write down my thoughts. I became critical of the way I wrote every single sentence. I convinced myself I couldn't merely write down what came into my head. The ideas had to sound more intelligent or sophisticated, which I could do by using big words and long sentences to sound as smart as my classmates. I never thought that my original ideas or word choices were appropriate for any part of my essays. Aware that the teacher might read the essay to the class, I wanted to make sure that I would present the best image of myself in my writing. I was willing to spend an enormous amount of time if it meant handing in a paper that read like the others. Therefore, I literally blocked off the nights of the week I would be writing. But although I had as long as I needed to work on papers, I couldn't avoid the time limits of in-class essays. Every time we were given forty-five minutes to write an essay in class, I ended up writing half of what I wanted to say and handing in a fraction of the writing my classmates did. You can't disguise yourself as a smart student when you pass in a paragraph and everyone else in the class has two pages.

Although I was still earning honors in my classes, I never felt that I was doing well enough. There was always someone I knew who was doing better and, in such a competitive environment, I learned to accept not being the best. Since kindergarten, my parents had pushed me to be the very best and stand out from the rest of my classmates. Once I arrived at Lewisburg, I warned my mom, "I don't know how well I'm going to be able to do in prep school." Seeing my worried expression and fearful eyes, my mom hugged me and said, "I know it's a hard school. I just want you to work hard and do well for yourself, not for me."

Once I finally realized that I would push myself just as hard even if another activity took up some of my time, I decided to try out for the baseball team my junior year. By making the junior varsity team, I achieved my first accomplishment outside of the classroom. I felt so proud to have made the team that I didn't even care if I played in the games at all. All I ever wanted was to be part of the team, as being an athlete in prep school meant popularity and face recognition.

By senior year, I finally knew how to play the academic game and spent more time on campus participating in the activities I wanted to do. I realized that the key to classes included two things: taking classes taught by the teachers with whom I performed well, and simply doing a good job on the first exam or paper. As a senior, I took complete advantage of the system that I knew worked. I had my academics under control; I knew exactly what I had to do in order to get a good grade from each teacher. Even in my senior year, I still had few friends, and not many people on campus knew who I was.

As senior spring finally rolled in, I became actively involved with the community service program led by the school's priest. Father P. is the most generous man I have ever met. In addition to teaching classes and providing the Catholic services, he cooked and invited people over to eat dinner at his house practically every night. I became involved with his mentorship project tutoring public junior high school students. The kid I tutored, Mike, had the potential to become a great student, but he found he could have more fun leading his friends into trouble. I still remember the day I met him at the public school gym with all the other junior high kids. Mike called Father P. over and pointed at me, saying, "I want him to be my tutor." Mike was an African American child in the same school system I had come out of four years earlier. He had the initiative and drive of a leader. Unfortunately, he never used that energy and leadership to get his work done or finish his application for admission to Lewisburg. For the first time, I had the chance to give back to the community that had helped me survive the Lewisburg experience.

My best friend, Ben, was at my side throughout prep school. He gave me the courage to meet new people and participate in social events. I always felt awkward around people when he was not with me. Although we were completely different, Ben and I complemented each other. While Ben helped me develop social skills, I helped him develop his academic skills. We relied on each other to survive throughout the four years of academic and social torture we faced at Lewisburg. Ben was the exact opposite of me; he was the all-American boy, over six feet tall, blond hair, blue eyes, and a laid-back attitude about everything. I, on the other hand, was a Latino immigrant with dark skin, black hair, brown eyes, and a serious attitude toward my academic work. Ben had the confidence and charm, and I had the knowledge to back up his smart talk. No matter how different we seemed together, we shared a key aspect in common. As day students from the same city, we came from similar socioeconomic backgrounds. We were definitely not part of the crowd whose parents were doctors, lawyers, or Lewisburg alumni. As financial aid students, Ben and I shared a completely different experience from all the boarding students and the wealthy day students. Although I never fit in to the social environment at Lewisburg, I never felt isolated because I had Ben as a friend. Every morning, I woke at dawn to walk downtown to the bus stop where Ben would be waiting for me. I still remember the early mornings when we stood waiting underneath the small sheltered bus stop as the sun rose over the river. From the time we got on the bus until we left for our first morning class, Ben and I would just talk about everything. Ben told me about his problems living at home with his grandmother, his job at the ice cream parlor, and his social life.

I think I learned everything I knew about the opposite sex in high school from Ben. I remember confessing once, "I really like Alicia but I don't even know how to let her know I'm interested." Ben gave me his usual wide smile because he knew how seriously I considered a crush on a new girl. He would always come up with some advice. "Why don't you spend some time with her helping her with Spanish class? We can come to the next dance and invite her." I always asked him questions I had about girls, dating, and sex. I began to develop an interest in girls after Ben began dating. When he shared his dating stories of dining out with a girl, I began to feel jealous because he was experiencing the feelings I had only talked about. Everything I thought and talked about regarding dating and women, Ben had the courage to go out and do, even if the girl rejected him. I never had the guts to flirt with a girl I liked, but Ben was confident about himself and had the type of personality that made girls laugh and talk to him.

As a poor Latino student, I never felt comfortable in the predominant white, wealthy environment of Lewisburg. The reason was not only the color of my skin but also the difference in culture. Although I felt isolated from the mainstream community, I never felt a need to look for the support of the school's small Latino and African American community. In the cafeteria, most of the black and Latino students always sat together in one corner of the dining hall. Although I knew some of the minority students, I never separated myself from the larger community. In turn, I think I also distinguished myself as an individual who did not belong to one particular group. The few friends I had were day students that attended the same classes as I did. I didn't really talk to them enough to tell them everything I was thinking about. Most of the day students knew me because I was the only dark-skinned Latino among them. I felt that Ben was truly the only person who saw past the color of my skin and stopped asking me about how tough it must be for me in a place like Lewisburg. From the first day we took the bus together, Ben wanted to get to know the person I had grown to be, not as an immigrant in the United States.

The day students often asked me, "Why are you friends with Ben?" They labeled him as an outcast because he didn't conform to their group standards. Ben never cared about how he dressed, mainly because he had no money to spend on the clothes that were in style. He never seemed to get his academic work done between working nights and weekends and taking care of his grandmother. We were best friends simply because we understood and lived in each other's situations. Knowing that he faced the same problems and circumstances made me feel like I was not the only one struggling through my adolescent years. He was the one person I placed my complete trust in. Even if he didn't have answers, at least I knew that we would be lost together in the trials of adolescent relationships.

During my four years at Lewisburg, I only faced a single blatantly racist episode, which pulled together my feelings of isolation and intimidation. I played on the junior varsity football team as a senior and I was one of two dark-skinned linemen. As we lined up two by two, I faced Tony, the only other dark-skinned lineman. We set up in our three-point stance in front of the tackling sled and I waited for the coach's whistle to signal us to push the sled. Before the whistle, I heard someone yell, "Here come the *brothers*." At the whistle, I slammed all my anger into the sled as if I was pushing the words back into my teammate's mouth. Although I was furious, I went straight to the back of the line. A day student friend came up to me after practice and said, "I told him that you weren't black but that you were

Hispanic. And he said, 'I guess I should have called him a spic, huh!'" Although I had been called "nigger" on two occasions by strangers, I had never experienced racism from a group of people I felt I was a part of, such as the members of my team. I never told anyone except Ben about the incident, and I never faced the teammate who made the comment. After that episode, I saw the campus with a new perspective; I knew I couldn't trust everyone in the so-called multicultural community of the prep school.

During the winter break of my sophomore year, my older brother José and I discussed our experiences in prep school. José and I shared a bedroom when he was home from school, and as we lay in our beds, I innocently asked him, "How is school going?" We never had the opportunity really to talk to each other about the one thing we shared in common, prep school. As we began to talk, I felt a sense of relief as he began opening up to me. With tears in my eyes, I told him how hard it was for me to do well in school, how I had no idea how to get a girl to like me, and how lonely I felt with all my siblings away at school. He never saw the tears roll out of my eyes in the darkness, but he knew how I felt. We shared all of our experiences, fears, and expectations, as if trying to get everything we had been holding back off our chests. He told me about his first girlfriend, how lonely he felt in school without me and our family, and how he never knew how to really talk to me when I was young. Throughout the winter, my brother and I spoke late into the night, trying to catch up with each other's lives. We had missed out on too much in a year and a half away from each other. During that winter break, I shared and learned more from my brother than ever before with any other family member.

Therefore, when the time came to choose what college I would attend, I decided I would not let the opportunity to be with my brother pass me by. I had the chance to get a good education anywhere, but I only had one brother to learn from and spend time together for what could be the last carefree years of our lives. Although it took me some time to adjust to the Dartmouth College environment, I finally got my goals straight with my brother at my side.

At the start of my freshman fall semester, I found it hard to make friends, so I immersed myself in the college's Latino community in order to meet people. I ended up learning more about myself than about other people and learned to proudly define who I am. During the first term, I joined the Latino theater group organized and run by other Latino students. After the first meeting of the group, I was cast in a play in the role of a streetwise, right-hand man to the main character. A week before opening night,

April, the girl who founded the group and was producing the play, came to see a rehearsal. After watching the first scene, she made us all stop and sit down for what turned out to be the talk that made me fully recognize who I am.

"Do you all realize what this play is about? Have you thought about the issues this play addresses?" she asked.

April looked each one of us in the eyes. Silence filled the auditorium. I had never stopped to think at all about what the play meant.

"I just want you all to know that this play is about you and me. This play talks about the things that haunt our Latino community at home and here at school. We all know what they are . . . or do we?"

I still had no idea what to say. I only felt guilty for not taking the play seriously.

"Ernesto shows the problems within the Latino community. Ernesto deals with an issue we all hate to talk about and even think about, but one that we have to deal with. Ernesto talks about the issue of skin color in our own community." April continued to stare into our lowered gazes. "Ernesto speaks about what it means to be black in the Latino community, and how we ourselves are ashamed of our own African roots. Do you all even realize that we have a black Latino in our cast?" April looked at me and I stared back at her. Never had I even heard those two words together: black and Latino. Until April said it, I had never recognized the color of my skin as being part of my identity. I looked around and realized that I was the only black Latino on stage in the auditorium, and, with the exception of my own brother, on the campus.

After April's final question the whole cast fell silent, and I knew I had to break the silence. "I guess I've never thought of myself as a black Latino. When I was young, my mom always took my brother and me to the barber to get our monthly haircuts. She always said that we looked better with short hair and that way we wouldn't have to deal with our afros," I said. Since I was a young child, my mother raised us to believe that we were Latino above everything else. She never mentioned the fact that two of her children were light skinned and two were dark skinned. Skin color had never been an issue when I lived on a Caribbean island. Until I reached the United States, and particularly college, I was not aware of the politics of skin color. Even in the Latino organization and community, I noticed I was the only dark-skinned male in the group. I didn't quite fit in the Latino community that was supposed to be a support group for me. The only other person in the Latino community at college who understood what I experienced every day was my own brother.

As I began to meet students outside of the Latino circle, I found the friends who have given me the confidence and the courage to go after what I wanted. When I joined a black fraternity, I found friends who pushed me to my limits but stood by me at all times. The brothers of the fraternity made me see myself in a new light. One night, a brother asked me to stop by his room to talk. As he walked up and down the room, he just smiled. "Have you ever looked at yourself, I mean really looked at who you are?" he asked. I just stood quietly because I didn't know how to respond. He said, "Look at yourself. You are a Latino man at one of the best colleges in the country. You have a good GPA, you are an athlete, and you have a job. Not many people can do all that at this place." I guess I have always done whatever it took to make it. In prep school, I had to stay at home in order to keep focused on my academics and avoid the elitist attitudes of the students. In college, I had to focus on academics by keeping myself busy in different areas of work and sports. I simply stared at him blankly. He realized he had not gotten his point across, and said, "I guess I'm going to have to break this down for you. You have the physique, the looks, and the mind to get everything you want on this campus. You have done it in class and on the field. And the only thing that's stopping you from going after women is your self-confidence. I'm here to tell you that just by looking at you, there is nothing that can stop you. When you realize that for yourself, you will understand what I have said." I left his room with a silly grin on my face. I knew I had received good news about how others perceived me, but I had no idea what to do with it. My first instinct was to run and tell my friends, but my friends might have thought I was incredibly conceited. "He's so full of himself," they would have said. And that's exactly how I felt. I felt full of my *self.* That brother made me step out of my body, look at, and judge myself. As a friend and a brother, what did I have to offer? I had more than I had ever imagined.

As I look back, I now know that I stood in between the black fraternity and Latino community. My worst fear came true: I was not part of any one group and never will be. As a black Latino on a small campus, I found a way to define and redefine my identity from the perspectives of both the African American and Latino communities. In my journey, I followed the voices that helped me reevaluate myself. Through those voices, I saw another piece of my "self," another piece of what it means to be a black

Latino. I just hope I can be a new voice for those who live between the lines.

Alessandro Meléndez is currently in his medical residency training in a Boston area hospital. After working for three years as a research assistant in basic science research, Alessandro chose to return to his island Puerto Rico for medical school where he graduated with honors. He has returned to the Northeast to continue the journey to his true identity. He continues to live somewhere between his island culture and the life determined by the color of his skin.

From as early as I can remember, and even well before then, I've been raised to see the world through a variety of lenses. I was born into a home that epitomized diversity. My father's background was that of a very poor Mexican American; my mother's was that of a fairly wealthy white woman from a predominantly black island in the French West Indies; and, Dora, my housekeeper-babysitter—or more accurately sister–second mother— was an illegal immigrant from Honduras. I grew up speaking English, Spanish, and French. My family's closest friends, men whom I referred to as uncles, were Iranian immigrants. My childhood neighbor and best friend was Jewish; another neighborhood friend was Lebanese. When I visited my mother's family in Martinique, I was constantly under the supervision of two black women who had roles in the family similar to that of Dora's in mine. I have grown up in a family and household that celebrates sameness, what is universal in people, not difference; the people who hold the dearest places in my heart come from a wide range of ethnic, racial, religious, linguistic, and socioeconomic backgrounds.

My family was and continues to be at the core of everything I do and every decision I make. My parents just celebrated their twenty-fifth anniversary and have served as the perfect role models, as individuals and as a couple, in my and my siblings' lives. My father, who was the first in his family to graduate from college, has balanced a successful career as an attorney and civic leader with being a husband, father, brother, and friend. My mother has also balanced a successful career as an optometrist with being a loving, devoted mother, sister, and friend. Both of my parents have been models of who I hope to be. Moreover, their strong relationship, as well as their strength and respect for each other as individuals, has greatly shaped how I view women and relationships. My father, whom I've grown up calling "Papa," is a strong, intelligent man, recognized for his leadership in all venues of his life. But he is also a very emotional man; every morning that I've woken up in our home, I've been greeted with a hug, a kiss, and an "I love you" from him. My mother, "Mama," is an equally strong, very intelligent, and beautiful woman. Growing up, my father was a mentor and disciplinarian while my mother was my confidant and the person from whom I asked for things or permission to do things; since I've left for college, their roles have melded and each provides so much of everything for me.

I am the oldest of four children. I have two younger brothers, Sebastien and Bryan, and a younger sister, Stefanie. Seb has been my best friend throughout much of my life, and Bryan and Stefanie have become better and better friends as our interests overlap more with age. I have a great sense of duty as the oldest sibling and set the best example I can for my brothers and sister—both because my parents have raised me to do so and because of the great love I have for them. I've often been accused by others of being too hard on myself, but I set high standards and have lofty expectations for my siblings—therefore, I must meet them myself.

A discussion of my family wouldn't be complete without including Dora. She became a part of our family when I was only eight months old; at the time, she was nineteen. Dora had hitchhiked, but mostly walked, all the way to Houston, where we lived, from Honduras in the hopes of making money to send back to her family. When she joined our family, I have to assume that she was an "illegal alien"—words that seem like such a cruel label to put on someone you love. Dora lived with my family until I was sixteen years old, when she left us to start her own. I have since become the godfather of her second son, Sergio, an honor I had never expected.

Until she left I spent almost all of my free time as a child with her. I remember being somewhere between five and eight years old and sneaking into her room late at night to watch Spanish comedy shows and soap operas. I remember how I helped her with her English as she prepared for some sort of citizenship test. Dora provided everything that my mother would have liked to while she was at work. I don't want to give the impression that my mother left us with a nanny while she pursued her career, however. Incredible as it may sound, my mom was able to balance her work and home lives so well that I can't think of one instance in my life when I felt as if she wasn't there for me.

Outside of my family life, school and sports seemed so simple until I changed schools just before the fifth grade. Up until then, I went to a tiny school in which entire grades were usually no more than fifteen students. I remember visiting St. Michael's, an upper-middle-class Catholic school, with my mom and being both excited and petrified about the notion of joining a class of sixty kids my age. I had felt like a big fish in the tiniest of ponds up until that point, and I wondered about how I would fare in my new school. Would I make friends? Would I be popular? Would I be a good athlete? What would it be like having more girls my age in class?

Before school even started, I met Cas, who would become my childhood best friend. He was a "designated liaison" and his job was to welcome me to St. Michael's. My having been paired with Cas was probably the single most defining moment in my childhood social life and development. Cas was a very popular, if not the most popular, kid at St. Michael's. He was loud, funny, and charming; he was only average looking and an average athlete, but his dynamic personality more than compensated for that. We hit if off instantly, and before I knew what had happened I was plugged into the "cool" kids' group. I attribute my social "success" as a youth to sheer dumb luck and association with him more than anything else. I wonder what would have happened had I not been paired with Cas. Would I have ended up spending time with the popular kids anyway? I was a fairly smart, athletic, decent kid, but I was and am extremely shy. I don't think it would have been difficult for me to go through life with only a few close friends and my family. Instead, I've always found myself with a large group of friends and an abundance of acquaintances. I can't say for certain which lifestyle I'd prefer, but I'm pretty sure it'd be the former. The latter has often made me feel very alone in crowded rooms, as they say.

As early as middle school, I began to struggle with accepting the social hierarchy. Because of academic tracking and a few extracurricular activities—particularly Boy Scouts and the trivia team—I found myself spending lots of time with "not so cool" kids. I remember the conflict of interests when Cas and company would want me to join them for a movie with the girls on the same night that Eliott, a social outcast, would want me to sleep over. Eliott, a scrawny little kid with freckles, a British accent, and a terrible stutter, had approached me immediately upon my arrival at St. Michael's. We became good friends, but over time it became more and more difficult to maintain my friendship with him. I couldn't tell Cas that I'd have to pass on the night at the movies with girls because I was spending the night at Eliott's, and God only knows what they would have said had I suggested Eliott join us. Looking back, I'm ashamed of how I acted, while at the same time I'm cognizant of how hard it is to do the right thing in that situation at that age. Although I was aware of what was happening, I wasn't ready to find my own voice, independent of the popular group.

The change in schools also forced me to deal with my Latino identity for the first time. Up until that point, I had never really had to think much about it—it just was. I had many fond memories of going to my father's old home to visit my grandparents. Although the neighborhood was poor, old, and somewhat frightening, I always felt safe once we pulled into the driveway. My grandmother died when I was about seven years old. As long as she lived she would always greet us at the front door with a big smile, hugs, and kisses. She seemed to always be wearing the Mexican equivalent of a sundress and her mesmerizing smile. Upon entering her home, we'd immediately be fed, hungry or not, and then we'd be sat down to play board games or let loose in the yard while the adults visited around the small kitchen table. Before leaving we were always treated to some *sandía*, aka watermelon—or if we really lucked out, ice cream from the ice cream truck that happened to drive by.

My holidays were spent with my aunts, uncles, and cousins from my dad's side of the family. When we were all very young, none of us were aware of any differences between us, and we all got along well. However, before long the stark contrast between my family's lifestyle and those of my aunts, uncles, and cousins became apparent, and awkwardness began to set in. We grew up in middle- and upper-class predominantly white neighborhoods; they grew up in lower-class Latino ones. We went to private schools; they went to the local public schools. They spoke, dressed, and acted differently. My dad's Mercedes stuck out in the driveway, which was otherwise full of minivans and pickup trucks, and I felt we tended to stick out in the living room in our polo shirts and khakis. My brothers, sister, and I were seriously outnumbered; we were the weird ones. I often felt as if my cousins were for some reason more Mexican than we were—or more accurately, that they felt that they were.

Between the signals I was getting from my peers at my school and my cousins at family gatherings, my Mexican heritage became somewhat of a secret, guilty pleasure. I remember Sundays when, rather than going to St. Michael's, we would go to St. Joseph's, in a poor Latino neighborhood, where I enjoyed the masses much more. Rather than falling asleep to the rants of a pretentious, stiff, guilt-instilling white priest with a year-round golf tan, I was inspired by the words of a robust, short, dark, Hispanic priest preaching about hope and faith. After the Mass, rather than going to the school gym for coffee and donuts like at St. Michael's, the St. Joseph's congregation would pour out into the courtyard for mariachi music and fresh tacos. I could sit and eat *chorizo con juevo* tacos and listen to mariachi music forever. After the fifth grade, though, I remember how this experience became a conflict. While I devoured my tacos and soaked in the sounds, I would always make sure that I couldn't be seen from the streets. My biggest fear was going back to school Monday and having a classmate tell everyone how he or she saw me at the poor Mexican church as they drove by.

During middle school, and even the beginning of high school, I found myself projecting various, audience-tailored identities. During the week at school and sporting events, I was who my wealthy white peers expected me to be; on weekends I was who my poor, Mexican American relatives expected me to be. While there were components of these fronts that differed, my fundamental values and characteristics did remain the same. Perhaps the most accurate way of describing my identity at the time was that of a young boy lacking his universal voice. I knew how I felt and what I wanted to say about things; I was just too concerned with approval to yet be my own person.

The stereotypes and jokes I heard at St. Michael's exemplified the opinions of the community at large toward Mexicans, who were portrayed as essentially lazy, drunk, fat, poor lawnmower pushers and dish boys. I couldn't understand these stereotypes in light of my own experiences and relationships, but I was in an environment in which they were the norm so I may have believed them to a certain extent, and I became embarrassed about my background. At my first soccer practice at St. Michael's they asked me where I had played the year before and I said St. Cyril's. "Oh, you played with all those damn Mexicans," they said. "We hate playing y'all because y'all do all that Mexican trick soccer shit." The "Mexicans" they spoke about weren't all Mexicans: some were from Colombia, Ecuador, Guatemala, and other Central American countries. But it didn't really matter in my new peers' eyes; one poor Latino was really no better or worse than another.

I remember how uncomfortable I felt the following year when I realized that some of my teammates were going to be from "the apartments," a housing project with poor Latinos who attended St. Cyril's. The year before, my teammates were all the kids from my neighborhood; but the new soccer commissioner had made a point of inviting all the kids from the apartments to play. Through the course of the season, I became close friends with many of them and often visited their homes. I remember the uncomfortable feeling of hearing them referred to as spics and how my new classmates and teammates had wished they would "go back to their own country." I said nothing; fitting in was much more important. I never was quite sure why I was so quickly accepted—after all I was just as "Mexican" as any of the other players at St. Cyril's had been. I assume it was simply because of the neighborhood I lived in and the cars my parents drove.

From the fifth grade all the way until my college applications, I seldom thought about being Latino. All of my closest friends were white; I attended a predominantly white middle school and an all-boys, predominantly white Jesuit high school. I always let the racist jokes slide, and to be honest, I'm not sure how many of my classmates knew or cared that I was Latino. I had told myself that it shouldn't matter; what matters is that we all get along and don't distinguish based on race. As for the jokes and racial slurs, I accepted those as slightly ignorant but by no means malicious.

The transition to high school wasn't too difficult for me. Through the course of my childhood I had always revered the Jesuit high school as a hallowed place where boys went on to become men. I had seen my cousin Stephen make the transition there. I heard about his successes and all the great friends he had made, and he told lively stories about all things high school; I was fascinated. Perhaps the best part about his attending Strake was my going to the major athletic events because of it. Since I didn't have any older siblings I was always intrigued to see older boys; I couldn't wait to be as big as they were or to be able to do the things they did. These guys, only a few years older, looked so strong and confident. I remember when they would walk by after the games, shoulder pads off, sweat and dirt dripping down their chiseled faces. I couldn't wait for my day to come.

When it did come, the muscles and stature did not. I woke up the morning of my first day of football practice looking pretty much the same as I had the day before. I was a tall, lanky, slightly above-average athlete. It didn't matter, though, because much more important were the social implications of the football practices, which began two full weeks before classes. The field and the locker room provided the perfect medium for a social hierarchy at an all-boys' school to be established. My group of friends from St. Michael's quickly established itself at the very top and handpicked those that would join. After-practice sleepovers quickly solidified relationships with the "new" guys.

By the first day of class, I already knew many of my two hundred new classmates. While football practices had served as the first socializing battlefield, lunchtime quickly became the second. I never once ate in the traditional cafeteria. The place to eat was in a room next to the cafeteria called "the foyer." Here there were only a few round tables, seating about twelve each. This was where all the most popular kids from all grade levels ate, and where we sat on our first day of school.

I remember so vividly how that hour went down. First, there was the seat saving for our closest friends who had classes farther away. Next, there was the acceptance or rejection of new guys who wanted to join us. I'll never forget when John came up to our table with his food tray and stood awkwardly next to an empty seat. It was clear how nervous he was and how badly he wanted to sit with us. John was an overweight black kid who wore glasses and was a mediocre football player at best. However, he had made a few jokes in the locker room that had made people laugh. I'm pretty sure that his being black was somewhat intriguing for my friends, especially since we'd never had a black classmate at St. Michael's. I'm pretty sure John was somewhat aware of this because he liked to refer to himself as the "black man" when making jokes and telling stories. So there he was; physically he couldn't have been any more different from us, but emotionally he was going through the exact same things as we were. After a weird silence and a few quick glances around the table, my friends decided that he couldn't sit with us. Several more kids suffered the same fate that day, and consequently there was a table next to ours of "fringe friends."

I remember the encounter with John so vividly because in retrospect I am terribly ashamed of my passive nature through it all. There wasn't much that distinguished me from John. It was the first day at a new high school for the both of us. He was nervous, as was I. He was one of the few black students on campus, I one of the few Latinos. The one pivotal difference: I already had the friends he so desperately wanted. I wondered what would have happened had that been my first encounter with these guys who were now my closest friends. Would they have let me take a seat at their table? Or had I just been lucky enough to meet them earlier in life in a much less hostile time and environment? At the time, I ignored the queasy feeling in my stomach and stared down at my food for fear of making eye contact with John before he walked away. I spent the first two years of high school in very much the same way.

I consider myself a very introverted person. I have always been very big on reflection and self-improvement. My father has been the ultimate role model in all regards; I admire the way he treats people and the way they respond to him. Growing up, though, I lacked a major component of what makes him who he is: courage. My mind was always in the right place, but the same cannot be said about my actions. I was never the one to throw the first insult, but I was never the one to stop them from being thrown either.

I remember a poster in one of my history classes that quoted Martin Niemoller. It read,

> In Germany they came first for the Communists and I didn't speak up because I wasn't a Communist. Then they came for the Jews and I didn't speak up because I wasn't a Jew. Then they came for the trade unionists and I didn't speak up because I wasn't a trade unionist. Then they came for the Catholics and I didn't speak up because I was a Protestant. Then they came for me— and by that time no one was left to speak up.

In a lot of ways, this is how I felt about the social world of adolescent boys, and I hated it. I had been raised to stand up for others; I just hadn't found the voice to do so. I spent my first two years of high school purposely trying to appear to be on the fringe of the circle of friends I belonged to. I needed the social security of being a part of that group, but I didn't want others to see me as they saw them.

A turning point in my high school life came on March 2 of my sophomore year. I remember the date specifically because for the next year and a half or so I would be reminded of it every 2nd of the month. Melissa had "come into my life" at a New Year's party. At the time, I merely asked my buddies who the new cute girl was and then went on about my business. Heidi was a very close female friend of mine, and over the course of the next two months, Melissa became Heidi's best friend and started showing up everywhere in my life—eventually Heidi was convincing me about how I really needed to date this girl. With the same nervousness and insecurities that I had had in middle school, I dreaded the notion of having a girlfriend and not having a clue what to do with her. I didn't have a complete grasp of the whole kissing thing; moreover, the whole "southern gentleman" thing was too firmly embedded in my mind for me to ever have the courage to move from base to base in the game of physical intimacy. But she was persistent. Perhaps more important, Heidi, who held the key to my heart but didn't know it, was persistent. I loved the attention and the possibility that such an attractive girl would be interested in me. At the same time, however, I was horrified, paralyzed by my insecurities.

On March 2, it finally happened. A week before, Heidi had told me that Melissa was giving up; I had to act quickly. I finally started calling her on a nightly basis. We talked for hours each and every night, not once confronted with a dull awkward silence. (I was confident on the phone, but if you put me in a room with a girl that I didn't really know, I instantly crawled into my shell.) In the wee hours of the morning of March 2, as I was falling asleep, I finally gathered my courage. Exemplifying just how courageous I was even at my best, I asked, "So what exactly do you want from us?" even though I knew full well what she wanted. She replied, "Well, I don't know . . ." After about fifteen minutes we somehow indirectly came to the conclusion that we were now dating. We said our good-byes and I promptly passed out.

A few hours later I found myself in the shower getting ready for school. I was nervous; I wondered if I should immediately regret having told Melissa that we could be boyfriend and girlfriend. Was it too late to call her before she went to school? I can't begin to describe how worried I was about how my friends would respond, even though this was the girl that they all had so badly wanted to date. Still, for some reason I was traumatized by the prospect of them ridiculing me, or telling me that I had picked a bad apple and sharing with me some new gossip that I hadn't caught wind of yet. It wasn't until lunch that word spread; more likely out of my paranoia than the reality of my friends' curiosity, I suddenly felt like I was a key witness in a major trial with groups of people coming at me with a barrage of questions. By the end of the day, everything had settled; I scrambled off to baseball practice, the field always being my sanctuary, and everything was okay. My friends, after some quick questioning, approved of the girlfriend while expressing some envy; the girls did the same, mostly in that fake kind of way that girls are so good at. I now had my first "real" girlfriend.

From then to the fall of my senior year, my life can very accurately be defined and described through my relationship with Melissa. Everything else became secondary. In her I found a confidant unlike any I had previously come across, including Heidi. Even though Heidi was my best friend, I saw her more as "one of the guys," and I had too big of a crush on her to ever share my insecurities. In Melissa, I found a very stereotypical, traditional Southern girlfriend. She was girly, loved to gossip, and was a social butterfly. I quickly won her parents over and soon had a home away from home. My parents hated this, and my father was particularly unexcited about Melissa as a person. But when I finally fell for Melissa, I fell hard.

Because of the emotional outlet Melissa provided me with, I valued my relationship with her more than with either my lifelong group of friends

or my family, though for two distinct reasons. When I became fully con-
sumed by Melissa I had already been growing apart from my friends. I
don't think I was ever able to forgive them, and more importantly myself,
for what had happened to John. Before dating Melissa, I never dared act
on such feelings for fear of finding myself isolated. Dating Melissa gave me
the confidence to act based on my own beliefs and values and served as the
catalyst for much of my adolescent growth and identity development. For
this I will forever be grateful to her.

Another reason my relationship with my friends had been steadily de-
clining was that they were all starting to drink and experiment with drugs,
and consequently their grades dropped and they started quitting sports. I
resented the hell out of them for it, especially Cas, my best friend. We grew
up competing against each other in everything, including sports, academics, and socializing. However, Cas quickly faded into mediocrity while
making his rise as a quasi social king. He blamed the deterioration of our
relationship on "that bitch Melissa," I on him being a pathetic druggie
drunk. Every weekend I went to parties I would see him, and it was always
awkward, as we never got beyond small talk. It didn't matter, though; I had
Melissa.

Socially, the biggest problem Melissa and I had was that my old friends
were her new friends, and she was first and foremost a social butterfly. Her
biggest fear in life, at least I thought, was missing the biggest or best party.
If there was a party, she needed to be there—just in case. We quickly found
out how fundamentally different we were in this regard. Summer meant
the possibility of a party every night. I didn't like parties; I thought the concept of a big party in and of itself was pretty stupid: a bunch of kids trying
to figure out how to handle alcohol and using it to have the courage to talk
to the opposite sex, not to mention to have the occasional macho man fight,
which boiled down to who had more friends. While I attended more than
my fair share of parties, rarely did I enjoy myself, and more often than not
I went so that my phone would stop ringing with the same usual suspects
hounding me to go out and "stop being such a loser." With Melissa, all I
wanted to do was go on dates and spend quality time with her. It felt like
a much healthier thing to do at the time.

After about six months, Melissa and I started getting frustrated with
each other because of our differences in opinions on partying. Physically,
our relationship was pretty immature as well. I think she shared the same
fears as I did about sexual activities. As I grew comfortable with her, I did
want to try new things and always wanted her to be honest with me and
give "tips" if there were any to be given. But Melissa was far less comfort-

able with the notion of communicating about sexual activity, so for the
most part we avoided communication. It didn't bother me much; I was
more interested in the personal growth that I was going through by simply having her. When our relationship slowly evolved into a series of fights,
I tried to deal with or at least ignore the problems; I was too immersed in
the process of finding my own voice through my relationship with her to
give it up.

When school started again junior year, my relationship with Melissa
continued to deteriorate. But I wasn't prepared to accept losing it; I still
relied too heavily on her. I learned as much, if not more, about myself
through the gradual falling apart of my relationship with Melissa than
through the actual relationship. I couldn't stand the notion of anything that
I was a part of not succeeding: more than losing Melissa, I hated the idea
of having been a part of a "failed" relationship. In my eyes, if we broke up
(especially if she was the one who broke up with me), then I had just squan-
dered over a year of my life; I couldn't let that happen. She kept treating
me poorly and I kept taking it. She kept breaking up with me and I kept
letting her back in at her convenience. It was all about control. If I broke
up with her, I could be on another date in a few days as happy as a beaver.
If she broke up with me, I would be at home fretting and constantly calling while she was on her own date. And every time it seemed as if I was
about to turn the corner and move on, she would come rushing back into
my life just to make sure she still had me where she wanted me.

I started to make a conscious effort to make new friends and get to know
each and every one of my classmates, and also to immerse myself in extracurricular activities. The turning point in my social life came with the
school elections at the end of the year. Running for student body president
provided a means through which I could gauge the success of my efforts
to get to know, and more importantly, befriend my school peers. However,
Cas was running for president too, and although we hadn't spoken exten-
sively in a long time, it was hard for me to run against him. I'll never forget the first day of classes freshmen year as we walked through the hall,
when Cas, outgoing and charismatic, looked at me and announced that
come senior year we'd be running this school. He'd be the president and
I the vice. He was the Batman, I was the Robin. I liked it that way; I much
preferred being the man behind the scenes, the brain behind the mouth.
But in this instance, it just couldn't be that way; I had to take the reins. Cas
and I didn't so much as speak through the course of the election after it became clear that neither would settle for being the other's vice president.

As election day approached, the campaigns very much took on the personalities of the candidates. Cas was calling all the freshmen, promising a huge keg party with lots of girls if he won. Brian, the third candidate, was running a very conservative, policy-oriented campaign. I made my campaign project me as right in the middle. I wanted to be the fun guy that the popular crowds would enjoy to hang out with but also the serious guy that the "nerds" would believe could take care of business. And in the end, I won. It was a monumental day in the defining of my self-perception: I no longer felt that I needed associations through which other people could define me. Moreover, I had indeed won the approval and the respect of my school peers. I had succeeded in achieving the goals that I had set for myself at the beginning of the school year—all with my dragged-out relationship with Melissa lingering in the backdrop.

During the summer after my junior year, I worked, played, started visiting colleges, and of course dealt with Melissa. By this point it was clear that we weren't going to be together, but we still struggled to completely stop dating. The key difference was that I was now fully confident in myself. I was the student body president, editor of the newspaper, and founder-chairman of the only community service organization on my school's campus, as well as a participant in various other activities, including baseball. I needed no one: not friends and surely not Melissa. This drove her crazy. She couldn't stand the idea of my being so confident and happy without her being a part of it. I, on the other hand, loved it. The tables had turned and she was going to have to deal with it.

Entering my senior year, I made new goals. In order of importance, first, I wanted to succeed in all of my extracurricular activities. Second, I wanted to take command of my social life and make the most of senior year. Third, I wanted to get into a great college. And finally, I would "play the field." I had spent the past year and a half locked down; it was time for me to see what running around was all about. On a college application, my senior year was pretty much the kind that those cheesy high school movies are made of. I was Mr. Everything at school, had a nice car and a great family, was pretty socially adept, and was now single. The high school world was my oyster.

Community service was the last essential element of my high school life and self-identity formation. Consciously or subconsciously, service became a medium through which I could deal with my Latinoness. I don't want to say that it was like penance, because I thoroughly enjoyed it, but there was definitely an element of obligation and even guilt involved. Every time I interacted with minority children, in the back of my mind I thought of my father. I hoped to provide something, anything, for a child who was coming from a situation similar to the one he had grown up in. Service for poor minorities was one of my methods for alleviating the sense of contradiction I felt when comparing my socioeconomic and ethnic backgrounds.

During my senior year, I had a life-altering experience through one of these service projects. Magnolia Park, where the service project was taking place, had always had a special, mysterious place in my heart. The colorful houses, spice-filled air, and loud *ranchera* music always made it an adventure to drive through on the occasional Sunday with my father. My great-grandparents, grandparents, and father had all lived in this historic immigrant neighborhood. They had been products of the Mexican Revolution, the Great Depression, and the postwar baby boom, and I wondered if they ever dreamed of me, their descendant, returning to their neighborhood as part of a student service project. The contrast of my returning as a giver of charity, and not as a recipient, struck me.

My mind raced as I assisted in preparing for the holiday distribution of food, clothing, and toys. While I quickly worked with the other volunteers to meet our start time, I watched the line of recipients form. It occurred to me that the Special Recreation Center was not unlike the ones my father had visited as a child in search of food, clothes, and vaccinations. I always remembered his tales of his youth as a poor Mexican American in a poor Mexican American neighborhood; but having grown up in a much nicer neighborhood and attended private schools with wealthy, predominantly white student populations, this important dimension of my heritage had always been foreign to me. His stories had been just that—stories—until today.

The line began forming at eleven in the morning, even though we were not planning on serving until three in the afternoon. The people waiting had kind, strong, and honest faces, not unlike those of my aunts and uncles. That day, I saw all the things I had failed to see before. The names and characters I had heard about growing up now had faces, and their struggles were put into a context for me. These people were waiting patiently for a cabbage, some carrots, stale bread, and a few used toys to offer their children for Christmas.

As all the other volunteers from school worked feverishly to make sure that everything was in order and ready to go for the afternoon event, I would find my friends—who had come only to fulfill the one-hundred-hour service requirement needed to graduate—hidden in a corner smoking cigarettes, or perhaps popping the balloons and inhaling the helium to make their voices sound funny. Daniel, one of my closest friends, was the primary recipient of my wrath. I pulled him aside after he made fun of me for being so uptight and gung ho about the service project. He crossed the line when he said, in front of our other friends, "Hey, David, why don't you fucking relax, man? We're going to get credit for the hours already; you don't need to give yourself a heart attack." I took him into the next room, and the sadness I felt hearing these remarks came out in the form of rage; Daniel was also Latino, and his father had come from a similar background to my father's. "Fuck you, Daniel, fuck you!" I screamed, unaware of where these emotions were coming from. "I don't see how you can sit around and suck helium out of balloons with those idiots when you know just as well as I do that our dads sat in lines just like the ones you see outside now. How fucking dare you, Daniel? You should be ashamed of yourself." I had never scolded my friends because of my perpetual fear of being accused of being "holier than thou," but I couldn't control myself this time. I stormed out of the room and manned my position in the line, helping to distribute loaves of bread.

That day cemented in my mind something that I had perhaps always tried to deny. I was different. Among the many things that made me different was my Latino identity. No longer could I deny it, and no longer did I want to be ashamed of it. That day I saw so much more honor, humility, and love in the faces of those waiting in line than in the faces of my selfish, ignorant, spoiled friends. In the end, I would much rather be associated with a poor Mexican than a rich white kid, regardless of the stereotypes.

College applications forced many of the things that I had kept in the back of mind to the forefront. I did enjoy 99 percent of the application process—especially the silent, secretive pleasure of being able to make known all of my accomplishments. I hated being recognized by people I knew personally, so there was a great deal of satisfaction in knowing that people outside my life would appreciate what I had done. But then there was that 1 percent that I disliked: the checking of a box identifying your ethnicity.

I think the affirmative action movement has had the single most significant impact on my conception of my identity as a Latino and whether or not I qualify. My parents had given me every advantage a child could ever wish for and had provided me with the best education available. And I did not want to get in to a college simply because I was Latino. I did not like the notion of one of my good friends not getting into a school of his or her choice because a minority student, perhaps less qualified, would get the spot. I understood the purpose and intentions of affirmative action but felt as if there were too many negative misconceptions that went with it. To me, it implied that minority students were not as capable as white students. I knew I was just as capable, if not more so, than many of my classmates, and I couldn't stand the notion of receiving acceptance to a college they were refused from and then hearing, "Oh, you just got in because you checked the Latino box."

There was a major ongoing debate as to whether affirmative action was fulfilling its goals or whether minority students coming from upper-class predominantly white educational backgrounds were simply abusing it. I was not asking for special assistance, but there was no box to check that said, "I am Latino but would not like to benefit from affirmative action." In many ways, I felt that being Latino was equated with poor and disadvantaged. I was neither, but I was Latino. Where did I fit into the equation? Why did it matter? By getting enough students who checked a certain box, would the college truly see itself as "diverse"? Would I be able to provide the diversity they sought?

I always felt that my background was something inherent, a part of me that resonated in all that I did and sought to be. Never before did I feel as though I had to wear it like a badge. I wanted to check "Other" and then write a long paragraph describing my uniqueness and challenge them to find another male student from Houston, Texas, whose mother was born and raised in Martinique; whose father's family immigrated to Texas from Mexico; whose housekeeper-sister–second mother was from Honduras; and who went to a Catholic middle school and a Jesuit, all-male high school. I was proud of my entire background—a background that no one other than my brothers could match. By forcing their applicants to check one of five boxes, I felt that they were stripping away any and all diversity that was worthwhile.

In the end, I checked the "Latino" box, and one of my essays did describe my struggle with establishing my self-identity as a Latino through the service project my senior year. I was accepted at Dartmouth by the head of minority recruitment and invited up for a special weekend for potential students. When I got there I soon found out that it was a weekend for minority recruits only. What the hell was going on, I thought? Why was there a constant need to focus on difference? Here was a school that was encouraging diversity yet at the same time separating minority students from white students. Nevertheless, the weekend went well, and I did indeed interact with an incredibly diverse group of people. I came home excited about those I had met and eager to return the following fall to continue to meet such interesting people.

As expected, when college acceptances began to come in and I got into schools that others had not, the comments began. I'll never forget a night when I was out with my friends and one of my classmates happened to be there; I was going to attend a school he had wanted to attend but was not accepted at. In a very snide tone he began to question all of my accomplishments: "How many times have y'all published the newspaper this year? Did you even do anything as student body president? I had a 3.75 GPA and you had what . . . a 3.2? Oh wait, but you said you were Latino, huh?" The anger I felt was difficult to control; Brad had no idea how much pent-up frustration he had just tapped into. My other friends quickly corrected him, but he had pushed that special button. "Oh wait, but you said you were Latino, huh?" Said? What the hell was he implying? Was I not? Who the hell was he to say what I was or was not? But at the same time, I couldn't help but question again. Would I not have gotten in if I had not checked the box? Why did being Latino have to be a burden, or a crutch? Why couldn't it just be a part of me, and that's all?

The fall of my freshman year at college was a time in which I learned a lot about myself and what it meant to be Latino to others and to myself. Just by being in New England I was much more aware of it. The culture shock that came with seeing a white man mowing his own lawn and a white woman housekeeping had a very concrete effect. Moreover, within a few days of setting foot on campus I was bombarded with e-mail from each and every group with which I could be affiliated. None stuck out more than the Latino organizations, probably simply because of my own paranoia. My being Latino had never entailed a conscious effort; now that I had gotten into this school as a Latino, did I have some sort of obligation? Was I to be the resident Latino on my floor? These questions did not seem so ridiculous when taking into account how segregated the campus appeared to me. I quickly found out the diversity of that marvelous prospective weekend would never be replicated in the rest of my college experience.

I hated the fact that there was affinity housing and organizations. It seemed as if everywhere I went black students were with black students, Latinos with Latinos, and so on. I thought that by segregating themselves in affinity housing and organizations those minority students had lost their right to complain about ignorance. Yes, they provided cultural activities such as dances and lectures, but in my opinion, by segregating themselves and therefore limiting the possibility of interaction with white students, I believe they eliminated the best means of curing ignorance and spreading diversity.

I think my appreciation of and definition of what my Latino background means to me differed fundamentally from the majority of the other Latinos at my college—at least the more visible ones. I appreciate my Latino background first and foremost for the cultural components, whereas at college the impression I got was that people appreciated it politically. I love the values that I associate with my Latino identity, such as the absolute, primary importance of family and of being honest and hard working. These are the things that make me proud of being Latino. I do not see my Latino background as a reason to run around and belittle every person who makes an ignorant derogatory comment, or to serve up tacos at Mexican heritage night.

My father has played a large role in the development of my understanding of what it is to be Latino. As I've mentioned, he was the only one of seven children to attend college, and he then went on to law school. He is a well-respected member of the community at large and a leader in the local Latino community. Growing up, I always struggled with how I perceived my father's role. He was and continues to be surrounded by influential and often wealthy white men but has a strong sense of where he came from and where he's been. I would see him in a tuxedo on his way to a gala one night and the next morning we'd be in a *taquería* for breakfast mingling in Spanish with whoever else was around. I couldn't figure it out. Was he a phony? Had he forgotten his roots and just pretended to still care around other Latinos? Or was he just a Latino that has learned to play the game by the "white man's rules in a white man's world"?

Eventually I realized and accepted the truth: my father is very proud of his roots and wouldn't deny them for the world; but to be successful at anything, you have to know how to pick your battles. He explained to me that, although there had been several times in his life when he had to bite his bottom lip to avoid conflict during meetings in which old, wealthy white men made ignorant comments, his being the only Latino on many of the boards he sits on is a major step for the Latino community. He taught me that it would be much easier to have a discussion with that person in private than it would be to shame him or her in public. A lot of times change comes one person at a time. My father did not deny his Latino background; instead, he just learned to control the emotions that came with it and developed a voice that was very much Latino but very patient. He was not a phony, he had not denied his roots; he just understood people, and understood that change takes time and involves a certain amount of finesse.

At college, any time I ran into another Latino student I would always feel a little uneasy. I wondered if they looked at me and wondered why I didn't go to meetings, or if they saw me as a sellout, like I felt my cousins might have done long ago. It bothers me less and less, though. I am coming to peace with my Latino background and know that as long as I am true to it and myself, no one can take it away from me or cheapen it in any way. I'm sick of feeling like I am not a true Latino simply because I was not poor or disadvantaged. I hope to eliminate that stereotype among any and all people that I encounter. Latinoness does not equal weakness. I want to be seen as successful, proud, and honest. And when people see that in me I want them to associate it with being Latino. But also with being Martiniquan, having a Jesuit education, being the oldest of four, and so on. I am not to be categorized and I never again shall allow myself to be. Next time I'm asked to check a box, maybe I will take the time to write out that long paragraph about who I am and tell them what they can do with that box.

After graduation, David Ralos spent two years teaching bilingual fourth-grade language arts in inner-city Houston as a Teach For America corps member. He then taught for a third year while helping open a new public school before moving on to graduate school on the West Coast to pursue a joint-degree MBA and ME. He hopes to spend the rest of his life improving the opportunities available for at-risk students in our public school system.

About the Editors

Andrew Garrod is Professor of Education and Director of Teacher Education at Dartmouth College, where he teaches courses in adolescence, moral development, and contemporary issues in U.S. education. He currently directs a teaching volunteer program in the Marshall Islands in the central Pacific and has conducted a research project in Bosnia and Herzegovina over a number of years. His recent publications include two coauthored articles "Forgiveness after Genocide? Perspectives from Bosnian Youth" and "Culture, Ethnic Conflict, and Moral Orientation in Bosnian Children," and the coedited books, *Souls Looking Back: Life Stories of Growing Up Black* and *Learning Disabilities and Life Stories.* With Robert Kilkenny he has coedited an anthology on growing up Asian American to be published by Cornell University Press. In 1991 he was awarded Dartmouth College's Distinguished Teaching Award.

Robert Kilkenny is Clinical Associate in the School of Social Work at Simmons College in Boston. He is coeditor of *Souls Looking Back: Life Stories of Growing Up Black* and of *Adolescent Portraits: Identity, Relationships, and Challenges*, which is in its sixth edition. With Andrew Garrod he has coedited an anthology on growing up Asian American to be published by Cornell University Press. He is the founder and Executive Director of the Alliance for Inclusion and Prevention, a public-private partnership providing school-based mental health, special education, and after-school programs to at-risk students in the Boston public schools.

Christina Gómez is Associate Professor in the Department of Sociology and Latino Studies at Northeastern Illinois University in Chicago. She received her doctorate from Harvard University in the Department of Sociology and completed her undergraduate studies and MBA at the University of Chicago. She is completing her book, *Latinos, Class, and the Boundaries of Whiteness*, which focuses on the racialization of Latinos in the United States. Her research focuses on identity construction, discrimination, and ethnic relations. Her recent publications include a coauthored article, "Assimilation vs. Multiculturalism: Bilingual Education and the Latino Challenge," and "Ethnic Relations, Class, and Latino Political Participation." She has been awarded various fellowships and grants including a National Science Foundation Fellowship, Ford Foundation grants, and Henry Luce Scholar Fellowship.